Edward J. Kameenui   Craig B. Darch

University of Oregon   *Auburn University*

INSTRUCTIONAL Classroom MANAGEMENT

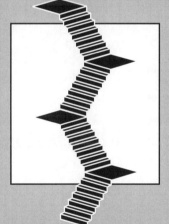

A Proactive Approach to BEHAVIOR MANAGEMENT

🚢 **Longman** *Publishers USA*

INSTRUCTIONAL CLASSROOM MANAGEMENT:
A PROACTIVE APPROACH TO BEHAVIOR
MANAGEMENT

Longman, 10 Bank Street, White Plains, N.Y. 10606

Associated companies:
Longman Group Ltd., London
Longman Cheshire Pty., Melbourne
Longman Paul Pty., Auckland
Copp Clark Longman, Ltd., Toronto

Sponsoring editor: Virginia L. Blanford
Production editor: Linda Moser
Cover design: Robin Hessel-Hoffman
Production supervisor: Richard Bretan

Library of Congress Cataloging-in-Publication Data
Kameenui, Edward J.
   Instructional classroom management : a proactive approach to
managing behavior / Edward J. Kameenui, Craig B. Darch.
       p.   cm.
   Includes bibliographical references (p.   ) and index.
   ISBN 0-8013-0636-1
   1. Classroom management. 2. Behavior modification. 3. School
discipline. I. Darch, Craig B. II. Title.
LB3013.K32 1994
371.1'024—dc20
                                                        93-10321
                                                        CIP

1 2 3 4 5 6 7 8 9 10-MA-9897969594

Contents

Preface

Instructional Classroom Management is about managing student behavior from an instructional point of view. It is based on a rather simple proposition: the strategies for teaching and managing social behavior are no different from the strategies for teaching reading, earth science, or mathematics. By their very nature, classroom and behavior management procedures are instructional, not merely behavioral or social, because they take place within the context of instruction and are designed to impart information. To impart information about how to behave, a teacher teaches, instructs, explains, directs, models, or otherwise communicates to a learner exactly how to behave and how not to behave. This process is no different from the process involved in teaching a concept, fact, or principle in mathematics or science. For all practical purposes, the teaching processes are the same—communicating information to the learner in ways that are clear, unambiguous, considerate, and passionate.

We developed this text for all teachers, who, by virtue of teaching, must manage the behavior of students in the classroom, in the hallway, or on the playground. The text offers an introduction and a set of general strategies associated with an instructional analysis of classroom and behavior management. As such, it does not provide an exhaustive analysis and description of all the principles and dimensions for designing a complete, step-by-step instructional classroom management plan. Instead, this text describes basic concepts and strategies to provide a sufficient starting point for thinking about instructional classroom management. In addition, we review several general strategies for rethinking and reorganizing a classroom to reflect an instructional classroom management approach.

NOTE TO THE READER AND INSTRUCTOR

We included several pedogological features to aid instruction:

Examples. Examples scattered throughout the text apply to both special or regular education contexts because many problems cut across programs, many special education students receive instruction in the regular classroom, and many special education teachers must now consult with regular education teachers about programs for students with special needs.

Advance Organizers. Each chapter begins with a chapter overview, which offers an organizational outline of the chapter content. The overview may be used to discuss key concepts before reading the chapter.

Chapter Figures and Tables. Figures and tables in each of the chapters present detailed information that enhances the narrative.

Chapter Summaries. Each chapter ends with a brief summary. Although the summaries are not detailed, they offer a general review of the main points in the chapter.

Chapter Activities. Each chapter summary is followed by three chapter activities. These activities require you to apply the content of the chapter to classroom situations. Several of the exercises require a visit to classrooms to interview teachers and administrators.

Suggested Readings. In addition to a reference list for the citations in each chapter, lists of current books and articles on various topics in classroom management are provided.

Acknowledgements

This text represents a collaborative effort over long distances and a long period of time, and with the assistance of many people. The idea for developing this book originated with Raymond O'Connell, who was our former executive editor. Ray guided our writing until the final draft and was always generous and supportive. The ideas central to an instructional classroom management approach belong to three of our colleagues, Geoff Colvin, Zig Engelmann, and Randy Sprick. Their work continues to stimulate us and deepen our understanding of instruction, behavior management, and the communication of ideas. We are grateful to Randy Sprick for chapter 10, in which he offers a detailed description for developing school-wide discipline policies. We are also indebted to George Sugai for his writing and thinking on these matters.

We are particularly grateful to the following colleagues, who continue to influence our thinking and writing about instruction: Doug Carnine, Marty Kaufman, Deborah Simmons, Gerald Tindal, and Hill Walker. Our editors at Longman Publishing Group, Ken Clinton, Stuart Miller, Hillary Henderson, and Chris Konnari were gracious with their assistance.

We are especially appreciative of Katie Tate at the University of Oregon, who provided us with valuable assistance in the preparation of the manuscript. The following reviewers contributed valuable insights during the preparation and review of the text:

Anne Bauer, University of Cincinnati

Paul Beare, Moorehead State University

Diane Berkell, Long Island University

Robert Carpenter, State University of New York at Binghamton

Joyce Choate, Northeast Louisiana University

W. N. Creekmore, Northeast Louisiana University

Howard Drucker, Cal Polytechnic—San Luis Obispo

Lawrence Maheady, State University of New York at Fredonia

Brenda Manning, University of Georgia

Don Marozas, State University of New York at Geneseo

Mary Melvin, Miami University

Richard Mesaros, California State University—Northridge

Larry Parker, Georgia State University

Marilyn Kay Stickle, Ball State University

Finally, our deepest gratitude goes to our families, Brenda, Bree, and Ani Kameenui and Gabriele and Eric Darch. Brenda Kameenui served as our personal editor for the text and her advice on words, commas, and gerunds was invaluable.

chapter **1**

Classroom Management and the Context of Instruction

INTRODUCTION

Authoritative and controlling approaches to classroom management appear to be, if not dead, at least dying a slow but certain death. Hard, scientific data to support this observation may be difficult to find, but if the public marketplace is a reasonable index of consumers' preferences, then the signs are fairly clear and compelling. Teachers, school administrators, and professional organizations, such as the Association for Supervision and Curriculum Development (ASCD), which

1

boasts a membership of at least 160,000, appear to have abandoned the old approaches to "discipline." Instead, educators appear to be embracing more reflective and self-directed approaches to discipline. These new approaches are known by various names: discipline with dignity (Curwin & Mendler 1988), cooperative discipline (Albert 1990), assertive discipline (Canter 1989), positive discipline (Nelsen 1987), developing capable people (Glenn & Nelsen 1987), and so forth.

These approaches appear to be popular despite the lack of "scientific evidence" to support their effectiveness at both the classroom and school levels (Chard, Smith, & Sugai 1992). The lack of scientific evidence notwithstanding, the popularity of the approaches appears to reflect a significant disenchantment with the old school of discipline, which sought control and lived by the maxim "Be firm and don't smile until January." Moreover, these approaches are based on the notion that human beings are thinking, feeling, problem-solving, social creatures who, when given a chance, are capable of self-reflection, self-direction, and self-management.

These approaches to classroom management ostensibly require teachers and school administrators to rethink their approach to solving perceived behavior problems in the school and classroom. These "new" approaches to behavior management require careful consideration in order to discern fad and fashion (Slavin 1989; Kameenui 1991) from substantive and effective management strategies. Nevertheless, the apparently high and sustained level of interest by educators in supposedly "new and better" approaches to classroom management is testimony to the complexities of both managing children's social and academic behavior in and out of the classroom, and the elusiveness of finding a method that works and fits each teacher's management and teaching disposition.

In this text, we too offer another approach to thinking about classroom and behavior management. We do it with some reluctance in light of the range of "new" approaches to classroom management noted earlier. However, our reluctance reflects in part the fact that the approach we offer is different, but not altogether unfamiliar. In fact, the procedures may look so familiar that they don't look at all different from the typical classroom practice of *behavior management*. These qualifiers notwithstanding, the approach we describe is greatly different conceptually, theoretically, and philosophically because it is concerned with *instruction* and is based on the instructional requirements for managing and organizing behavior. While the general requirements of instruction are obviously familiar to practitioners, what may be the most challenging is the subtle, yet enormous shift in how teachers think about instruction in the context of managing children's social and academic behavior.

Literary folklore claims that Mark Twain once remarked, "The difference between the almost right word and the right word is really a large matter—'tis the difference between the lightning bug and the lightning." The difference between behavior management (or a strict behavioral approach to classroom management) and instructional management is significant, not unlike the difference between the lightning bug and the lightning. Specifically, a one-word, semantic change (e.g., *lightning bug* vs. *lightning*) may appear to be subtle and insignificant, but it represents in fact a very significant change in meaning. Likewise, the semantic difference between behavior management and instructional management is also a subtle but significant change in thinking about instruction, children's behavior, teaching, and the context of instruction itself. In fact, the difference is perhaps best captured in the words *reactive* and *proactive*.

In this text, we argue that the primary difference between an instructional approach to classroom management and *all* other approaches (notice: *all* other approaches; not some, or a few, but all), including the new approaches listed earlier, is that an instructional approach is *proactive*. This means that *before* an action or problem occurs, ***the teacher teaches carefully and strategically all that is required so that students will have the information necessary to behave appropriately.*** More importantly, the teacher's teaching systematically sets up numerous opportunities for reinforcing what's been taught and directly communicating to students how well they are doing as reflective and problem-solving school citizens.

Teaching carefully and strategically all that is required for students to behave appropriately doesn't sound too different from what most, if not all, teachers are doing right now. However, the shift in a teacher's focus and thinking on a day-to-day basis is significant and necessary if instructional management is to succeed.

The basic assumption of the instructional classroom management (ICM) approach that we propose in this text is that teachers must first *teach* students how to behave in *every* circumstance for which the teacher expects appropriate behavior. This may appear to be a tall order, but it's not; in fact, it represents exactly what we expect of ourselves as teachers—to teach. More importantly, the opportunities to create new ways of behaving are initiated by the teacher, who by teaching takes advantage of those opportunities to reinforce newly taught behaviors, actions, and events.

In contrast to a proactive instructional approach to classroom management are those that can be characterized as behavioral, psychological, and social approaches to classroom management, all of which are basically *reactive*. In reactive approaches, the teacher intervenes only *after* an inappropriate action occurs—for example, after a child shouts out an answer, or after students come into the classroom in a noisy and disruptive manner, or after students are caught cheating on homework. The list is indeed endless. In short, the teacher simply "acts back" and fails to prepare the learner for opportunities to demonstrate successfully skills taught *before* "appropriate behavior" is expected or prompted by the environment. Although an instructional approach is concerned with teaching and not simply reacting to problems, it is difficult to appreciate fully how different this approach is from traditional approaches to classroom management.

Many of the requirements of effective classroom management are obvious and are known intuitively and experientially by teachers and school administrators. For example, we know about the importance of (a) developing and setting rules on the first day of school; (b) establishing acceptable limits of social behavior in the classroom, school halls, bathroom, playground, school bus, and cafeteria; (c) praising acceptable behavior while providing explicit and sometimes immediate consequences for unacceptable behavior; (d) providing consistent consequences for unacceptable behaviors when they surface; (e) maintaining clear and consistent expectations of student behavior throughout the entire school year; (f) creating and nurturing a positive, engaging, and safe classroom environment that encourages students to take academic risks and doesn't punish them for making mistakes; and so forth.

However, what is less obvious is that these same procedures that are known intuitively by teachers and school administrators are more than simply classroom and behavior management procedures. They are, first and foremost, *instructional procedures*. When teachers manage [i.e., handle, direct, govern, control, see *The Random House College Dictionary*, p. 811] social behavior, they assume that students have been taught or know instinctively how to act (or not act), react, move, respond, acknowledge, gesture, and, in general, behave. If students don't know (i.e., the information is not understandably clear, and the student is left without a sense of certainty) how to behave, then they must be taught how to behave or meet the expectations of the environment that is placing demands on them. In the absence of this information and teaching, the "management" of human beings who don't know how to behave is, at best, chaotic. Therefore, managing social behavior is not simply a matter of managing students' behavior within a social context through the timely delivery or withdrawal of praise (reinforcers) and reprimands (punishers).

For all practical purposes, classroom management is instructional management. But this way of thinking about classroom management is often lost or ignored in the research, even when it is made by those who have studied this subject in a substantial and serious way. For example, in interviews with classroom teachers, Brophy and his colleagues (cited in Wong, Kauffman, & Lloyd 1991) found that "teachers rated by their principals as more effective in dealing with chronic behavior problems reported using interventions that *teach* students how to behave. That is, they said they usually tried to teach misbehaving students something about how to behave appropriately, not just assert their authority or control over students" (p. 109, emphasis added). Clearly, the role of teaching is profoundly important in classroom and behavior management approaches. However, what's been missing from the genre of classroom management approaches is an approach that has as its core and foundation, teaching or instruction. As Figure 1.1 shows, instruction is the anchoring concept in instructional classroom management.

Whether a teacher is preparing a unit with an academic focus, or planning to teach students a specific aspect of the classroom management program, the basis for each is instruction. Simply, the teacher must consider instructional variables such as task history, response form, task schedule, and task complexity when planning instruction. The instructional focus of the Instructional Classroom Management approach differentiates it from other behavior management approaches.

Context of Instruction

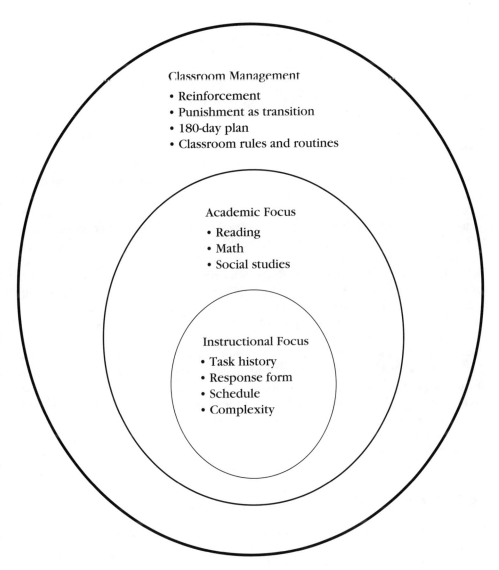

Classroom Management
- Reinforcement
- Punishment as transition
- 180-day plan
- Classroom rules and routines

Academic Focus
- Reading
- Math
- Social studies

Instructional Focus
- Task history
- Response form
- Schedule
- Complexity

FIGURE 1.1 Relation of classroom management to instruction

MANAGEMENT AND THE CONTEXT OF INSTRUCTION

Classroom management *always* takes place within the context of instruction—a context in which information (Toffler 1990) is always changing hands or being clarified and exchanged between the teacher and students, between student and student, and between teachers and administrators and parents, and so on. In this context, the teacher designs and sends a message to a student about what is acceptable and unacceptable behavior. The message could be straightforward and simple, such as, "Thanks for parking your bike at the bicycle rack," or the message could be general and abstract, such as, "You are expected to use respectful language at all times in school." If the message is reasonably clear, the student receives the message and interprets it based on his or her experience, disposition, background knowledge, prior learning history, and the immediate social context. In short, the student attempts to assign meaning to the message. In the process of instruction, the teacher is responsible for sending clear, unambiguous messages to students, not only about unfamiliar academic concepts, such as those in science (e.g., learning about friction and machines), reading (e.g., discerning the theme of Jack London's "To Build a Fire"), math (e.g., finding prime factors), and social studies (e.g., learning why the Mormons moved to Utah), but also about what are assumed to be "familiar" concepts of acceptable social behavior in the school environment (e.g., "You are expected to use respectful language at all times in school"). The substance of these messages, as well as their clarity, frequency, intensity, accuracy, and sincerity, comprise the *process of instruction*. Therefore, the teacher must design the communication of these messages in ways that increase the probability that students will receive clear and unambiguous signals about how to behave, both socially and academically. For some students, this instruction need only be completed once or twice to change behavior successfully. However, for some students, such as students with behavior disorders who have a history of acting-out, the instructional procedures must be intensive, ongoing, and carefully designed.

ORIENTATION OF THE TEXT

The information on the instructional approach to classroom management provided in this text is introductory. This text offers a starting point for thinking about instructional classroom management and several general strategies for rethinking and reorganizing regular and special education classrooms to reflect an instructional classroom management approach.

Our orientation in this text is on the instructional process for managing behavior and not only on the management process for merely reinforcing (increasing), shaping (gradually increasing), or punishing (decreasing) behavior. We do not view or treat classroom management as a set of conditions and activities that is separate and distinct from instruction. When teachers manage, they also teach or communicate information to students about how to behave (or not behave). By thinking about classroom management and classroom instruction as being parts of the same process, overall, teaching is likely to be clearer, more focused and balanced, more sustaining, and more enriching for both teachers and students over the course of an entire school year.

The approach we offer in this text assumes that the teacher first teaches students, thoroughly and carefully, how to behave. In essence, the teacher provides all the necessary information to students about what is appropriate in both the school and classroom settings. Although managing and controlling student behaviors are part of the instructional management process, our primary emphasis is on instruction, not management. At first glance, this difference in emphasis may seem small, uninteresting, and perhaps trivial, but it is not. As noted earlier, the differences between behavior management and instructional management are profound.

THINKING ABOUT BEHAVIOR MANAGEMENT

One important difference between instructional classroom management and behavior management is how so-called behavior or management problems are conceptualized or thought about (Kameenui & Simmons 1990). Specifically, Colvin and Sugai (1988) argue that educators (i.e., administrators, teachers, teacher trainers) often approach instructional problems differently from social behavior problems. For example, when a student makes a persistent error on a complex reading comprehension skill, such as identifying the main idea in a passage, we could engage in a range of instructional strategies. We might prompt the student to scan and reread a particular passage in the story (Carnine, Silbert, & Kameenui 1990), or we might engage in a facilitative questioning procedure (Carnine, Stevens, Clements, & Kameenui 1982) to assist the reader to think through the various propositions in the passage. Following this teacher assistance, we might provide more practice and review for the student on a range of passages. If the errors persist, then additional remedial steps can be taken to diagnose the problem and rearrange the teaching presentation or lesson and the schedule of instruction in ways that allow the student to succeed.

All of these steps are taken to ensure that the child will succeed, because the teacher has conceptualized the problem or student's error as an academic learning problem and not as a management one. In contrast, when a social behavior problem occurs, we frequently respond in a very different way. When a student breaks a classroom rule, such as calling out an answer without raising a hand, the instinctive response is to "punish" the rule breaker by using a verbal reprimand (e.g., "You need to raise your hand; c'mon you know the rules!"). In some cases, we might even ask the student to leave the room (e.g., "How many times have I told you to raise your hand? I think it's time for you to sit out in the hall and think about how to behave the right way"). The underlying assumption of these approaches is that the negative consequences are likely to change the child's future behavior. Specifically, by removing the student from the class-room, the student will behave appropriately in the future in order to return to the classroom. The approach is clearly reactive, not proactive. In many cases, when one negative consequence doesn't work (e.g., verbal reprimand), the teacher typically increases the level of negative consequences (e.g., exclusion-ary time-out, detention) (Sugai 1992).

Of course, the responses to any kind of perceived misbehavior vary consid-erably from teacher to teacher. For example, one teacher may choose to ignore the inappropriate behavior, while another teacher chooses to praise a behavior that is incompatible with the misbehavior (e.g., praise a student who raises a hand), and still another teacher may choose to acknowledge the behavior with a long, stern, nonverbal glare at the bewildered violator. No matter how different the apparent responses are in their physical action (e.g., verbal praise, glare), they are the same in at least four very important ways. The responses are all: (a) reactive (i.e., the teacher acts only after the behavior occurs); (b) predicated on the assumption that the learner already *knows* (i.e., understands clearly and with certainty) how to respond appropriately; (c) the learner is *capable* of responding appropriately; and (d) the negative consequence will increase the likelihood that the inappropriate behavior will not surface (or will surface less frequently) in the future.

Table 1.1 summarizes the differences between the approach to academic problems and the approach to social problems as described by Colvin and Sugai (1988).

Can't versus Won't Problems

The basic difference between an instructional approach to an academic error and a noninstructional approach to a social error is how we think about it. When a learner makes an academic error (e.g., learner can't name the thirteenth presi-dent of the United States), we usually think about it as a *can't* problem; that is, we assume the learner simply doesn't know the answer and, therefore, can't respond correctly (Kameenui & Simmons 1990). We make the reasonable assump-tion that it's impossible for the learner to come up suddenly with the answer, just as it is impossible for the learner to walk through a concrete wall. The assumption is well founded and we give it no second thought. The primary solu-tion to the learner's lack of knowledge is to tell him or her the answer, or to develop a teaching strategy or problem-solving sequence that will communicate the skills needed to answer the question that was previously deemed unanswer-able by the student.

On the other hand, if a learner misbehaves, we usually assume that the prob-lem is a *won't* problem; that is, the learner knows how to behave or knows the correct response but simply chooses not to behave appropriately or respond correctly. The image that comes to mind is of the learner standing firm and replying, "No, I won't do it. I *can* do it, but I won't!"

TABLE 1.1 A comparison of approaches to academic and social problems

Frequency of Error	Procedures for Academic Problem	Procedures for Social Problem
Infrequent	Assume student is trying to make a correct response.	Assume student is not trying to make a correct response.
	Assume error was accidental. Provide assistance (model-lead-test).	Assume error was deliberate. Provide negative consequence.
	Provide practice. Assume student has learned skills and will perform correctly in the future.	Practice not required. Assume student will make right choice and behave appropriately in future.
Frequent (Chronic)	Assume student has learned the wrong way.	Assume student refuses to cooperate.
	Assume student has been taught (inadvertently) the wrong way.	Assume student knows what is right and has been told often.
	Diagnose the problem.	Provide more negative consequences.
	Identify misrule.	Withdraw student from normal context.
	Adjust presentation. Focus on rule. Provide feedback. Provide more practice and review.	Maintain student removal from normal context.
	Assume student has been taught skill and will perform correctly in future.	Assume student has "learned" lesson and will behave appropriately in future.

Understanding the difference between a *can't* problem and a *won't* problem is important because a misdiagnosis can cause serious management and learning problems, in the short run and in the long run. Specifically, if we treat a can't problem as a won't problem (i.e., we assume the learner *can* do what we're asking, when in fact the learner can't), then we end up unfairly punishing the learner and losing any trust necessary for effective instruction. In contrast, if we treat a won't problem as a can't problem (i.e., we assume the learner can't do what we're asking, when in fact the learner *can*), then we end up unfairly reinforcing the learner's prior history of deception and agitation. Moreover, we end up losing any authority necessary to effective instructional management. In addition, we allow the learner to avoid substantial learning responsibility.

By thinking about and approaching social behavior errors or problems from an instructional point of view, we guard against the potential misdiagnosis of both can't and won't types of problems because we engage in a set of decision rules that examines a child's misbehavior within an instructional context. By viewing potential behavior problems as instructional, the teacher knows what skills have been taught, reviewed, and mastered, just as a teacher knows what specific reading or mathematics skills or operations have been taught, reviewed, and mastered. Specifically, a teacher wouldn't require a child, for example, to work multidigit subtraction problems involving renaming if the teacher knew that the student had not mastered the component prerequisite skills (e.g., knowledge of basic facts, numeral identification, the concepts of more than and less than) (Kameenui & Simmons 1990). By knowing what has been taught, what needs to be taught, and what the learner already knows, the teacher avoids the pitfalls of both can't and won't problems.

Schwartz and Lacey (1982) argue that, "How we understand an event can have a dramatic impact on what we do about it" (p. 2). Certainly how we *think we understand* a problem influences how we act on that problem. As noted earlier, if we understand a problem to be a *can't* problem, we are likely to act differently than if we understand the same problem as a *won't* problem.

To appreciate the instructional approach to classroom management, consider the problem of lying. Lying is not generally thought of as an instructional problem (Kameenui & Simmons 1990). Instead, it is typically viewed as representing a devious social misbehavior, akin to a fundamental character flaw. The problem of lying is a tricky one to "manage" for at least three reasons: (1) it generally represents a low frequency behavior, (2) it is difficult to discern where truth ends and lying actually begins, and (3) we typically respond to episodes of lying only *after* a child has lied. As Sprick (1981) points out, children typically lie to avoid punishment or gain attention.

To punish a child for lying is to make at least one very clear assumption: The child knows what it means to tell the truth. Interestingly and not surprisingly, rarely is this assumption ever tested. A child who lies may simply not know what it means to tell the truth in much the same way a child who misreads the word *paint* may not know how to read *ai* vowel combinations in the middle of CVVCC words (C = consonant, V = vowel). In other words, what is perceived, accepted, and treated as a won't problem (i.e., not telling the truth), may actually be a can't problem (i.e., not knowing what it means to tell the truth). In short, no matter how much a child wants to tell the truth, the child simply doesn't know what it means to tell the truth; that is, under what conditions the truth and nothing but the full truth is to be told and the full range of circumstances that are associated with truth telling.

Kameenui and Simmons (1990) provide a partial beginning teaching sequence to teach the skill of telling the truth. The teaching sequence consists of the teacher requiring a learner to perform some rather obvious and unchallenging tasks, such as picking up a pencil on a desk or walking to a spot in the classroom and returning to the teacher. The teacher frames the teaching sequence by telling the learner that he or she will be asked to perform some silly actions and report the actions by telling "exactly what he or she did." After performing a request (e.g., picking up a green pencil and returning it to the teacher), the teacher asks the child to describe the act exactly (e.g., "I walked over to your desk and picked up the green pencil and brought it to you."). After the child describes exactly what was done, the teacher responds with a rule: "When you tell someone exactly what you did, you are telling the truth. You just told me exactly what you did, so you told me the truth."

Although the "truth telling" teaching sequence is incomplete and represents only the beginnings of an instructional strategy for this significant problem, it demonstrates that the way we respond to a management problem depends in part on how we come to understand and represent the problem.

Personal Teaching Efficacy and Instructional Management

As we noted, the actions we take as teachers depend in large part on how we choose to understand a problem, whether it's a problem of lying or decoding single syllable words. The knowledge of teaching—knowledge of subject matter (e.g., science, reading), pedagogy, instructional procedures—that a teacher brings to the classroom is certainly important to being an effective teacher. However, a teacher's perception of his or her ability to affect how children learn and behave is also important. A teacher's personal teaching efficacy (Smylie 1989), that is, a teacher's judgment of his or her capacity to significantly influence how children learn, appears to be based on the teachers' beliefs regarding the process and outcomes associated with teaching. For example, Smylie (1988) found that a teacher's personal teaching efficacy was influenced by the "concentration" of low-performing students in the classroom. That is, the higher the number of low performers in the classroom, the less certain teachers felt about their ability to influence learning and achievement.

Based on Smylie's study and the research on teacher efficacy (Gibson & Dembo 1984), it appears that what teachers believe about their ability to make a difference in what students learn and how they behave is important. If teachers believe they can make a difference, they usually do. A teacher's "psychological state," as Smylie noted, and more specifically what a teacher believes about the learner, the teaching context, and the teacher's role in the schooling process appears to influence student performance. In the next section, we examine some of the beliefs and assumptions that are associated with an instructional approach to classroom management.

ASSUMPTIONS ABOUT INSTRUCTIONAL MANAGEMENT

We propose a set of beliefs that we consider to be important to an instructional approach to classroom management. We characterize these beliefs as assumptions because they represent the premises upon which an instructional approach to classroom management is built. These assumptions provide the teacher with a foundation for managing children within the broader context of instruction. By holding to these assumptions, we believe that teachers will be able to identify behavior problems in ways that translate into instructional solutions.

What is important is not only the assumptions, but also the process of reflection and professional commitment implied by these assumptions—a process in which the teacher selectively and intentionally drives some pedagogical or philosophical "stakes" into the ground and announces, "These are my beliefs. They are important to me as a professional and a teacher and will serve to guide my performance as a teacher." In a sense, the assumptions reflect the teacher's commitment to the teaching profession and to *all* children, irrespective of their diverse learning and curricular needs.

The assumptions are developed in two different areas of the teaching and schooling context that include the learner and the teacher. For each context, three assumptions are described. Of course, more assumptions can be developed about each context, but for this text's purposes, we begin with these. The assumptions presented here are merely representative of the considerations teachers should give to each context.

The first set of assumptions concerns the learner and examines how the teacher should view the learner.

Assumptions about the Learner

The first assumption we make about the learner is:

Assumption 1: The learner should always be treated with respect.

This assumption represents a truism in education, but it is one that is easily forgotten when serious behavior management problems begin to surface, or when a learner, saddled with a history of academic or social failure, continues to make very little progress in school. In situations such as these, the temptation to "blame the learner" is great, and the effort required to overcome the predisposition to simply give up on the learner is even greater.

Treating the learner with respect when he or she is behaving appropriately is not a challenge. However, when the learner is disruptive, abusive, deceptive, inconsiderate, threatening, menacing, or in the colloquialism of the modern street culture, "in your face," then it is certainly a challenge to treat the learner with respect. Specifically, respectful treatment means at the very minimum, not responding to inappropriate behavior by physically or verbally assaulting a student. In some rare cases, students may need to be physically restrained, but even under these conditions, the restraining must be conducted in a professional manner that respects the student. Unfortunately, situations that involve verbal or physical threats are very difficult for teachers, because the "heat" of the moment typically prompts teachers to respond in a heated way, which is understandable. However, these are unusual circumstances that require "unusually" controlled responses from teachers.

Assumption 2: Every learner has the capacity to learn.

An instructional approach to classroom management requires, at the very minimum, that teachers hold to the assumption that every learner has the capacity to learn. Notice that the assumption says "every learner" and does not refer to "some" learners or the "average" learner. In this case, *every* means each individual in the classroom, irrespective of accompanying social and educational labels, prior school history, family circumstance, or daily attire. Simply, every individual has the capacity to learn what is being communicated in the classroom. In the absence of this assumption, an instructional approach to classroom management that is based on clear and effective communication of information is meaningless. If the information is not acquired, retained, or recalled by students, then both the content and delivery of the information must be reexamined by the teacher to ensure that *all* learners acquire, retain, and recall the information. However, the burden to communicate the information clearly and effectively in this case is placed on the teacher, not the student. In short, the teacher makes every effort to explore the instructional remedies that are available within his or her province, and in doing so, refrains from blaming the learner for failure in teaching or learning.

This assumption represents another truism or slogan that is frequently and vociferously cited in educational circles. Holding to this assumption, however, is not easy and will require an instructional tenacity that thinks about students' performance in a different way. Specifically, it will require framing problems in terms of instruction and not in terms of a learner's ability, learning style, motivation, predisposition, or learning history. As Kameenui and Simmons (1990) note, "To assume that a problem is inherent in the learner leaves the teacher without any influence, because the problem is framed as being outside of the teacher's province of control (i.e., in the learner's head)" (p. 13).

Assumption 3: The learner's behavior is purposeful, strategic, and intelligent.

It seems that a rather basic human predisposition is the need to feel valued. As such, human beings engage in activities and events that are likely to be rewarding to them in both the short term and long term. However, one of the oddities of human behavior is that we often repeatedly engage in behaviors that do not appear to be rewarding and valued. This is particularly true of children who have significant histories of academic and social failure. For example, a child who has failed repeatedly, as the child who has succeeded repeatedly, learns from the experience and understands, in a shrewd and perceptive way, the circumstances of his or her own failure and what works best for him or her in a particular context. If a behavior or a series of behaviors that lead to some kind of punishment is repeated by a learner, it is safe to assume that the consequences of the behavior are valued or reinforcing for the learner in some way. A specific example is that of a child who does something that appears to be "crazy," such as hitting a teacher. While this behavior may appear to be crazy, it is for the learner purposeful, strategic, and intelligent, primarily because in the long run, the learner fundamentally changes how the environment will respond. In this particular case, the learner notices readily that the teacher places less academic and social demands on her, avoids potentially troublesome situations, and simply leaves her alone. What initially appeared crazy might be viewed as purposeful and intelligent by the learner.

By viewing the learner's behavior as purposeful, strategic, and intelligent, we position ourselves in a way that is reflective and allows for problem solving, because it broadens the context in which responses to a child's behavior are considered. By viewing a response as intelligent, instead of crazy, we are immediately prompted to problem solve by considering the ways in which the specific response best serves the learner. Likewise, we are positioned to determine how best to respond to the perceived unintelligent behavior in an equally purposeful, strategic, and intelligent manner.

Assumptions about the Teacher

The assumptions described in this section relate to how teachers should view their profession, their role as significant forces in the lives of children, and themselves.

Assumption 1: The teacher makes a difference in how, what, when, and why students learn.

Most people are able to identify by name a teacher who made a profound difference in their schooling experiences. This difference, however, can be profoundly good or profoundly bad. Ernest Boyer (1990), the former U.S. commissioner of education and current president of the Carnegie Foundation for the Advancement of Teaching, noted that, "The harsh truth is that teaching in this nation is imperiled. There are poor teachers, to be sure, and one bad teacher is more dangerous than one bad surgeon, because a surgeon can only hurt one person at a time. But good teachers outnumber the bad . . ." (p. 3).

Not surprisingly, what makes a teacher "good" or "bad" is constantly debated, even though some characteristics of good teachers (or bad teachers, for that matter) are intuitive and straightforward. Interestingly, the research on teachers' perceptions of their ability to make a difference in children's learning suggests that what teachers believe about their role and ability to bring about change influences how and what they teach. For example, Smylie (1988) notes that "Teachers' perceptions of their own ability to affect student learning have been associated with their choice of classroom management and instructional strategies" (p. 6). Specifically, teachers are more likely to change their behavior to improve their classroom practice if they believe that they are instrumental in student learning. In order for teachers to feel instrumental in their students' learning, they must be certain of their practices, and they must hold a high sense of "personal teaching efficacy"; that is, they must believe that they have the capacity to directly affect a student's performance. Simply put, if teachers feel competent and confident in their teaching tools and instructional strategies, they are likely to make a profound and positive difference in how, what, when, and why students learn.

The Nonreciprocal Laws of Expectations state that negative expectations yield negative results. The corollary of this law suggests that positive expectations yield positive results. If teachers believe they can make a difference in children's school performance, then they very likely will.

In addition to teachers' beliefs, the recent research on staff development also suggests that several other conditions are necessary to bring about significant and sustained educational improvements. These include, for example, (a) the importance of strong support for teachers from both principals and superintendents (Berman & McLaughlin 1977), (b) collegial support (Little 1982), and (c) strong instructional leadership at the school and classroom level. While support of teachers at every level of the school process is important, the substantial convergence of the research continues to support one clear and simple fact: Teachers engaged in the teaching process do make a difference. Similarly, *not* teaching also makes a difference. If we were to dispense with the teaching of beginning reading or of mathematics altogether, would there be any question as to outcomes?

Assumption 2: Good teaching involves creating as many opportunities as possible for successful learning.

Most models of school learning include as an important component the opportunities that schools provide for learning. The logic to these models is rather straightforward: The quantity and quality of learning opportunities are related directly to successful student performance in school. For example, Carroll's (1963) economics model of the school learning process argues that "the learner will succeed in learning a given task to the extent that he spends the amount of time that he *needs* to learn the task" (p. 725).

The assumption we propose acknowledges that teaching involves creating opportunities for successful learning. Of course, these opportunities go beyond the typical teaching schedule in which specific blocks of time are allocated for the teaching of basic subject matter (e.g., reading, mathematics, social studies). An instructional approach to classroom management requires that teachers maximize both the "scheduled" and the "unscheduled" opportunities for learning. More importantly, however, this assumption requires a different way of thinking about managing and organizing instruction. For example, consider a definition of positive reinforcement, which Wolery, Bailey, and Sugai (1988) define as "the contingent presentation of a stimulus following a response that results in an increase in the future occurrence of the response" (p. 235).

Definitions of positive reinforcement from a behavioral perspective on classroom management are not likely to vary greatly. For the most part, positive reinforcement has two essential but limiting features: (1) the power of a reinforcer can only be determined by what happens to a child's response in the *future*, and (2) the teacher's response always *follows* the student's response. These two features are noteworthy because they bring into clear perspective the possible limitations of a behavioral approach and, concomitantly, the advantages of an instructional approach to classroom management. Specifically, if we are concerned with increasing the likelihood that a response will occur again in the future, then the more opportunities we create to influence the learner's behavior, the more likely the target behavior will occur in the future. Instructional classroom management requires the creation of as many as possible opportunities for successful learning.

The other feature of a behavioral approach is that reinforcement always *follows* the learner's response, which suggests that the learner must "emit" a response in order for reinforcement to take place. In short, reinforcement, when viewed from the consequent side of the operant model and not the antecedent side, is *reactive,* not proactive. An instructional approach to positive reinforcement acknowledges this feature by (a) first teaching students what should be reinforced; (b) increasing the opportunities to practice what was taught, which also involves reinforcement; and (c) priming the context for reinforcement through a set of "preteaching" or "precorrection" and "framing" instructional procedures. These procedures and the analysis of reinforcement will be discussed further in chapter 3.

Interestingly, these two positive reinforcement features represent the hallmarks of a behavioral approach to managing behavior. By understanding the requirements and dynamics of reinforcement, we can appreciate the power of instruction and how reinforcement enhances successful learning.

Assumption 3: Effective teaching enhances what the learner already knows and enables the learner to do things that could not be done before.

This assumption is borrowed from Kameenui and Simmons (1990), who recognize "the often unacknowledged and unspoken power and influence a teacher holds in the teaching context" (p. 10). The assumption clearly underscores the importance of the schooling process and is predicated on the simple proposition that schools are designed to take a learner from a state of "unknowing" or partial knowing to a state of full and complete "knowing." This analysis is admittedly an oversimplification of the complexities inherent in the processes of teaching, learning, and schooling. However, to understand the full measure of these complexities requires occasionally applying some "simplifying assumptions" (Carroll 1963, p. 724).

In a simple but poignant way, this assumption captures the potential excitement and power of what successful teaching is all about, that is, the simple notion that we can come to know something entirely new that was simply not known before. Or we can come to know something more fully that once was known in only a partial way. This new state of knowing is limitless and obviously includes the full range of human experience and knowledge—from reading simple words (e.g., *sat, am, bit*), to understanding the complexities of words such as contronym, eonomine, and hendiadys; from naming a pair of pliers as a tool, to identifying it as a first-class lever; from knowing nothing of Shakespeare's play *King Lear*, to explaining its significance as a tragedy; from identifying an event, to understanding its significance in terms of probability theory. The list is endless.

SUMMARY

In this chapter, we presented a rationale for what we characterize as an Instructional Classroom Management approach. We argued that when teachers manage behavior, they also teach. Behavior management procedures are by their very nature, instructional procedures, because management always takes place in the context of instruction. The basic assumption of this approach is that teachers must first teach students how to behave in every situation for which appropriate behavior is expected. We recognize that this shift in thinking about management as instruction is not easy. It will require teachers to examine the assumptions they make about the learner, the context of instruction, and the significant role that teachers play in the daily lives of children.

CHAPTER ACTIVITIES

1. Discuss the differences between instructional classroom management and other approaches to classroom management.
2. Describe the differences between solving academic problems and social problems for (a) infrequent errors and (b) frequent errors.
3. Develop your own set of assumptions for instructional classroom management, the learner, and the teacher.

SUGGESTED READINGS

Brandt, R. (1990). Restructuring: What is it. [Special issue]. *Educational Leadership, 47* (7).

Grossnickle, D. R. (1990). *Preventative discipline for effective teaching and learning: A Sourcebook for teachers and administrators.* Reston, VA: National Association of Secondary School Principals.

Major, R. (1990). *Discipline: The most important subject we teach.* Lanham, MD: University Press of America.

Reynolds, M. C., & Lakin, K. J. C. (1987). Noncategorical special education: Models for research and practice. In M. Wang, M. C. Reynolds, & H. Walberg (Eds.), *Handbook of special education: Research and practice* (pp. 331-356). New York: Pergamon.

chapter 2

Prominent Approaches to Classroom Management

INTRODUCTION

In the first part of this chapter, we describe the essential elements of effective classroom management. By looking critically at current classroom management approaches, we are best able to develop new, more powerful and versatile approaches to managing student behavior in the classroom.

In the second part of the chapter, we examine four current, popular approaches to classroom management: (1) Behavior Modification, (2) Assertive Discipline, (3) Teacher Effectiveness Training, and (4) Cooperative Discipline. Following a description of each approach, we evaluate each method according to the essential elements of an effective classroom management program described earlier. After a discussion of the characteristics and theoretical basis for each of these classroom management approaches, we present the assumptions upon which each of the approaches is based. In addition, we highlight an example of how each management approach is generally used by teachers. Finally, we conclude each analysis with a discussion of the advantages and disadvantages of the classroom management approach.

ESSENTIAL ELEMENTS OF EFFECTIVE CLASSROOM MANAGEMENT

What characterizes the most effective classroom management program and what should teachers look for when they consider using it? The guidelines in the following list give an overview of the important characteristics of an instructional classroom management program and the questions teachers might ask when considering various approaches. As we noted, an approach must be effective in controlling behavior, useful and easy to implement, adaptable to different teaching situations, and appropriately aligned with the teacher's ongoing instructional program. The four guidelines are: (1) effectiveness, (2) usefulness, (3) adaptability, and (4) alignment to instruction. Specific questions for each guideline are also provided. The application of each guideline allows the teacher to assess the overall effectiveness of a management approach. The extent to which a management procedure meets standards under each of the guidelines will determine the utility of that approach. A discussion of each of these characteristics is presented in the following list.

Guidelines for Evaluating Classroom Management Approaches

Effectiveness
- Are students taught appropriate behavior with reinforcement?
- Is there adequate time provided for learning?
- Is the management program proactive? Does it prevent problems?
- Is there a link between effective instruction and management?
- Is punishment used only as a transition tool for the teacher?

Usefulness
- Is the approach useful for the 180-day school year?
- Is the approach programmatic?
- Is the approach useful in a variety of learning contexts?

- Is a framework for instructional assessment of the classroom required?
- Is the teacher given specific guidelines on how to implement the instructional management techniques?

Adaptability
- Can regular and special education teachers use the approach?
- Can the approach be used with students of various age and ability levels?
- Can teachers with different orientations use the approach?
- Is the program adaptable to different content areas?
- Are guidelines provided for managing academic and nonacademic activities?

Alignment with Instruction
- Does the approach utilize techniques of effective instruction?
- Will the management program increase academic performance?
- Is disruptive behavior considered a problem of instruction?
- Is appropriate behavior specifically taught to students?
- Are there guidelines for how to manage extreme forms of disruptive behavior?

Proactive Management Techniques
- Are students taught to behave in the classroom?
- Are management procedures implemented before behavior problems occur?
- Are students taught a set of classroom rules and routines?
- Are tasks analyzed for potential learning & behavioral problems?
- Are assessment procedures used to monitor performance?

Effectiveness

In a recent article about effective instructional techniques, Anderson and Armbruster (1990) discussed how teachers should first consider both the task and the learner before introducing an instructional activity. The teacher must, they stated, "provide just the right amount of coaching or support so the students will succeed at performing the target task, but only by stretching their competence. With too little challenge, students will not achieve maximum growth; with too much challenge, they will become discouraged and dependent" (p. 403). Effective classroom management is characterized by a balance between instruction and management. Teachers can achieve this balance by integrating classroom management into their regular academic program, and by thinking that instruction is the solution to disruptive behavior. Teachers must use an instructional model that is flexible and adaptable for students with different abilities. It is important that a classroom management approach be generalizable to different teaching contexts. The most effective classroom management approach is one that not only controls disruptive behavior, but increases student academic performance as well.

Usefulness

The most effective classroom management program is implemented by teachers for the entire school year and for every instructional context. Ideally, the system is started the first day of school and continues each month of the school year. This system allows for program adjustments based on the time of the school year and the objectives of the teacher. Also, a useful management system should be effective in controlling all types of disruptive behavior, from mild disruption, to the most severe behavior problems. In addition, the approach must be user friendly, that is, relatively easy for the teacher to implement during instruction. The most powerful classroom management approaches are useless to teachers if they are excessively complex. A useful program provides the teacher with specific guidelines for implementation. In this sense, useful management programs are similar in design to many curriculum programs because they address the details of instruction.

Adaptability

Because of the complex nature of classrooms, a classroom management program must be adaptable to different circumstances. If a system is not flexible enough to be used in a variety of classes and contexts with students of different abilities, then the program will be of little use to teachers. Consequently, an adaptable program must provide a thorough assessment of the learning environment. This allows the teacher to tailor the management program to individual classroom needs.

Alignment with Instruction

Another guideline teachers should consider when evaluating a management program is whether the program can be integrated into the teacher's daily teaching activities. Teachers need to consider whether the management program helps them improve the overall performance of the students, including social behavior and academics. An important consideration for teachers is whether or not the system utilizes sound principles of instruction. If a management program is not aligned with the instructional program, a teacher will not maximize the student's academic achievement. It is important for a teacher to note whether the classroom management system can be easily integrated into daily teaching in the content areas.

Proactive Management Techniques

The final guideline consideration is whether an approach allows teachers to proactively manage their classrooms. For example, are procedures in place to decrease the probability that behavior problems will occur in the classroom? Also, at the beginning of the school year, are students presented with specific class-room rules? Are students taught specifically how to follow all rules and classroom routines? By implementing each of these components, an approach more effectively stresses prevention over remediation.

In the next section of the chapter, we review four current and popular approaches to classroom management. Following each description, we evaluate the approach using the four essential elements previously described.

POPULAR APPROACHES TO CLASSROOM MANAGEMENT

Behavior Modification

Behavior modification is a familiar term to most practitioners. However, it is also known by various other names, such as applied behavior analysis, behavioral analysis, M & M therapy, and so on. In general, the terms refer to the various methods derived from learning theory that are used to modify student response. Behavior modification is characterized by the practical application of the principles of operant conditioning, made popular by B. F. Skinner (1971), and it is widely used in education.

The first use of behavior modification with children occurred in the 1960s and continued to be developed and refined in the 1970s. Application of behavior modification to some of society's most difficult problems characterized the discipline in the 1980s. Early use of behavior modification was designed to "verify that the principles of operant conditioning that were shown to govern animal behavior also governed human behavior" (Rusch, Rose, & Greenwood 1988, p. 35). Once this relationship was established, the practical application of behavior modification to the problems faced by the mentally retarded, delinquents, and the emotionally disturbed was demonstrated.

Not surprisingly, behavior modification is especially prevalent in special education. Baer (1988) described the important link between behavior modification and special education: "The application of behavior analysis is almost always educational, in the best and broadest sense of the word; and special education is the branch of education that most requires an applicable analysis of behavior in order to teach" (p. ix). Other learning theory approaches, such as classical or respondent conditioning, are derived from a different theoretical base than behavior modification and have a less prominent role in education.

Theoretical Basis and Characteristics. The basis of behavior modification is that learning results from an interaction of the behavior and environment. The environment includes all events, activities, and situations that precede and follow a response. Conditions that occur just prior to a behavior such as classroom organization, instructional materials, and teacher directions are called *antecedents.* In short, how a teacher arranges the antecedents and the consequences that follow a behavior will determine the future occurrence of that behavior. *Behavior* is defined as any observable, measurable event or action. Using behavior modification, teachers are able to increase appropriate behavior or decrease inappropriate behavior either by adjusting antecedent conditions or by applying reinforcers or punishers.

In the language of behavior modification, the *contingent* application of *consequences* is of primary importance. Consequences refer to actions, events, or words that follow a behavior and are defined only by their effects on that behavior. Consequences can increase, decrease, or have no effect on a behavior.

Reinforcers are consequences (i.e., actions, events, words) that follow and strengthen the behavior of a student and increase the likelihood that the behavior will occur in the future. A teacher who uses positive reinforcement will use a variety of reinforcers (e.g., verbal praise, points, M & M candy) to increase appropriate behavior. At first, reinforcers are most effective if they are applied continuously and immediately *after* the behavior occurs. Such applications make the delivery of the reinforcers "contingent" on the behavior that is demonstrated. Specifically, reinforcement depends on the kind of behavior that is displayed. If an appropriate behavior is demonstrated, then a reinforcer is likely to follow the behavior. If an inappropriate behavior is exhibited, then a reinforcer is *not* likely to follow the behavior.

Like reinforcers, punishers refer to events or actions that follow the occurrence of a behavior. However, a punisher is defined as such only if its application results in *decreasing* the probability that the behaviors will occur in the future. Therefore, if a teacher uses verbal praise to increase students' on-task behavior and the behavior does not increase, then in this instance, verbal praise is *not* a reinforcer. What is a positive reinforcer for one student may not be a positive reinforcer for another student. Punishment is also defined by its impact on a student's behavior. A consequence that decreases a behavior of one student (e.g., verbal reprimand) may have little or no effect on another student.

A behavior modification program incorporates four general procedures: First, the teacher must identify a problem. For example, the teacher might determine that a student has a poor *self-concept.* Second, the problem must be analyzed and explained in terms of observable and measurable behaviors (Baer 1988). For example, a teacher would be required to operationally define self-concept using clear and measurable terms. Specifically, self-concept might be defined as the frequency with which a student smiles, volunteers answers in class, or makes positive self-statements during class.

The third general procedure of behavior modification is that a teacher must systematically arrange the learning environment and apply reinforcement and punishment procedures to modify (i.e., increase or decrease) the occurrence of the behavior in question. The teacher may devise a program that increases or strengthens the frequency of certain behaviors that are already present. Or, the teacher could decrease or weaken the frequency of an inappropriate behavior, or teach an entirely new skill or behavior that the student has never demonstrated (e.g., teaching expressive language to a severely disabled child). Finally, the teacher must record the number of times the behavior occurs to determine the effectiveness of the behavior modification program.

Assumptions.   The underlying assumption of behavior modification is that all behavior, acceptable or unacceptable, is learned. Behaviorists believe that learning is determined in part by the feedback the student receives from the environment. Therefore, a child who is viewed as willful and difficult to manage in the classroom is not considered by a behaviorist to have a genetic predisposition toward disruptive behavior. Instead, the behaviorist assumes that the student can be taught appropriate alternative behaviors.

By applying this assumption, behaviorists believe that students can be taught appropriate behavior, while inappropriate behavior can be reduced and replaced with more acceptable alternatives. Based upon these assumptions, the teacher plays a prominent role in the management of student classroom behavior. Teachers are considered to be in the best position to control consequences directly within the classroom and to teach students appropriate classroom behavior. Less direct approaches to changing student behavior, such as psychoanalytic counseling, are not considered viable options for addressing disruptive behaviors.

Duke and Meckel (1984) point out that just as the conduct of students is controlled by the principles of behavior modification, the teacher's behavior is similarly influenced: ". . . the teachers who utilize Behavior Modification may need to consider their own behavior and how it may be subject to reinforcement from the classroom environment" (p. 16). The underlying assumption is that a prominent feature of behavior modification programs is for the teacher to assess how his or her behavior is influenced, and perhaps controlled, by student behavior.

Even though the behavioral approach focuses on observable and measurable behavior, it does not exclude the role or diminish the importance of the neurological aspects of learning. Wolery, Bailey, and Sugai (1988) stated that "it makes sense to assume" that learning has a neurological basis, and the developmental aspects of learning must be acknowledged when planning an instructional program. However, individuals who are designing and implementing behavior modification programs place "primary emphasis on observable behavior as well as the observable antecedents and consequences to behavior" (p.10).

EXAMPLE: A BEHAVIOR MODIFICATION PROGRAM

Ms. Johnson, an elementary school teacher, has a student named Sara who has a habit of calling out answers during class discussions, often before the teacher has a chance to select students. Ms. Johnson considers this a problem because she is not able to assess the knowledge of the other students in the class. These students also find Sara's behavior obnoxious and perceive her as trying to dominate class discussions.

Ms. Johnson decides to implement a behavior modification program. First, she targets the class in which Sara's disruptive behaviors are most frequent. In order to establish the rate of Sara's call-outs, she decides to count them for several days. When the rate of her call-outs is documented and the stability of the behavior is established, Ms. Johnson develops a two-part intervention plan. First, Ms. Johnson decides to ignore Sara's answers each time she calls out, regardless of whether the answer is correct or not. The teacher is very careful not to respond to Sara's frequent call-outs during social studies. This means that Ms. Johnson must refrain from giving Sara any form of attention, verbal, visual, or physical. If Sara does call out an answer, Ms. Johnson immediately selects another student, who has appropriately raised his or her hand, and states: "Thank you for raising your hand. I appreciate how you follow the rules during class discussion."

In addition to ignoring all call-outs, Ms. Johnson praises Sara each time she raises her hand or waits to be called on before giving an answer. When this occurs, the teacher is very specific in her praise to Sara: "Sara, thank you for raising your hand and not calling out your answer." Throughout class, Ms. Johnson continues her data collection and counts Sara's call-outs. At the end of the class, the teacher records the number of call-outs on a graph that shows the frequency of call-outs before and after the intervention. Ms. Johnson is pleased to note that after implementing the praise-and-ignore strategy, Sara's call-outs decreased significantly.

Advantages and Limitations.   Following is a discussion of the five evaluation guidelines.

Effectiveness.   Literally hundreds of journal reports attest to the effectiveness of behavior modification as a management tool for teachers. Teachers who are motivated and have a background in behavioral training are adept at using behavior modification effectively. Other teachers with less training may find implementation of behavior modification programs more difficult. Because teachers are required to identify the problem to be modified, behavior modification provides teachers a strategy for observing and monitoring behavior in their classrooms. Behavioral programs are well suited for modifying disruptive classroom behavior. These programs are particularly useful for modifying noncompliance and aggressive behaviors. There is also evidence that behavior modification programs can be effective in providing teachers a blueprint for changing more complex academic problem behavior. One potential limitation of behavior modification programs, however, is that the same program is sometimes used for all students in the classroom. While it is possible for a teacher to have several behavior modification programs implemented simultaneously, this requires organization and careful monitoring.

Usefulness.   Teachers who work with disabled or low-performing students will find behavioral programs useful for eliminating disruptive classroom behavior. Behavior modification programs can be useful for preventing behavior and learning problems if they are implemented at the beginning of the school year. The typical behavior modification program is probably less useful when teachers are interested in developing generalization and transfer of skills (Engelmann & Carnine 1982). Another limitation is that most behavior modification programs are not designed to be implemented for the entire 180-day school year and are sometimes used reactively; that is, teachers use specific management techniques only in response to disruptive behavior.

Adaptability. Behavioral procedures can be used to help students of all age and ability levels. The specific guidelines for these programs can be modified to fit most problems that teachers face in a typical school day. Behavior modification programs adapt well to special education and remedial programs. The research literature is replete with examples of behavior modification programs adapted successfully for all types of students, regardless of their learning or behavioral problems. However, if a teacher is not well trained in using behavior modification procedures, he or she may find it difficult to adapt this approach to the classroom.

Alignment with Instruction. The majority of behavioral programs are developed in response to disruptive behavior with consideration given to how the teacher can best apply consequences. There is less emphasis on how problem behavior may be caused by inadequate instruction or poor organization. Teachers who use behavior modification procedures look less to the curriculum and instruction as the causes of misbehavior and more to aspects of the environment that reinforce the disruptive behavior. Consequently, some behavior modification programs are not integrated into an instructional program.

Proactive Management Techniques. In our view, one limitation of the behavioral approach is that it does not require teachers to analyze tasks to determine those that might foster behavior problems. The focus of most behavioral approaches is remediation rather than prevention.

Assertive Discipline

Canter and Canter (1976) define an assertive teacher as "One who clearly and firmly communicates her wants and needs to her students, and is prepared to reinforce her words with appropriate actions. She responds in a manner which maximizes her potential to get her needs met, but in no way violates the best interests of the students" (p. 9). The structure of Assertive Discipline provides a framework that fosters the teacher's effectiveness in communicating to students the limits of their behavior in the classroom and clearly establishing consequences for disruptive behavior. Canter and Canter developed Assertive Discipline because they felt that teachers were not being adequately trained to respond effectively to disruptive behavior. Assertive Discipline requires teachers to take control of their classrooms by (a) utilizing an assertive teaching style, (b) specifying the types of behaviors that are expected, as well as those that will not be tolerated, and (c) developing a plan for increasing appropriate behavior and decreasing inappropriate behavior.

According to Canter and Canter (1976), teachers develop conceptualizations of the causes of misbehavior that, in reality, serve only to limit their effectiveness in properly managing behavior. As Canter and Canter have indicated, teachers often attribute classroom behavior problems to factors that are beyond their control (e.g., emotional disturbances, brain damage, inadequate intelligence, inadequate parenting, low socioeconomic status). By accepting these as the main causes of inappropriate behavior, teachers do not empower themselves, according to Canter and Canter, to influence positively student behavior; that is, teachers do not accept the idea that they have the right to set firm limits and that students need the limits.

Theoretical Basis and Characteristics.   Canter (1989) feels strongly that many professionals have misinterpreted Assertive Discipline by assuming that the key element is providing negative consequences for misbehavior. The key to effective Assertive Discipline, Canter states, is "catching students being good" and applying positive consequences for appropriate behavior (p. 58). Assertive Discipline is based on a balance between the rights of teachers and the rights of students. For example, while the teacher has the right to determine and request appropriate behavior from students, students also have the right to choose how to behave and to know the consequences that follow their behavior (Canter 1989).

Assertive Discipline incorporates the principles of Canter's assertion training program by helping teachers improve their personal and professional relationships. Teachers are taught to (a) communicate their expectations clearly, (b) attend to both positive and negative student behavior actively, and (c) use consequences for both appropriate and inappropriate student behavior persistently. The Assertive Discipline approach has three major program characteristics: (1) the discipline plan, (2) consequences for misbehavior, and (3) positive discipline. Each of these components is discussed below.

The Discipline Plan.   The teacher presents the class rules to students at the beginning of the school year and describes the consequences for rule violations with use of the discipline plan. This is an important feature of Assertive Discipline because, without this plan, teachers rely on spur-of-the-moment consequences for treating student misbehavior, often causing them to negotiate and explain every consequence to misbehaving students. As Canter (1989) points out, "That is not an effective way to teach" (p. 59). By adhering to the discipline plan, Canter argues that teachers can be more consistent with discipline. The discipline plan is sent home to parents at the beginning of the school year to inform them of the teacher's behavioral expectations. This explicit communication to students and parents delineates the roles and responsibilities of each participant in the learning process, allowing teachers to enlist parental support in managing the most disruptive student behaviors.

Consequences of Misbehavior.   The feature of Assertive Discipline that is the most well known, and probably the most misunderstood, is the method the program uses to deliver consequences for student misbehavior. A misperception of

Assertive Discipline is that the teacher stands in front of the class, discussing rules and consequences, and writing students' names on the board when they misbehave. In response to this misperception, Canter (1989) states, "Assertive Discipline is not a negative program, but it can be misused by negative teachers" (p. 59). In Assertive Discipline, positive reinforcement for appropriate behavior should be used in conjunction with negative consequences. Canter suggests that teachers limit the number of consequences used for misbehavior and include only those with which the teacher is comfortable, and which he or she finds appropriate for the situation. Consequences are delivered in a systematic manner.

When Assertive Discipline was first introduced, the technique most frequently used was that of putting the offending student's name on the board, along with corresponding check marks. This method, it was thought, allowed for explicit communication to the disruptive student about his or her behavior. It also provided the teacher with a record of the misbehavior. However, according to Canter (1989), many teachers started to use the public display of names as a singular means of controlling students. Also, some students found it reinforcing to have their names displayed publicly on the board. Canter suggests that record keeping be less public and that teachers use instead a notebook to record the students' names.

Positive Discipline.   It is important that teachers reinforce appropriate student behavior when using Assertive Discipline. Without the vigilant use of reinforcement, Assertive Discipline is not effective and teachers can expect their management program to become negative, both for them and the students. It is important to use positive discipline with both elementary and senior high school students. However, it is suggested that teachers make adjustments for the age and ability differences of students in the delivery of positive reinforcement. Canter suggests that teachers use a three-step approach to positive discipline: instruction, practice, and correction.

Assumptions.   Assertive Discipline is based on several assumptions about the teacher's role in classroom discipline. A key to Assertive Discipline is the belief that the way in which a teacher disciplines a student will directly influence the behavior of all students in the class. It is through positive influences, not negative consequences, that teachers can best affect the behavior of students in the classroom. It is also assumed that the teacher's attitude is vitally important in the success of Assertive Discipline. Through the use of Assertive Discipline, teachers can gain the skill and confidence to identify (a) the type of classroom he or she wants, (b) the obstacles in the classroom that prevent successful management, and (c) the plan needed to overcome the obstacles.

The assertive teacher systematically *teaches* students expected classroom behavior by establishing clear parameters of appropriate behavior. Once this teaching is complete, the teacher is expected to follow through consistently with specific consequences. Teachers who are assertive in their responses to appropriate behavior best communicate to students the classroom expectations.

Positive assertions form the core of effective classroom management in the Assertive Discipline approach.

Finally, Canter and Canter (1976) developed Assertive Discipline with the understanding that this approach "will not provide a teacher with a blueprint for every difficult classroom problem" (p. 13). Instead, Assertive Discipline is most appropriate as one of many options teachers have when deciding on a classroom management approach.

EXAMPLE: AN ASSERTIVE DISCIPLINE PROGRAM

The teacher who decides to use Assertive Discipline institutes the program on the first day of the school year. His or her first task is to develop the discipline plan. As an initial step, the teacher reflects on his or her expectations of how students should behave in the classroom. Next, the teacher identifies certain behaviors in the classroom that are intolerable and specifies consequences for rule infractions.

The teacher's next step is to develop positive discipline practices. The teacher first instructs students how to follow critical directions, which requires that he or she specify what is expected from students in each learning situation. Because of the ability ranges of students in most classrooms, the teacher often incorrectly assumes that all students know what is meant by the direction, "Everybody stay in your seats." During this first critical phase of positive discipline, teachers state the classroom rules and clearly *model* what is meant by each rule. Students are then asked to restate the rules and demonstrate their understanding of the teacher's classroom behavior expectations.

Once the teacher discusses and models the classroom rules, students practice following those rules under the teacher's careful guidance. During this practice, the teacher focuses attention on those students who *are* following the directions and praises them for their efforts. This positive approach increases the likelihood that these students will continue to follow directions. It also provides a positive model to students who have not yet learned to comply with classroom rules.

Once the teacher is assured that students have a clear understanding of the rules, negative consequences are applied to misbehavior. If a student breaks a classroom rule while a teacher is presenting a lesson, the teacher gives the student a verbal warning and writes the student's name into a record book. For the next rule infraction, the student is verbally reprimanded and receives the next level of consequence (e.g., five minutes after school). A check mark is then placed beside the student's name in the record book. A third infraction brings with it another reprimand and yet another level of consequence (e.g., ten minutes after school). If there is a fourth rule violation by the same student, the teacher informs the student of his misconduct and follows up with a phone call to the student's parents. If the misbehavior continues, an administrative action is taken, and the student is sent to the principal's office. It should be noted that because the discipline plan and negative consequences are determined beforehand and the students are informed of consequences for any misbehavior, teachers are not required to explain their consequences, nor are they to engage in negotiating with the student, which wastes valuable teaching time.

Advantages and Limitations

Effectiveness. While there are numerous teacher reports on the effectiveness of Assertive Discipline, there are no controlled research studies that have demonstrated its effectiveness (Chard, Smith, & Sugai 1992). Consequently, teachers should be skeptical of the numerous anecdotal reports about Assertive Discipline. However, because Assertive Discipline is predicated on a set of "teacher rights," teachers gain a feeling of control in their own classrooms. In addition, because communication plays such a prominent role in this approach, students are provided with an understanding of classroom expectations. This results in fewer misunderstandings between the student and the teacher, which may contribute to the effectiveness of this classroom management approach.

Usefulness. Assertive Discipline can be used for the 180-day school year. This allows the teacher to administer a classroom management program prior to behavior problems. However, the approach requires teachers to use the same procedures for the entire school year. One significant limitation of Assertive Discipline is that a comprehensive monitoring system is not provided for the evaluation of learning and behavior outcomes. The lack of careful monitoring, especially with disabled students, can pose both practical and administrative problems for the teacher. Assertive Discipline is sometimes misused by teachers who focus on only negative consequences. This negative focus causes the classroom to become an aversive learning environment, both for students and teachers alike.

Adaptability. One advantage of Assertive Discipline is that the procedures can be used by either general education or special education teachers. These procedures are likely to be effective for all students, irrespective of their diverse learning and curricular needs. Because there are clearly articulated guidelines to be followed, teachers of all training backgrounds can use Assertive Discipline in their classrooms. However, one limitation that teachers have reported when using Assertive Discipline is that it does not accommodate students of different ages. For example, the severity of the consequences is the same for younger students and more mature students, limiting the adaptability of Assertive Discipline for many teachers.

Alignment to Instruction. A significant limitation of Assertive Discipline is that it does not consider one of the major sources of misbehavior, poorly designed instructional programs, as a contributor to classroom disruption. For example, if a student's unmanageable behavior is caused by misplacement in a reading program, Assertive Discipline is not effective for rectifying the problem. It does not provide a mechanism for the teacher to evaluate critically the role of curriculum in classroom management. One could argue that Assertive Discipline is not intended or designed to address instruction, but this simply acknowledges the need for an approach that considers management of instruction as well as behavior.

Proactive Management Techniques. Assertive Discipline does not provide teachers with specific guidelines on proactive management techniques. While students are presented classroom rules at the beginning of the year and the consequences for not adhering to them, this approach does not provide guidelines for teaching students these skills. Another glaring problem is that Assertive Discipline has no assessment component to help teachers evaluate their classroom for potential behavior problems. Consequently, management in this approach is largely reactive.

Teacher Effectiveness Training

Thomas Gordon developed *Teacher Effectiveness Training* (TET) in 1966, and it has become widely used as an in-service training program for teachers throughout the country. The procedures that make up TET derive from the Parent Effectiveness Training program developed by Gordon and his associates. Proponents of TET feel that the quality of the teacher–learner relationship is more crucial than "what the teacher is teaching, how the teacher does it, or whom the teacher is trying to teach" (Gordon & Burch 1974, p. 3). This approach focuses on how the teacher develops communication with the students to foster effective links between the teacher and students.

Theoretical Basis and Characteristics. The philosophy of TET is that the relationship between the teacher and students is based on the nature and history of their interactions. In TET, classroom discipline and academic instruction are considered separate processes that require teachers to be competent in both to be effective. Gordon feels that teachers often equate discipline with threats of punishment and should instead use less-coercive means to control their classrooms. An effective teacher–student relationship is (a) open, (b) caring, (c) interdependent, (d) independent, and (e) mutually supportive.

The teacher develops communication by using active listening techniques in the TET model. Gordon and Burch (1974) feel that active listening is the basis for effective teaching because it allows "for clarifying, promoting inquiry, creating a climate where students feel free to think, discuss, question, and explore" (p. 178). Teachers may also use classroom modification to prevent problems. Systematizing and enriching the environment are several modifications among an array of options that teachers can elect to use. The use of a "No-Lose" method of resolving conflicts in the classroom is another important feature of TET. In this approach, teachers use a specified problem-solving strategy to negotiate conflicts.

Assumptions. The TET model assumes that teachers cannot develop effective learning environments using coercive methods of behavior control. Gordon and Burch (1974) state that "Criticism and negative evaluation tend to inhibit rather than promote change" (p. 29) and that in order to establish an effective relation-ship with students, the teacher must take the primary responsibility for develop-ing communication. To that end, teachers talk with students and listen carefully to their concerns in order to negotiate equitable solutions to problems that arise in classrooms. It is also assumed that most teachers, in their attempt to establish classroom control, use authoritarian techniques to control students' behavior. TET proponents feel that teachers who use coercive, power-play tactics often con-tribute to the negative atmosphere of schools that promotes conflicts rather than resolves them.

EXAMPLE: A TET MODEL

Mr. Lance, a seventh-grade science teacher often has students work in groups to prepare materials for science experiments. During this group activity, Mr. Lance uses the time to test several low-performing students individually for mastery on the daily lecture material. These quizzes require about five minutes for each student to complete. When Mr. Lance conducts the quizzes, he asks the student groups to talk quietly and not distract those taking the test. On one particular day, one of the groups working on their science project is disrupted by the giggling and talking of another group. The interaction between Mr. Lance and the group of disruptive students follows:

MR. LANCE: Hey Jim, could your group work more quietly? We are trying to complete this quiz, and it's difficult with all the noise.

JIM: We are trying to complete our assignment before the end of class. If you want us to work together, then we have to talk.

MR. LANCE: That's great that your group is concerned about completing the assignment and working together. You are right that I have asked all the groups to work as a team to complete the assignment.

JIM: Yesterday we worked together, and you didn't say that we couldn't talk when we broke into groups. It's not just our group that is talking. The others are making noise too.

MR. LANCE: I think we have a problem here. I understand that you want to complete the work by the end of the period and that working together is part of the assignment. On the other hand, I have to give quizzes to three more students and it is difficult for them to concentrate when you guys are talking and making so much noise. Do you have any ideas about how we can solve this problem?

JIM: Well, I guess that we could not talk as loudly while you are giving the quizzes. Also, is it okay if we move some of our materials to the other side of the room and do some of the work there for the rest of the class?

MR. LANCE: That would be great, Jim. Really, I don't mind if you guys talk, just keep it down so the people who are taking the quiz have a chance to concentrate on the material. When I'm done giving the quizzes you can move your group back if you want. Thanks for helping out!

Advantages and Limitations.

Effectiveness. Although many teachers report the effectiveness of TET, there is a limited research base to support these claims. The TET model is probably least effective in solving discipline problems that are a direct result of poor instructional programming. For problems that are a result of inadequate communication between the teacher and the students, the teacher can probably effectively use the TET model.

Usefulness. Teachers who learn the TET model will find these procedures useful in a variety of nonteaching situations, such as parent conferences and meetings with school administrators. However, because this model requires the teacher to assume the role of counselor, teachers may find the techniques described in the approach unusual and difficult to apply in their classrooms. One advantage TET has is that the procedures can be applied in a variety of teaching situations, from elementary classrooms to senior high school programs.

Adaptability. Many components of the TET program can be applied to a variety of instructional contexts. For example, active listening can help the teacher better communicate with students, regardless of the students' abilities or grade levels. Guidelines for TET use are general, so teachers who are familiar with these procedures can adapt them to their individual teaching situations.

Alignment with Instruction. The most severe limitation of the TET model is that teachers are not trained to consider the instructional program as a potential cause of classroom management problems. Instruction and classroom management are considered separate processes in TET. This limitation renders this approach too narrow in scope. The TET model provides teachers with only an indirect approach for solving discipline problems that result from faulty teaching or faulty curriculum design.

Proactive Management Techniques. Another limitation of TET is that guidelines are not included for development of proactive management strategies. Because TET's focus is on the teacher–learner relationship and not on the instructional content or teaching methods, there is little chance that this approach can be used to proactively manage behavior problems. The lack of instructional guidelines relegates TET to that group of reactive approaches to classroom management.

Cooperative Discipline

Another approach to discipline is based on the work of Alfred Adler and Rudolph Dreikurs. This approach is based largely on the premise that misbehavior should receive natural or logical consequences, and that if a teacher understands a student's motive for unacceptable behavior, the teacher will be better able to design an effective plan to help the student. Training in this approach is based on a number of books by Dreikurs such as *Discipline without Tears* (1974) and *Maintaining Sanity in the Classroom* (1982). A new program entitled

Cooperative Discipline (1990) by Linda Albert is also based largely on the work of Dreikurs and Adler. In discussing this approach, Albert's Cooperative Discipline program will be used as a model.

Characteristics and Theoretical Basis. The Cooperative Discipline model is based on three basic concepts. The first of these underlying concepts is that students choose their behavior. Although environmental conditions may invite a particular behavior, the student is free to choose how to behave. Once the teacher understands that student behavior is based on choice, the teacher can begin to influence a student's decisions about how to behave.

The second basic concept is that the goal of student behavior is to fulfill a need to belong. Students choose different behaviors to feel a sense of importance and belonging in different environments such as clubs, teams, or home. When a teacher recognizes a student's need to belong, he or she can help a student choose appropriate behavior to achieve a special place in the classroom.

The third concept underlying Cooperative Discipline is that a student misbehaves to satisfy the need to belong. However, the student's efforts have not been successful, and he or she is now trying to achieve one of four immediate goals: (1) attention, (2) power, (3) revenge, or (4) avoidance-of-failure. Knowledge of what the student is trying to achieve with the misbehavior allows the teacher to take appropriate action.

These three underlying concepts are used to devise a thoughtful, rather than an impulsive, reaction to a student's misbehavior. This is accomplished by a Five-Step School Action Plan, which serves as the procedural heart of Cooperative Discipline. Each step is described below.

Step 1: Pinpoint and describe the student's behavior
The first step of Cooperative Discipline requires that the teacher develop an objective view of the problem. A teacher can easily make subjective judgments or assumptions about the student, such as the student is lazy or unreliable. However, the teacher must get past a subjective view of the problem and describe the problem objectively. An example of an objective view of a problem behavior might be the following: "Thomas fails to hand in two to three assignment each week." An objective definition of the problem focuses on what actually happens, not how the teacher feels about what happens.

Step 2: Identify the goal of the misbehavior
Once the teacher has identified the problem behavior, he or she now has the necessary information to make a judgment about what the student is trying to accomplish with the misbehavior. The teacher determines if the student is seeking attention, power, revenge, or avoidance-of-failure.

Step 3: Design specific intervention techniques
The intervention should be based on what the student is trying to achieve with the misbehavior. For each of the four goals, suggested procedures are given on how the teacher might respond to future incidents

of the misbehavior. For example, if the student is trying to get attention, the teacher might minimize the behavior by ignoring it, or he or she might distract the student by changing the activity. If the goal of the misbehavior is to seek power, the teacher might use time-out or set a consequence, such as the loss of an activity. For each of these four goals, Cooperative Discipline suggests a variety of appropriate response techniques.

Step 4: Select encouragement techniques to build self-esteem

The interventions for the moment of misbehavior are viewed as a stopgap measure that will not prevent the future occurrence of the misbehavior. To do this, the teacher must plan interventions for helping the student feel more capable. Specific techniques are suggested that may help the student connect more with classmates or feel like a contributing member of the class. The rationale is that when the student's self-image improves, he or she has less need to misbehave to create a sense of belonging.

Step 5: Involve parents as partners

Specific suggestions are given for increasing parental involvement and support. All of the previous steps are strengthened if teachers, students, and the parents participate in the plan. Information is provided on productive parent-teacher conferences and on how to develop a "Home Action Plan."

EXAMPLE: A COOPERATIVE DISCIPLINE APPROACH

In a middle school classroom, a student named Elliot chronically says hurtful things to the teacher. One day when reviewing an assignment, Elliot reads vocabulary definitions that are correct but are sarcastic and rude toward the teacher. The goal of this type of behavior is revenge because the definitions are designed to hurt and anger the teacher.

There are six guidelines for avoiding and diffusing confrontations:

Guideline 1: Focus on the behavior, not the student.

Guideline 2: Take charge of negative emotions.

Guideline 3: Avoid escalating the situation.

Guideline 4: Discuss the misbehavior later.

Guideline 5: Allow the student to save face.

Guideline 6: Model nonaggressive behavior.

At the time of the incident, the teacher informs Elliot that he will need to speak to her after lunch. This delay avoids escalating the situation at the time of the incident and lets the student know that the behavior will be dealt with at another time. Before the conference, the teacher acknowledges to herself that the student's behavior hurt her feelings. By doing so, the teacher takes charge of these emotions and doesn't become negative or hostile toward the student.

At the conference, the teacher describes the student's exhibited behavior. She informs him that he did the assignment correctly, but that it is not acceptable to insult her. She acknowledges the student's wit and informs him that it is acceptable to be funny, but it's important to understand the correct time and place for being funny. As the discussion continues, the student and teacher work out two possible options for getting credit for the assignment. One is to redo the assignment and eliminate the disrespectful parts. Another option is that if the student really wants to be funny, he can prepare a skit to present to the class that will demonstrate respectfully his knowledge of the vocabulary assignment. The third option is to choose not to redo the assignment and receive a failing grade.

In a reasoned and respectful way, the teacher has acknowledged the student's power and wit and has allowed the student to save face. If the behavior continues, the teacher may need to try additional interventions suggested in the program for dealing with power and revengeful behaviors.

Advantages and Limitations

Effectiveness.   One of the biggest advantages of this approach is that it offers the teacher specific and practical suggestions on how to respond to misbehavior in both proactive and reactive ways. Specific suggestions are given for what the teacher might do at the moment of misbehavior and what he or she can do at a later time to improve the student's self-image.

Usefulness.   One advantage that teachers will find in using Cooperative Discipline is that the procedures can be used with students of all age and performance levels. If the procedures are used properly, the teacher can avoid escalating the troubling behavior because Cooperative Discipline has specific guidelines for avoiding and diffusing confrontations with students.

Adaptability.   This approach offers alternative techniques if the teacher's first effort is not successful. There is an acknowledgement that every situation is unique, and one approach will not be effective with every student. This makes the Cooperative Discipline model adaptable to a variety of teaching situations.

Alignment to Instruction.   The most significant limitation of this approach, as with others, is that it does not offer the teacher specific information on how to organize the classroom and how to use instruction to teach students how to be successful.

Proactive Management Techniques.   Because the focus of Cooperative Discipline is on the individual behaviors of the student, this approach is not designed for proactive classroom management. Cooperative Discipline does not consider the teacher's instructional program or classroom organization as a potential cause of disruptive behavior. Consequently, teachers who use Cooperative Discipline respond reactively to classroom disruption.

SUMMARY

In Figure 2.1, we summarize our evaluation of the four classroom management approaches discussed in this chapter based on the five essential elements. We have used a three-level evaluation system: A management approach is evaluated as either (1) fully meeting guideline standards, (2) partially meeting guideline standards or (3) not meeting standards.

None of the approaches discussed in this chapter meet the standards for all five of the evaluation criteria. Of the approaches discussed, the behavioral approach is the strongest. However, when alignment to instruction and proactive

FIGURE 2.1   Adequacy of current classroom management approaches

	Behavior Modification	Assertive Discipline	Teacher Effectiveness Training	Cooperative Discipline
Effectiveness	Fully	Does not	Does not	Partially
Usefulness	Fully	Does not	Does not	Partially
Adaptability	Partially	Partially	Partially	Partially
Alignment	Partially	Does not	Does not	Does not
Proactive	Partially	Does not	Does not	Does not

● Fully meets standards

◐ Partially meets standards

○ Does not meet standards

management techniques are considered, even this approach is less than adequate. Cooperative Discipline has some research evidence supporting its effectiveness, but further research is necessary. Similar to the behavioral approach to management, Cooperative Discipline is not adequately aligned to the instructional program, nor is it proactive in design. Finally, we have judged Assertive Discipline and Teacher Effectiveness Training as inadequate on four of the five evaluation criteria. Teachers who use these two approaches will not be able to sufficiently increase academic performance and improve social behavior of students.

In the chapters that follow, we present the specific components of the Instructional Classroom Management approach, a management program designed to be incorporated into a teacher's daily instructional activities. We will provide the reader with guidelines for assessing the instructional environment and for using punishment as a transition tool and reinforcement as a teaching tool. The reader will find guidelines on managing persistent forms of disruptive behavior and developing schoolwide discipline policies and procedures.

CHAPTER ACTIVITIES

1. List and discuss the theoretical basis, the characteristics, and the assumptions for each of the behavior management approaches that were discussed in this chapter: (1) Behavior Modification, (2) Assertive Discipline, (3) Teacher Effectiveness Training, and (4) Cooperative Discipline.
2. List and discuss the advantages and disadvantages of the Behavior Modification approach for each of the five guidelines for evaluating classroom management: (1) Effectiveness, (2) Usefulness, (3) Adaptability, (4) Alignment with Instruction, and (5) Proactive Management Techniques.
3. Discuss how each behavior management approach described in this chapter could be used in a special education resource classroom.

SUGGESTED READINGS

Charles, C. M. (1992). *Building classroom discipline*. New York: Longman.

Curwin, R. (1988). *Discipline with dignity*. Alexandria, VA: Association for Supervision and Curriculum Development.

Kaplan, J. S. (1991). *Beyond behavior modification: A cognitive-behavioral approach to behavior management in the school*. Austin, TX: Pro-Ed.

chapter 3

Instructional Dimensions of Classroom Management

INTRODUCTION

According to Berliner (1988), classroom management is the "area that the press and the public love to criticize teachers about, and it is the area that teachers have the most fear about when they begin to teach" (p. 321). However, he argues that "We have made unbelievable strides in the last decade, having learned many of the techniques used by teachers that lead to smooth-running, on-task, cheerful classrooms" (p. 321). Indeed we have made "unbelievable strides." For example, there is little disagreement about the importance of systematically arranging and organizing the classroom (Paine, et al., 1983) in ways that improve student task engagement and performance (Brophy & Good 1986), as well as student completion of clearly articulated learning tasks (Evertson 1989). In fact, more than a decade ago, Rohrkemper and Brophy (1980) argued that the research had produced a "largely consistent knowledge base identifying effective group management techniques and linking them to teacher success in maximizing student engagement in academic activities and achievement on standardized tests" (p. 1).

The research by Rohrkemper and Brophy (1980) on teachers' strategies for dealing with problem behaviors reveals some interesting findings. The researchers found that teachers who were judged as high-ability teachers for handling difficult students (a) used more rewards; (b) provided more supportive behavior, including more comforting and reassuring of students; (c) used punishment less than other teachers; and (d) were more likely to involve students in their own behavior change. These skills that characterized high-ability teachers more than 10 years ago are no less important now. In fact, the features of an instructional classroom management approach to problem behaviors are in part derived from the past research on classroom management and the research on teacher effectiveness, which attempts to clarify the relations between student outcomes and what the teacher does in the classroom. As Good (1979) stated, "Teachers' managerial abilities have been found to relate positively to student achievement in every process-product study conducted to date" (p. 54). The importance of this research notwithstanding, instructional classroom management's reach is broader than teacher behavior and student outcomes because it also incorporates an analysis of task and instructional variables.

A PROACTIVE APPROACH

We noted in chapter 1 that a critical feature of an instructional classroom management approach is that it is proactive. Simply put, one acts *before* a problem occurs instead of *reacting* to problems. As Gettinger (1988) states, "Proactive means to act in advance, to design a plan of action that affords an individual maximum control of a situation" (p. 228). A proactive approach to classroom management "anticipates and prepares for a situation through a plan to achieve control of the situation" (Swick, cited in Gettinger 1988, p. 228).

Gettinger (1988) describes three "distinguishing characteristics" of a proactive classroom management approach: (a) it is preventative, (b) it integrates methods that "facilitate appropriate student behavior with procedures that promote achievement through effective instruction" (p. 229), and (c) it emphasizes group dimensions of classroom management. Proactive classroom management, Gettinger

(1988) argues, "represents a broader approach to effective management than either behavioral or instructional management alone" (p. 229).

Although we agree with Gettinger's (1988) analysis of proactive classroom management, the implication that instructional management is not a broad approach is debatable for one simple reason: No one has delineated clearly and substantially the details of an instructional approach to classroom management. Therefore, to argue that a particular approach is not broad enough requires knowledge of the intricate requirements and details of that approach. This text is the first to delineate such details, at least at an introductory level.

A proactive classroom management approach doesn't require a teacher to anticipate and prevent every problem that surfaces in the classroom. There is simply no way to anticipate some problems. But a proactive approach to instructional classroom management means establishing a frame of mind or way of thinking about behavior that solves problems *before* initiating an exchange or a lesson with the learner.

Our perception of a proactive approach to classroom management usually includes the following characteristics of a teacher's behavior:

1. Identifies, teaches, and posts rules for appropriate behavior in the classroom.
2. Periodically reminds students of the rules for behaving appropriately.
3. Creates and maintains a positive, warm, and supportive classroom environment in which students feel comfortable and academically engaged.
4. Greets students at the classroom door before class begins.
5. Arranges the physical space and materials in the classroom to prevent disruption and distractions and maximize student task engagement.
6. Systematically rewards (e.g., verbal praise) students for demonstrating appropriate behavior in the school setting.
7. Establishes a clear and consistent routine for moving about the classroom and carrying out general classroom routines and activities.
8. Works with other teachers to insure quick and quiet transitions between classes and positive behavior management of students.
9. Facilitates the learning process by mediating and controlling learning activities and making adjustments in the instruction.
10. Accommodates student needs by adjusting schedules and lesson demands on a case-by-case basis.

The items in this list as a whole represent a proactive approach to classroom management primarily because they involve actions the teacher carries out either before or during a lesson to prevent a problem from surfacing. A proactive approach to classroom management, however, must extend beyond the general planning, management, and monitoring of students' social behavior. It must also consider the dimensions of the instructional process that are related to students' learning and academic performance. In short, a proactive approach addresses the very learning and teaching tasks and activities that often set the occasion for serious behavior problems. Moreover, a proactive approach to instruction requires identifying those dimensions of a task or the instructional process that may be troublesome for a learner *before* the learner is required to engage in the target task or lesson.

To appreciate the difference between a reactive and a proactive approach to classroom management, consider the following example. It should be noted that prior to starting the lesson, the teacher carried out some of the ten activities listed earlier as representing a proactive approach to classroom management. Specifically, the teacher (a) reviewed the rules with Jon and readily recited them (e.g., "I will keep my eyes on my work. I will give every task my best effort"); (b) created and maintained a positive, warm, and supportive classroom environment; (c) arranged the physical space and materials in ways that helped prevent Jon from being distracted; and (d) praised Jon when he demonstrated the appropriate behaviors. In spite of these attempts to be proactive, the lesson ended when Jon's verbalizations about his new puppy became excessive, and the teacher stopped the lesson and had Jon sit quietly with his head down on the desk. The teacher also did what was necessary *before* the lesson to ensure that the rest of the class was working on an independent activity, which allowed the teacher to work with Jon.

EXAMPLE: A REACTIVE APPROACH

Jon is a third-grader and is posing a problem for his third-grade teacher because he is very active, both physically and verbally. He is also falling behind in mathematics. The teacher has scheduled the task of counting by 5's, which requires Jon to state the facts orally (e.g., 5-10-15-20-25-30). The teacher introduces the task, and the following interactions take place:

TEACHER (T): Hi Jon, how are you?

JON (J): Did you know I got a new puppy?

T: Oh you did?

J: Yes, I got it for my birthday, and it has brown and white spots all over. It wiggles its . . .

T: Okay, Jon. Let's get back to work. Today we're going to count by 5. What are we going to do, Jon?

J: We're going to count by 5. My puppy is really cute, you know.

T: Yes, we're going to count by 5. Let's start, listen, 5-10-15-20-25-30. Your turn . . . You count by 5. Start with five and stop at 30.

J: 5-10-15-20-25-30. Do you have a puppy?

T: Listen, Jon. I'll count by 5 again. 5-10-15-20 . . .

J: Do you have a puppy? My puppy is really cute.

T: Listen again, 5-10-15-20-25-30.

J: My puppy has brown and white spots all over it.

T: Jon, I need you to count by 5. Get ready . . . count.

J: 5-10-15. . . . Do you have a puppy?

By most accounts, the teacher's efforts in the example represent rather reasonable attempts to teach Jon an important skill. She didn't waste valuable instructional time and began the task immediately even though Jon was more interested in talking about his new puppy. She focused on the task, ignored Jon's comments about his puppy, and tried to keep Jon focused. However, in spite of her efforts, the task deteriorated and Jon became relentless in his verbalizations. The teacher was simply unable to curb Jon's talk about his puppy and decided to place him in an "in-class time-out" situation.

The teacher's efforts to be proactive were sabotaged by her failure to consider one important variable—the instructional task and the response requirements this task made of Jon. In this case, the teacher prepared an instructional task that by all accounts was reasonable except in this particular circumstance. The task simply was the wrong one to teach at the time. Specifically, the task of requiring Jon to state a verbal chain (e.g., 5-10-15-20-25-30) from rote memory (Kameenui & Simmons 1990) contributed to Jon's excessive verbalizations. Because of Jon's penchant for being active both physically and verbally, the verbal task of counting by 5's simply fueled his verbalizations. The task provided Jon with an opportunity to practice not only the chain of math facts, but also his strategy of using verbal tasks to become disengaged from academic work. A more appropriate task would not require any verbalizations, such as a written task in which Jon would produce a sustained written response. By giving Jon a written task to start the lesson, the teacher would have minimized the probability that Jon would have engaged in the excessive verbal behavior. Simply put, a written task would have required Jon to write, not talk.

Matching the instructional task and Jon's performance requires intimate knowledge of at least two important sets of variables: (1) Jon's past behavior in a range of instructional conditions; and (2) the intricate requirements of the task, such as the response requirements placed on the learner. The instructional approach to classroom management considers the full range of task dimensions and the instructional context in the development of strategies for managing children's academic and social behavior.

TASK DIMENSIONS OF INSTRUCTIONAL CLASSROOM MANAGEMENT

There are six dimensions that are considered in the Instructional Classroom Management approach: (1) history, (2) response form, (3) modality, (4) complexity, (5) schedule, and (6) variation. Table 3.1 gives the definitions and examples of the task dimensions.

TABLE 3.1   Definitions and examples of task dimensions

Task Dimensions	Features and Examples
1. **Task history:** The status of a task and the extent to which the task has been taught before, and the likelihood that the learner will be familiar with it.	**New**—novel and never seen before **Familiar**—introduced previously but not mastered **Old**—mastered and established
2. **Task response form:** The manner in which students are required to respond to the task or teacher.	**Yes/No**—answer yes or no **Choice**—select an answer from multiple-choice **Production**—produce a response
3. **Task modality:** The mode of response required of the student.	**Oral**—verbal talk **Motor**—physical manipulation **Written**—writing a response
4. **Task complexity:** The extent to which a task involves multiple steps, new concepts, unfamiliar procedures, and so on.	**Easy**—task not complex **Hard**—task complex
5. **Task schedule:** The amount of time allocated to complete a task.	**Abbreviated**—task scheduled for short periods of time **Extended**—task scheduled for long periods of time
6. **Task variation:** The sequence in which easy or hard tasks are scheduled within a lesson.	**Varied**—Easy and hard tasks are varied one after another. **Unvaried**—Tasks are not changed in sequence.

Task History

The notion that learners have a learning history is well accepted. A student's learning is comprised of the full range of past events related to schooling and learning, such as acquiring information, responding to school demands, interacting with teachers, performing on tests, studying and collaborating with peers, writing reports, and completing daily assignments. Task history is concerned with assessing the learner's familiarity with a particular task. In other words, the task can be new and novel to the learner, or it can be an old task for which the learner has a great deal of background knowledge and even a high level of familiarity, if not automaticity.

New tasks present learners with a different set of problems and challenges from old tasks. Specifically, new tasks require a fundamentally different kind of teaching than old or even familiar tasks. The teaching of new tasks (i.e., social skills, concepts, algorithms, operations, rule relationships, stories, or principles) assumes that the learner has little or no competency for performing the tasks. The learner may have some background knowledge or prerequisite skills related to the target tasks, but for all practical purposes, the assumption is that the task is new and unknown to the learner. In a sense, the learner is in a state of "unknowing" about the task, and it is the teacher's responsibility to move that learner to a state of "knowing." Because the learner has had no instruction on the new task, the teaching must be carefully planned and all dimensions of the task must be considered, especially with a concern for the learner's potential response to the task. The more the learner knows about a task (e.g., a known, mastered task), the more demands we can place on the learner. Similarly, the less the learner knows about a task (e.g., an unknown, novel task), the fewer demands we can place on the learner. New tasks are the most difficult for learners and may set the occasion for problem behaviors.

Old tasks are tasks that have been taught and mastered by the learner. In a sense, these are mastery-level tasks that require little cognitive effort because the learner has had extensive practice on them and is fairly automatic and fluent. Typically, old tasks are scheduled for periodic review and practice and are used to assess the learner's retention or recall of what is already known. The teacher can reasonably assume that the learner understands the requirements of an old task.

A familiar task is one that has been introduced to the learner but has not been mastered, and therefore requires further instruction, review, and practice. The degree to which the task is familiar to the learner depends on several factors that include, for example, (a) the adequacy with which the task was previously taught; (b) the amount of time between successive presentations of the task to the learner; (c) the learner's retention and recall of the task; (d) the sameness in content, form, context, and response demands between successive tasks; and (e) the criterion level of student performance on tasks presented previously.

Gauging student's level of mastery across tasks is difficult and will require an evaluation and assessment system that is sensitive to students' daily classroom performance. The range of assessment tools and strategies is extensive and beyond the scope of this chapter and text. However, determining if a task is new, old, or familiar to the learner is fairly straightforward and sets the stage for considering the full range of task dimensions that may cause potential social behavior problems. By knowing the task history, the teacher will be alerted to potential problems and can adjust expectations about a learner's performance on the task.

Task Response Form

Learners demonstrate their general knowledge of the world by providing overt, observable responses to specific tasks. Not surprisingly, these responses can come in various forms, ranging from audible grunts designed to acknowledge something, to thoughtful, prosaic essays intended to persuade someone. Students' responses can come in the following forms:

1. **Yes/no choice response**-The teacher presents a question that requires a simple yes or no response from the learner. For example, the teacher asks, "Was Millard Filmore the twentieth president of the United States?" The student responds by answering, "No."
2. **Multiple-choice response**-The teacher presents a question that requires selecting an answer from a set of possible responses that are provided to the learner. For example, "Tell me if Millard Filmore was

the thirteenth president, the fifteenth president, or the twentieth president of the United States." The student selects an answer, "Millard Filmore was the thirteenth president of the United States."

3. **Production response**–The teacher asks a question for which the student is required to generate a response from "out of the blue." For example, the teacher asks, "Who was the thirteenth president of the United States?" The student responds by stating, "Millard Filmore was the thirteenth president of the United States."

The three types of responses can be placed on an easy-to-hard continuum in which yes/no choice responses are the easiest response form and production responses are typically the hardest. Multiple-choice response forms fall somewhere in the middle on the easy-to-hard continuum. The response forms vary in the amount of information provided to the teacher or person asking the question, and the amount of prompting and cueing carried by the response form. A yes/no choice response provides minimal information about what the learner knows because the learner has an equal chance of getting the answer right or wrong. In contrast, a production response potentially offers extensive amounts of information about what the learner knows because the learner is given little information about the correct response.

When planning a task, the teacher must determine the most appropriate response form for the student. As with other task dimensions, the selection of the response form will depend on a range of considerations. For example, if the teacher plans to teach a *new task* (i.e., task history) that may be difficult for the learner, a yes/no choice response may be the best response form to use initially. The yes/no choice response is a generally weak response form because the learner has a 50 percent chance of getting the answer right. Moreover, the structure of the questions is such that all the learner is required to do is listen and merely choose the correct response by noting yes or no. In contrast to a new task, if an old task were being taught, then it might be more reasonable for the teacher to require the learner to provide production responses, because the task is likely to be familiar, if not already mastered by the learner. Of course, in the academic domain (e.g., reading, mathematics, social studies), the desired outcomes and the learner's background knowledge are also important variables to consider when selecting the most appropriate response forms.

Task Modality

In addition to the form of a response, the modality of the response is also important. Specifically, a production response can be given orally, in writing, or motorically (e.g., student uses an augmentative communication device to select words or phrases to produce a statement). Like task response forms, task modes can be placed on an easy-to-hard continuum, in which the easiest mode of response is likely to be a motor response and the hardest mode of response is a written one. A written mode requires the learner to orchestrate "a host of skills that eventually result in a permanent product, a product that displays to the audience the thoughts and competencies of the writer" (Kameenui & Simmons 1990, p. 422).

Examples of different task modalities are as follows:

1. Oral: The student tells the teacher the name of the thirteenth president of the United States.
2. Written: The student writes the name of the thirteenth president of the United States.
3. Motor: The teacher gives the student a worksheet in which five written choices are given. The student circles the answer or indicates that Millard Filmore was the thirteenth president of the United States.

The difficulty of the response modality varies from learner to learner, and the selection of the best mode depends again on the learner, the desired outcomes, the task history, and so forth.

Task Complexity

As noted in Table 3.1, task complexity is concerned with the extent to which a task requires the learner to complete a series of steps that are either new or unfamiliar. If the task is new and involves a series of steps that are complex and require the learner to apply unfamiliar terms, information, or skills that are not mastered, then the task is likely to be hard for the learner. In contrast, if the task involves one or two steps, mastered concepts, skills, or knowledge, then the task is likely to be easier for the learner. As with other task dimensions, the complexity of a task can range from easy to hard.

The complexity of a task can be made easy or hard by a number of other variables not directly related to the particular task. For example, the clarity with which the task is presented, described, and "framed" (Kameenui & Simmons 1990) prior to requiring students to complete it, can also influence the complexity of a task. Specifically, if the task is not framed properly and expected outcomes and response forms are not clear, then the task will be difficult for the learner to complete successfully. If an unfamiliar task is presented immediately after the completion of another complex and difficult task, then the successive presentation of two difficult and unfamiliar tasks is likely to cause problems of fatigue and motivation.

Frequently, the complexity of a task is made easy or difficult by the number and kinds of concrete examples presented as a means of explaining or demonstrating the new task. For example, if a new concept is taught using only one or two examples, then the task is likely to be difficult for the learner. If a range of greatly different examples is used to teach a new concept, the task is also likely to be difficult. Tasks that are difficult, confusing, and unclear set the stage for serious behavior problems. Therefore, task complexity is an important instructional variable to consider when developing and designing a proactive instructional classroom management system.

Task Schedule

The time allocated and scheduled to teach and complete a task can influence the difficulty of the task and consequently cause behavior problems. Tasks can be scheduled for extended periods of time, or the time allocated to complete a task can be brief or abbreviated. For example, a task can be scheduled for an extended period of time, such as 45 minutes or an hour. By allocating this extensive time for a particular task, the teacher is making the following set of assumptions:

1. The task is not new but familiar to the learner.
2. The learner has all the component or prerequisite skills necessary to complete the task.
3. The task is of moderate difficulty; that is, it is not so easy that it will be boring to the learner, or so difficult that it will be frustrating or punishing.
4. The extended time is necessary for the learner to practice independently a set of skills that is related to an important educational outcome.
5. The response form of the task is production or a mixture of choice and production responses.
6. The mode of the task is written or a mixture of modes (e.g., oral, motor, and written).
7. The task history is such that the major components of the task are familiar to the learner and established in the learner's repertoire.
8. The expected outcome of the task is substantial, clear, and aligned with educationally valid goals for the learner.
9. The task is sufficiently engaging and motivating in ways that will maintain the learner's attention and increase the probability that the task will be completed successfully.
10. The task involves multiple steps and components that require extended periods of time to connect in order to demonstrate knowledge of a particular knowledge base or domain.

A task scheduled for an extended period of time should not be so difficult as to be punishing, or so easy as to be trivial to the learner. For example, a teacher could schedule 45 minutes to teach third-grade students how to work complex division operations. Such a teaching schedule is not likely to lead to much success, especially for low-performing students who have difficulty staying engaged for long periods of time. Ten minutes into the teaching routine, off-task behavior is likely to become a problem. Even if the teacher scheduled 20 minutes of teaching and 25 minutes of independent seatwork, the amount of real learning is likely to be problematic. Tasks scheduled for extended periods of time must be carefully planned with specific outcomes. In summary, extended periods of time allocated to teach a task or skill must be designed to consider the full range of task dimensions listed in Table 3.1.

In contrast to an extended schedule is a variable schedule in which a range of tasks, possibly even a greater number of tasks, is scheduled for brief periods of time. In other words, instead of scheduling the teaching of a new math operation of 45 minutes, the teacher may schedule it for 10 minutes, followed by 15 minutes of work on a writing task that is familiar to the learner. Similarly, the writing task is followed by 5 minutes of work on a rote task in which students work in pairs to memorize the names of the new countries in eastern Europe. Following this task, the teacher returns to the new math task that was previously introduced and reviews it for another 10 minutes. Finally, the teacher uses the last 5 minutes to check students' independent literature reading. In contrast to a traditional schedule of 45 minutes allocated for teaching and working on mathematics only, this variable schedule is comprised of five distinct sets of activities involving four different academic tasks. The proposed schedule consisting of abbreviated time slots for a range of academic tasks follows:

Ten minutes—introduce new math operation involving complex division

Fifteen minutes—complete writing task on story elements

Five minutes—review names of eastern European countries

Ten minutes—review previously introduced math task

Five minutes—check status of literature reading

It is important to note that is this is an ideal example. In reality, teachers must account for transition time between activities, which may require fewer switches between tasks. There are several advantages to a schedule of abbreviated activities. First, the variety of academic tasks (e.g., mathematics, reading, writing, geography) is likely to maintain the learner's attention and task engagement, because there is little redundant information and activity. The unpredictability from task to task also holds the learner's attention. Second, the abbreviated tasks represent succinct, obtainable goals. A task can be started and completed in a concise time frame that will offer students a sense of accomplishment. Furthermore, students are likely to feel reinforced and refreshed after completing a series of tasks, in contrast to enduring a long assignment for which the beginning and ending points are long forgotten.

Finally, a schedule of abbreviated activities allows students to review in a cumulative way information that was previously introduced, because the teacher is engaged in teaching multiple strands of skills, rather than just one skill or content area. Specifically, a new task introduced on Monday can be reviewed in various abbreviated chunks of time (e.g., 5 minutes one day and 10 minutes the next day) every day of the week. This differs from a traditional schedule that teaches a new skill for 45 minutes on Monday and reviews it on Tuesday (if at all), before moving on to the next task and skill.

Task Variation

When multiple tasks are presented in a lesson, they create a sequence. This sequence can be varied or unvaried, which means that the sequence of tasks can be comprised of both easy and hard tasks, or all easy tasks or all hard tasks. While it is unlikely for a lesson to be comprised of only easy or only hard tasks, a sequence of tasks can be comprised of two or more difficult (or easy) tasks. The primary concern with presenting difficult tasks back-to-back is that they set the occasion for frustration and failure, and perhaps behavior problems. A better alternative is to vary the sequence of tasks so that the presentation of difficult tasks is followed by easy or moderately difficult tasks. This varied sequence of tasks is especially important for low performers.

An example of a varied sequence of tasks was given earlier in the section on task schedule. The task variation is most important for students who experience academic learning problems and are at risk for behavior problems. For average learners who are not at risk for academic learning problems, task variation may not be necessary. Eventually it will also be necessary for low-performing students to respond to an unvaried sequence of tasks (e.g., a series of difficult or demanding tasks).

APPLICATION OF TASK DIMENSIONS TO CLASSROOM MANAGEMENT

Identifying, isolating, and describing the task dimensions of classroom management represents only part of an Instructional Classroom Management approach. These task dimensions must be considered within the full context of instruction. First, all instruction takes place within a temporal framework. Specifically, Kameenui and Simmons (1990) call for designing instruction within the following three phases of instruction: *Before Instruction, During Instruction,* and *After Instruction.* Designing instruction for the Before Instruction phase is different from designing instruction for both the During and After Instruction phases. The same analysis applied by Kameenui and Simmons (1990) regarding the design and development of instruction within a temporal framework can be applied to instructional classroom management.

Before Instruction

All of the task dimensions listed in Table 3.1 and described previously should be considered in this phase of instruction, which comes before a lesson or task is presented to the learner. Consideration of task dimensions can take place just before a lesson is taught, or well before school begins. What is important is that the task dimensions are considered *before* a lesson is taught and demands are placed on learners to respond.

Adjustments in task dimensions may require extensive adaptations to the particular curriculum program being used. For example, a commercial mathematics curriculum program may introduce a new operation or skill by requiring students to work with manipulatives for an extended period of time. Using manipulatives for teaching math concepts requires a great deal of instructional time. For example, Evans (1991) compared an algorithm-only strategy with a manipulatives strategy and found that students took an average of three times longer (i.e., average time of 75 minutes) to reach criterion level using manipulatives than an algorithm-only strategy.

For low performers, manipulating 100 or more objects (e.g., pasta, cubes, toothpicks) is not easy and presents serious challenges that may result in students becoming frustrated with the manipulatives. Low-performing children have a difficult time focusing on a task, selecting a strategy that's effective, carrying out a strategy, sticking with a strategy, and adjusting their use of a strategy to solve a problem. These difficulties in the context of using manipulatives are compounded because students are required to keep track of many loose objects, arrange the objects into specified groups, and make the association between a symbolic system and the concrete objects. Orchestrating all these actions and objects can be very frustrating, especially when the objects fall onto the floor, and the learner falls farther behind the group.

The following task dimensions as a group create what could be characterized as the most difficult task scenario:

Task History:	New
Task Response Form:	Production
Task Modality:	Written
Task Complexity:	Hard
Task Schedule:	Extended
Task Variation:	Unvaried

A task that is new, hard, presented for an extended period of time and with little variation in the sequence, and requires a written production response is likely to set the stage for potential behavior problems. On the other hand, if a task is old, easy, presented for a brief period of time and with great variation in the sequence, and requires only a yes/no oral choice response, then it is less likely to cause serious behavior problems. However, if the task is too easy, students may not take it seriously because it won't be cognitively challenging.

In the Before Instruction phase, the teacher must examine the dimensions of each task and determine the balance most appropriate for the learner and the design of the task (i.e., it is aligned with the goals and expected outcomes of the lesson). Designing the proper mix of task dimensions depends on the outcomes specified for the learner in the particular skill or content area. In general, however, special consideration should be given to the learner's performance when introducing a *new task*. It may be best to ease into a new and complex task by planning an easy response form (e.g., yes/no or choice), mode (i.e., oral), and an abbreviated but unvaried schedule (e.g., three–ten minute presentation). The sequence of task may be unvaried if the teaching is kept to a brief period of time. Once the new task is introduced, the learner could be required to make a more difficult response form (e.g., production) in subsequent lessons, using a more difficult mode (e.g., written) for a longer period of time. These considerations of the dimensions of the task are likely to *prevent* behavior problems associated with difficult academic learning situations.

We consider the Before Instruction phase to be the most important phase because it sets the foundation for what the teacher will do during the other two phases of instruction. Specifically, what the teacher designs and plans in the Before Instruction phase should unfold as planned in the During Instruction phase, which should be evaluated in the After Instruction phase. The extent to which the teacher's planning results in the desired outcomes for both the learner and teacher is considered after instruction. Changes in the lesson and task dimensions must be considered again in the Before Instruction phase.

In addition to considering the dimensions of a task, the teacher should also attend to other instructional requirements during this phase, including the rules and expectations of how students are to behave during instruction, a plan to respond to potential behavior problems, and so on. These requirements for all three phases of instruction are developed in chapter 4.

During Instruction

The During Instruction phase is concerned primarily with the delivery and ongoing management of the lesson. While all of the task dimensions should be scrutinized during this phase, the most important ones are the response form, modality, and schedule. If the task is either new or old, the teacher must monitor the degree to which students are facile in the prescribed response form and mode. Moreover, the amount of time allocated to complete the task must be monitored to determine if more time is needed, or if too much time was allocated. If a problem in any of the task dimensions is diagnosed, then the teacher must determine if it is a "can't" problem or a "won't" problem. In general, it is best to adapt the task so that the task dimension that is causing the problem is made easier for the learner. For example, if the production response form is too difficult, it could be changed to a choice response form. If the written mode is too difficult, an oral or gestural response could be used. In some cases, it may be necessary to stop the task altogether and present an entirely different task, preferably an established task or a task that is "neutral," that is, neither too easy, nor too difficult for the learner.

It is unlikely that only one response form or one mode will be used during an entire lesson. Instead, a range of response forms and modes could be used. The juxtaposition of response forms and modes will require the teacher to monitor students' responses and determine if the response form requires changing.

After Instruction

The primary purpose of an After Instruction phase is to recognize the importance of evaluating and reflecting upon the results of a lesson or teaching sequence. During this phase, the teacher should examine the student's performance and evaluate the six task dimensions in light of that performance. If adjustments are necessary, they should be made for the next lesson or teaching sequence. However, in general, wholesale and dramatic changes should be avoided. If dramatic changes are necessary, then the lesson and selection of task dimensions were poorly planned in the first place. It may be best to present the task again to the learner before making changes in the design of the lesson.

As a general rule, the appropriateness of a task dimension depends on the learner's performance on the task, and not on a logical analysis of the task independent of the learner's performance. Making adjustments in the full range of task dimensions within a proactive classroom management approach is based on the teacher's knowledge of his or her craft and the learner's instructional needs. While the principles of designing instruction are derived from a substantial body of research (Engelmann & Carnine 1982; Kameenui & Simmons 1990), the analysis we offer in this text is based on experience and logic. For example, logic and experience call for easing into a new and complex task by using an abbreviated schedule and easy response forms. However, if the learner is capable of handling a longer period of instruction and a more difficult response form and mode during initial instruction, then these task dimensions should be used. The design of a lesson plan and the selection of task dimensions depend on the teacher's judgment of the learner's capability.

It would be a serious mistake to design task dimensions that are easy for the learner because it may communicate to the learner that learning is not challenging. Moreover, the learner will not learn anything if not challenged cognitively and emotionally. On the other hand, learning need not be a punishing and frustrating experience. It can be exciting if the proper cognitive tension is created by designing task dimensions appropriate to the learner's ability and the educational outcomes.

SUMMARY

In this chapter, we defined and described six task dimensions. The purpose for examining these dimensions is based on the premise that the nature, structure, and demands of a task can set the stage for serious behavior problems. For example, tasks that are new and complex are likely to be more difficult than tasks that are mastered and simple. Similarly, tasks that are taught for an extended period of time and require a written production response are more difficult than tasks that are presented briefly and that require a choice response from the learner. By attending to the task dimensions and designing tasks appropriate for the learner, social behavior problems associated with difficult tasks can be avoided.

In addition, we described how the dimensions of tasks are considered within a temporal framework that consists of three phases of instruction: Before Instruction, During Instruction, and After Instruction. We argued that the Before Instruction phase requires special consideration because it is here that teachers select and design tasks appropriate to the learner's level of competence.

CHAPTER ACTIVITIES

1. Discuss the characteristics of a proactive approach to classroom management.
2. Define and give an example of the six task dimensions of instructional classroom management.
3. Discuss how the dimensions of tasks are considered within each of the three phases of instruction.

SUGGESTED READINGS

Algozzine, B., & Maheady, L. (1986). In search of excellence: Instruction that works in special education classrooms (special issue). *Exceptional Children, 52* (6).

Becker, W. (1986). *Applied psychology for teachers: A behavioral cognitive approach.* Chicago: Science Research Associates.

Roberts, C., & Zubrick, S. (1993). Factors influencing the social status of children with mild academic disabilities in regular classrooms. *Exceptional Children, 59* (3) 192-202.

chapter 4

A Temporal Framework for Instructional Classroom Management

Chapter Overview

INTRODUCTION

In the previous chapter, we described the instructional dimensions of classroom management and introduced the three phases of instruction—Before, During, and After Instruction. In this chapter, we examine the features and intricate requirements of each phase of instruction. As we noted previously, the management of academic and social behavior occurs within an instructional context. Management also takes place in real time; that is, what the teacher does in the face-to-face interaction with children represents only one of the three phases of instruction. Moreover, what the teacher does during instruction should be aligned both with what the teacher planned before instruction, as well as the expected accomplishments of the lesson anticipated after instruction.

ALIGNING THE PHASES OF INSTRUCTION

As with most events that occur outside the classroom and school, teaching follows the arrow of time and unfolds in a fairly predictable direction. By thinking about teaching in a temporal framework comprised of the Before, During, and After phases of instruction, the organization of management strategies within the context of instruction becomes clearer.

Too often the primary focus of teaching is on what the teacher does during instruction. It is during instruction that the teacher actively engages the learner and attempts to move the learner from a state of unknowing or partial knowing to a state of full or more complete knowing. This is the phase, as the saying goes, where the rubber meets the road and the integrity of the teaching content and the teacher–student interactions is often tested. However, while the during phase of instruction is important, it is by no means more important than the other two phases of instruction. In fact, is it arguable that the before phase of instruction is more important; after all, during instruction the teacher merely "delivers" and implements what was designed and planned before instruction. Of course, it is also arguable that the after phase of instruction is most important because what the teacher plans and delivers in the Before and During phases of instruction are guided by the outcomes that are expected in the After phase of instruction.

Obviously, no one phase of instruction is more important than another. The three phases are interdependent, which means that one phase of instruction and management cannot be planned independently of the other phases. All three phases must be conceptualized as independent but contiguous and connected organizational units. As Figure 4.1 indicates, the links between the phases of instruction cannot be left to chance but must be orchestrated if the goals and objectives for individual learners are to be accomplished.

BEFORE INSTRUCTION: DESIGNING INSTRUCTIONAL CLASSROOM MANAGEMENT

The Before Instruction phase sets the stage and establishes the foundation for sound instructional classroom management. The teacher must set the stage for a proactive, not reactive, instructional approach to managing student academic and social behavior. The teacher must also establish the foundation for building and

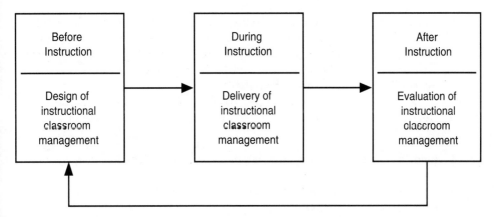

FIGURE 4.1 Instructional context

refining an Instructional Classroom Management approach for the entire school year. The teacher sets the stage by how he or she thinks about classroom management, how he or she talks about it to students, teachers, parents, and school administrators, and how he or she anticipates and responds to problems in the general school environment and the classroom.

In the list below, we identify five categories of activities that should be considered in the Before Instruction phase. Within each category, we identify several essen-tial features of a proactive Instructional Classroom Management approach. The list of features in each category is not exhaustive, but it provides a starting point for teachers to think about the kinds of considerations associated with bothinstruction and management.

Before Instruction Phase

Student Outcomes
1. Define the specific instructional objectives and student learning outcomes that are expected to be accomplished at the end of the lesson.

Task Design
1. Review and determine the appropriateness of the dimensions of the target task for the learners.
2. Modify selected task dimensions to accommodate learner's needs.
3. Allocate sufficient instructional time for each task and schedule time in ways that maximize student performance.
4. Identify tasks and component skills that require preteaching.

Management Plan
1. Identify the rules for how students are to behave in the classroom and during instruction.
2. Teach the rules for behaving appropriately in the classroom and during instruction.

3. Develop a plan for responding to unanticipated but potentially serious behavior problems during instruction (e.g., fights, disruptive tantrum).
4. Determine best use of physical space and seating of students during instruction that will maximize student performance and access to instruction and teaching materials.
5. Develop a plan for monitoring student behavior during instruction.
6. Develop a system for recording student errors during instruction.

Reinforcement Plan
1. Identify the appropriate dimensions of reinforcement for each specific task.
2. Develop a plan of reinforcement that will maximize student performance during instruction.
3. Develop a plan for responding to academic errors in which correct responses are reinforced and corrective feedback is provided.

Transition Plan
1. Identify the least intrusive procedures that will be used to decrease inappropriate behavior and increase appropriate behavior.
2. Develop and practice management procedures to ensure proper and effective implementation during instruction.
3. Develop an individual plan that is linked to a schoolwide discipline plan for responding to serious behavior problems.
4. If necessary, develop prompts and cues for thinking about punishment as a transition tool.

Student Outcomes

The desired student outcomes agreed upon before instruction begins set the focus for the following phases of instruction and determine, in part, the instructional tools and strategies that the teacher will use to move the student from a state of unknowing or partial knowing to a state of full or more complete knowing. Teachers must select the instructional tools and materials that are designed to ensure that the target skills and tasks are in fact taught. In many cases, the instructional materials will need to be modified to ensure that the outcomes will be accomplished.

Student outcomes can be stated in broad or narrow terms. Although it's neither feasible nor necessary for teachers to spell out in writing detailed student outcomes for each instructional lesson, we recommend that teachers have a very clear idea of the kinds of academic or social outcomes they want to accomplish by the end of each lesson. Without a clear idea of the expected student out-comes, the focus and execution of the lesson is in potential jeopardy, especially when behavior problems occur and disrupt the lesson. By targeting specific student outcomes ahead of time, the teacher will be able to gauge the extent to which the outcomes may set the stage for behavior problems or instructional difficulties. Once this is determined, the teacher can take the necessary steps to prevent those problems.

Designing Instructional Tasks

As noted in chapter 3 on task dimensions, the design of instructional tasks holds great potential for influencing student and teacher performance during instruction. Before instruction begins, tasks that are scheduled to be taught should be reviewed and the six task dimensions (e.g., history, response form, schedule, variation, modality, complexity) should be examined. Of course, these task dimensions cannot be scrutinized independent of the student outcomes. For example, if the outcomes and instructional objectives call for written production responses from the learner, then those task dimensions must be targeted for instruction.

In addition, if a task is new and the learner's responses are likely to be fragile, the teacher must be prepared to make changes in selected dimensions of the task (e.g., switch to a different response form, vary the sequence, complexity, modality, or schedule of the task). If the task is an established one, then the student's performance is not likely to be problematic (unless the task is too easy) and the teacher's readiness to change task dimensions is less significant. This readiness to make changes in task dimensions is an example of the proactive approach required in instructional classroom management. It is also important for the teacher to take note of the kinds of changes in task dimensions that are necessary during instruction, and the extent to which certain dimensions set the occasion for problem behaviors.

One of the most important features of the Before Instruction phase is the allocation and scheduling of instructional time for each task. A traditional schedule usually consists of 30 to 45 minute blocks of time that are allocated for reading, mathematics, science, and so on. In such a block schedule, a teacher typically teaches a lesson in reading, for example, and requires students to complete independent seatwork associated with the reading lesson. Because all of the teaching and learning activities are associated with reading, there is little variation in content and task demands. This kind of traditional schedule often sets the stage for behavior problems because the content and student response requirements are often predictable and redundant, which in turn leads to boredom and off-task behavior.

In contrast to a traditional block schedule is one in which several different topics, skills, or content areas are taught back-to-back in abbreviated time segments. The following schedule is designed for a second-grade class. Instead of teaching a reading lesson for 45 minutes, the allocated time would be scheduled as follows:

9:00–9:10   Review of specific errors made in previous reading lesson involving blending skills—oral small group production responding; medium-to-hard task. (10 minutes)

9:11–9:16   Review family of math facts—oral, production, individual responding; easy-to-medium task. (5 minutes)

9:17–9:32   Creative writing involving development of problem to be solved by main character—written, production response using structured story grammar writing sheets; hard task. (15 minutes)

9:33–9:36   Oral recitation of the capitals of selected states—production responses; easy task. (3 minutes)

9:37–9:45   Individual oral reading on student-selected book—oral production responding; one-to-one with teacher; easy-to-medium-hard task. (8 minutes)

The schedule consists of five different sets of activities that are to be taught in different blocks of time. The different tasks are unpredictable in sequence and their variation is likely to keep students engaged, motivated, and refreshed. This kind of schedule minimizes the amount of fatigue that is often associated with a block schedule in which the same content or topic is taught for an extended period of time. This schedule may not be feasible, but it may be used on a selective basis for students with behavior problems who have a difficult time attending to a task for long periods of time.

A final strategy for preparing instructional tasks is the planned use of preteaching. In this strategy, the teacher targets an academic or social skill that is likely to be a problem for the learner. In doing so, the teacher "primes" or prepares the learner to respond to a particular task by providing the learner with already taught information that will allow the learner to respond successfully. The preteaching strategy is especially useful for tasks that are new, complex, and potentially troublesome to the learner. An example of a preteaching strategy is given in Figure 4.2.

The task dimensions in Figure 4.2 justify the use of a preteaching strategy because the task is new, complex, and requires a written production response. Even though the task is taught immediately prior to the independent worksheet, the use of the preteaching strategy supports the student's transfer of the newly taught strategy in a context and format different from the teacher's oral and written demonstration on the blackboard. Although the preteaching strategy example in Figure 4.2 is specific to a newly taught task, it can be used for a range of new or old academic tasks.

In Figure 4.3 (see pp. 64–65), we apply the preteaching strategy to a motor task. In this case, the tasks involve walking through the halls to the library. As in most preteaching situations, the teacher has already taught students the skills required to perform the task, namely, that of walking quietly through the hallway. In Figure 4.3, the teacher decides to preteach going to the library because it is the beginning of the year and this is the first time the second-graders will make the trip to the library. For this particular task, the task dimensions are similar to the academic tasks in Figure 4.2. For example, the task is new and requires students to make an oral, motor-production response. Similarly, the task is easy

---

Task: Subtract two-digit subtrahends from two-digit minuends that require renaming in the one's column (e.g., 53 − 26 = ___)

Task history: New

Task response form: Production

Task modality: Written

Task complexity: Hard

Task variation: Unvaried

Task schedule: 35 minutes, unvaried

(The teacher has just completed teaching students the new task and distributes a worksheet of 15 problems for students to complete independently. Some of the problems require renaming, some don't.)

Teacher: Everyone, the problem on the board is the same as the first problem on your worksheet. Could someone read the problem for me? (Teacher calls on Craig.)

Craig: Fifty-three minus 26.

Teacher: Good job, Craig. Yes, 53 minus 26. Remember, some problems will require you to rename, so read each problem carefully and check the numbers in the one's column and decide if you have to rename. Get started.

(The teacher monitors the independent seatwork by moving around the classroom checking students' work.)

FIGURE 4.2 Preteaching strategy—academic activity

and not varied in its schedule or sequence of examples, which means the task is being taught in isolation and not in the context of other tasks or another lesson.

Four general conditions exist for which a preteaching strategy may be effective.

1. Preteach rules for how to behave before making the transition to a new context that may be unfamiliar (e.g., visiting another teacher's

FIGURE 4.3 Preteaching strategy—nonacademic activity

Task: Walk through the school hallways to the library.

Task history: New

Task reponse form: Production

Task modality: Motor/Oral

Task complexity: Easy

Task variation: Unvaried

Task schedule: Ten minutes, unvaried

(The teacher has taught the class the requirements for walking to the library. The class is about to visit the library.)

Teacher: I need everyone's attention before we leave for the library. I want to take a minute to talk about how I want you to behave walking down the hall to the library.

Teacher: What are some things I want you to remember when you're walking down the hall to the library?

A child volunteers: We should walk quietly.

Teacher: Good, but what does it mean to walk quietly?

Another child answers: It means not talking.

Teacher: Exactly, very nice. So when you walk quietly, is it okay to talk quietly or whisper?

Another child answers: No, it's not.

Teacher: What's another thing to remember when you're walking quietly down the hall to the library?

Another child volunteers: We should keep our hands and feet to ourselves.

FIGURE 4.3   (continued)

Teacher: That's right. Watch me. (Teacher flails arms back and forth to each side.) Am I keeping my hands to myself?

Same child answers: No you're not, because you can hit someone with your arms and no one can pass you.

Teacher: Good job. Alton, show me how you keep your hands to yourself when you walk down the hallway.

[Alton stands up and walks toward the front of the class and keeps his arms and hands close to his sides.]

Teacher: That's excellent, Alton. That's exactly the right way to walk quietly down the hall to the library.

Teacher: Before we leave for the library, I want to review quickly the rules for walking quietly down the halls. (The teacher quickly restates the two rules.) Now, I want you to prepare to go to the library. (The teacher walks around the class while students prepare to visit the library.) I'll know by your quiet waiting and your library books ready on your desk that you are ready to line up. (The teacher waits until it is quiet.) Very nice. Please line up to go to the library.

classroom), unknown (e.g., field trip), potentially ambiguous or troublesome (e.g., situations that have caused problems in the past, prior to going to a school assembly) for students. If there is any ambiguity, preteach the necessary behaviors or skills.

2. Preteach an already taught component skill prior to working a new and complex skill (e.g., the teacher points to the *a* in the word *rate* and applies a rule for reading these word types, "Remember when you read this word, you say the name of this letter").
3. Preteach *before* reentering class after an engaging and highly reinforcing activity (e.g., awards assembly, field trip).
4. Preteach after long absences and holidays.

In order for students to be successful at complex, higher-order operations, the component steps and pieces of the complex operations must be identified and taught. Frequently, however, serious behavior problems surface during difficult lessons and activities because students are required to think about and work complex operations for which they are not adequately prepared.

Designing a Management Plan

The *management plan* is the most traditional aspect of instructional classroom management. It is designed to control the movement of activities in the classroom in ways that allow bodies to move through space with a minimum amount of friction and unnecessary contact. A sound management plan addresses five different areas of concern: (1) rules for behaving appropriately in the classroom, (2) a systematic strategy for responding to potentially serious behavior problems, (3) efficient and effective use of physical space, (4) a system for monitoring student behavior, and (5) a system for recording student academic and social errors.

Identifying and Teaching Rules.   Rules are developed to inform students, from the very first day of school, of what the expectations are for behaving in classroom and school settings. Rules serve as the procedural anchoring points for both the teacher and the learner. They specify for the learner exactly what the teacher expects under most, if not all, instructional conditions. Specifically, the rules should describe for students the behaviors (i.e., gestures, language, physical movement) to perform under certain conditions. For example, if the conditions involve walking down the hall to the library (as described in Figure 4.3), then the rules will specify the behaviors (e.g., walking quietly, keeping hands and feet to your side).

If the conditions involve small-group, oral reading, then the rules should specify the required behaviors. For example, "When someone is reading, follow along with your eyes." The conditions for the rule are "when someone is reading," and the required behaviors are to "follow along with your eyes."

Rules can be very specific (e.g., "No touching others with your hands or feet at any time"), or they can be quite general (e.g., "Be kind to others."). The level of specificity required of rules depends on several factors, including the (a) teacher (e.g., experienced vs. inexperienced), (b) student cognitive level (e.g., high performers or low performers), (c) time of year (e.g., beginning or end of year), (d) school context (e.g., classroom, recess, bus, general school environment), (e) nature and history of schoolwide discipline (e.g., poor schoolwide discipline policy and history of serious behavior problems), and so on. In general, rules should be designed to meet the needs of the teacher, students, and instructional requirements. However, rules aren't developed in a vacuum, they require thought and careful planning. Kameenui and Simmons (1990) offer five general questions that guide teachers' thinking about rules and expectations:

1. What do I want my classroom to be like?
   Do I want my classroom to be highly organized with everything in its place most of the time?
   Do I want my classroom to be quiet most of the time?
   Do I want my children to be active and interactive with each other most of the time?
   Do I need to have things quiet or can I tolerate a great deal of activity?

2. How do I want children to treat me as a person?
   Is it acceptable for children to take issue with me and correct me when I am wrong?
   Is it acceptable for children to raise their voices even when they are right and I am wrong?
   Is it important for children to always, no matter what the circumstances, respond to me in a courteous manner?
3. How do I want children to treat each other as human beings?
   Is it acceptable for children to speak roughly or rudely to each other?
   Is it acceptable for children to laugh at each other's mistakes?
   Do I want children to be kind to each other and speak to one another with gentle voices?
4. What kind of information or values do I want to communicate to students about being an adult, an educator, a woman, or a man in today's society?
   Do I want to demonstrate a strong work ethic in which hard work is seen as important and necessary to succeeding?
   Do I want children to know that making mistakes is natural to the process of learning?
   Do I want children to respect the process of asking questions, no matter how silly or stupid the questions seem to be, and do I want to encourage children to ask questions?
5. How do I want children to remember me when the last day of school finally ends and I am no longer a part of their daily lives?
   What image do I want children to have of me when they think of me?
   What feelings do I want children to have when they think of me in their later years? (p. 476)

As Kameenui and Simmons (1990) state, "There are no right answers to these questions. The answers are personal to each teacher and are shaped by a teacher's teaching and life experiences. The answers, nevertheless, should reflect the teacher's genuine attempt to provide students with the best educational context possible" (p. 477). Posing these questions before the beginning of the school year ensures that ample time and consideration will be given to them.

Whatever the conditions, it is not feasible for rules to be of such remorseless specificity that they cover all possible behavioral conditions. More important than the rules themselves is the actual teaching of the rules and the examples and negative examples of an action the teacher uses to communicate the rules' requirements. The teaching of rules communicates to students what is important and valued.

Designing a Reinforcement Plan

In chapter 6, we describe the features of reinforcement and their correspondence with the dimensions of tasks. We conceptualize reinforcement as activities associated with increasing valued behaviors. Moreover, because the most frequent interactions a teacher will have with students are instructional interactions, then instructional interactions must be viewed and treated as reinforcement opportunities. By increasing and ultimately maximizing instructional opportunities, we likewise maximize reinforcement opportunities. Effective teaching naturally sets the occasion for reinforcement by leaving less to chance. Part of effective teaching is designing a reinforcement plan that considers not only student behavior, but also the dimensions of the task and the pattern of errors associated with specific tasks and student performance.

A carefully designed reinforcement plan aligns the dimensions of a task (e.g., history, response form, modality, complexity, schedule) with the dimensions of reinforcement (e.g., intensity, schedule, type, timing). For example, a brand-new task will require a different kind of reinforcement than will an old, familiar, well-established task. Specifically, a familiar task should require reinforcement that is delayed, less intense, and less frequent. In contrast, a new task may require a range of reinforcers (e.g., social, tangible, activity) that are delivered, immediately, more frequently, and with greater intensity. Chapter 6 describes the details for developing a reinforcement plan.

Designing a Remediation Plan

The purpose of the remediation plan is to acknowledge the need for "remediating" or correcting behavior problems that occur. Such a plan is in contrast to the proactive and preventative instructional strategies that serve as the basis of the instructional management approach advocated and described thus far. However, when problems can't be prevented, then it is imperative for teachers to have a very clear understanding of the procedures for decreasing the problem behavior; these procedures are commonly known as punishment procedures. Wolery, Bailey, and Sugai (1988) define punishment as "a functional relationship between a stimulus or event and a decrease in the occurrence of a behavior" (p. 336). In general terms, when the teacher presents or withdraws a "stimulus," and the target behavior *decreases*, punishment has occurred. In spite of the galaxy of meanings associated with the word, punishment (e.g., time-out, yelling, wall sits), the technical definition of punishment refers to the relationship between events in the environment (e.g., what the teacher says and does) and the resulting decrease in the target behavior. Therefore, if a target behavior decreases in the future, then the preceding events could be characterized as "punishing stimuli" (see chapter 7 regarding punishment). As Kameenui and Simmons (1990) point out, "Punishment and reinforcement are not defined by the actions of the teachers or school administrators, but by the reactions of children" (p. 481).

Only by understanding the technical requirements and features of punishment, is it possible to implement remediation strategies for correcting behavior problems. However, an instructional management approach conceptualizes punishment or remediation strategies as "transition" strategies or tools. If used correctly, punishment can be an effective tool for decreasing or stopping inappropriate behaviors. However, merely stopping a misbehavior is not enough because it does not provide the learner with information about how to behave appropriately. Punishment or remediation strategies must move a child quickly from a punishment context to a positive context of reinforcement and instruction. But the movement must be swift. By thinking about punishment as a transition tool, the teacher is in a mindset to move quickly from instruction "through" remediation and back to instruction and reinforcement.

Finally, the use of punishment procedures should be linked to a schoolwide discipline plan (see chapter 10). Punishment or remediation procedures should not be used in isolation, but instead in the broader context of school goals and expectations.

DURING INSTRUCTION: DELIVERING INSTRUCTIONAL CLASSROOM MANAGEMENT

The During Instruction phase in an instructional management plan is concerned with three categories of activities: (1) managing instruction, (2) delivering instruction, and (3) modifying instruction. The features in each category are as follows.

During Instruction Phase

Managing Instruction
1. Present and reinforce the rules and expectations at the beginning of the session of how students are to behave during instruction.
2. Preteach task requirements as necessary.
3. Monitor students throughout the instructional session by providing prompts and feedback when necessary.
4. Record persistent academic errors.

Delivering Instruction
5. Present information at a pace that maintains student attention and engagement.
6. Provide students with ample opportunities to respond.

Modifying Instruction
7. Make adjustments in the task dimensions (e.g., task modality, response requirements, task complexity), based on student performance.
8. Take note of academic errors and implement correction procedures consistently and appropriately.

Managing Instruction

The pace of presenting information and monitoring student performance during instruction can be very demanding, especially when we consider the hundreds of interactions that occur in the classroom every day. In order to orchestrate an effective, efficient, and engaging delivery of instruction, a well-established and well-designed instructional management plan must be in place. Specifically, the teacher must have confidence in the intended instructional tools and management strategies. The management of behavior during instruction is anchored to four dimensions of managing instruction: (1) presenting and reinforcing the rules to ensure clear expectations of student behavior, (2) preteaching difficult task requirements to ensure successful performance, (3) monitoring student performance and providing prompts and feedback when necessary, and (4) recording persistent errors in an effort to gauge the effectiveness of the teaching presentation.

The presentation of rules and expectations are essential to sound instructional classroom management because the expectations, when clearly specified for learners, set the ground rules for their responding to the instruction and the specific task requirements. Although it is widely acknowledged as important, the teaching of rules in clear and unambiguous terms is not easily accomplished. The general practice is for teachers merely to recite the rules by telling them to students. This practice is based on the assumption that students already know how to behave and that the teaching of what's already known is simply not necessary; in fact, it may appear redundant and in some cases, silly. However, although the assumption may be a reasonable one, it is not necessarily correct. The fact is that although some students may know how to behave under certain instructional conditions, it is unlikely that all students will know how to behave under all instructional conditions when the teacher, and not someone else, is present. More importantly, even if students know how to behave during instruction, it is important that the teacher clarify and affirm those expectations to establish a personal presence and to communicate the importance of the expectations and rules.

Rules should be taught during the first two to three instructional sessions (i.e., small group, large group, class lectures) in the first week of school. By teaching the rules at the beginning of the instructional session and school year, and by continuing to reinforce the rules throughout the year, the teacher communicates to students the importance of the rules in his or her general instructional management plan. However, the communication of the teacher's expectations depends not only on the frequency with which they are communicated, but also on the clarity with which they are taught. Specifically, the teaching of rules should be designed and delivered in the same way that any other skill, concept, operation, or academic piece of knowledge is designed and communicated. It is inadequate merely to tell students the rules. Teaching the rules of correct behavior requires (a) a clear statement of the rules, (b) the selection of positive and negative examples of each rule, (c) the presentation of examples of the rules in which positive and negative examples are appropriately juxtaposed, (d) the immediate and delayed assessment of students' knowledge of the rules, and (e) opportunities to practice the rules in the natural contexts (e.g., classroom, hallway, library) in which they will be applied. An example of a rule-teaching sequence is described in Figure 4.4 (see pp. 72–73).

In the example on teaching rules, the task is a new one and requires students to make oral, production responses to a fairly easy task. In addition, the teaching sequence on rules requires the presentation of concrete examples, both positive and negative, which are designed to communicate the boundaries of the expected behavior (e.g., speaking kindly to others). The design of the teaching sequence for teaching rules is no different than one that would be designed for teaching a concept.

As noted earlier, the preteaching of complex tasks is an effective strategy for preparing learners to respond successfully to difficult task requirements (see pages 62-65). For example, new rules can be pretaught immediately prior to their application.

Another important instructional management strategy involves the use of prompts and feedback as a means of monitoring student performance during instruction. There are a range of teaching prompts that include (a) verbal—written and oral, (b) facial, and (c) physical. The use of a particular prompt depends on a number of factors that vary according to the dimensions of the task (e.g., new or old, easy or difficult), the learner (e.g., age and developmental level), the learner's performance (e.g., working and completing the task), and the context of instruction (e.g., small group, large group, classroom, library). For example, during the first few weeks of school, it's appropriate for the teacher to use verbal and gestural prompts to remind students of the rules and teacher expectations (e.g., "Jennifer, I appreciate how you are staying on task and working on your writing assignment." The teacher gestures by getting John's attention and by pointing to John's paper. "John, I need you to work on your writing assignment").

It is important to record persistent student errors during instruction. Error patterns should inform the teacher about the nature of the instruction in general, and the specific task and management requirements. However, persistent errors cannot be managed adequately during instruction other than through a general correction procedure that involves modeling the correct response, assisting the child with the production of the response, if necessary, and requiring the learner to produce the response independently. Persistent errors require a fundamental adjustment in the design of the instruction, which must be considered in the Before phase of instruction. Specifically, persistent errors signal the following potential limitations on the part of the student and the teaching sequence: (a) lack of prerequisite knowledge and component skills to complete the target task, (b) inability to produce a complex response requirement, (c) inability to understand the task requirements, (d) lack of reinforcement, (e) fatigue, and so forth.

If errors during an instructional session are too frequent, the teacher should stop presenting the target task and switch to a neutral (i.e., not too easy or difficult) task with an entirely different set of task requirements (e.g., oral instead of written responses, choice instead of production responses). To continue presenting a task that is too difficult for students will more than likely lead to serious behavior problems. Once the teacher has determined the problems inherent in the design and delivery of the difficult task, then the requirements of the task or lesson can be taught separately, prior to reintroducing the entire task again.

FIGURE 4.4 Format for teaching rules

Task: Speak kindly to others

Task history: New

Task reponse form: Production

Task modality: Oral

Task complexity: Easy

Task variation: Unvaried

Task schedule: Five to seven minutes, unvaried

(It's the first day of class, and the teacher has spent the first 30 minutes greeting her third-grade class and discussing her expectations, the academic content and skills that will be covered during the year, and general procedures for moving about in the classroom and school.)

Teacher: I need everyone's attention. I want to take a minute to talk about how I want you to behave in and out of this classroom. Here's a rule I'd like you to follow when you are talking and working with each other. The rule is "Speak kindly to others." What's the rule to follow when you're talking and working with each other?

Student: Speak kindly to others.

Teacher: Yes, the rule is "Speak kindly to others."

(At this point, the teacher may want to solicit examples from students of what it means to speak kindly to others. In addition, the teacher may want students to generate *negative* examples of speaking kindly to others [e.g., speaking harshly and in an abrupt manner]. Following the examples volunteered by students, the teacher should continue with the following steps.)

Teacher: I'll show you exactly what I mean by the rule, Speak kindly to others. (Teacher approaches a student and looks directly into the student's face and speaks in a kind and direct tone.) "Joshua, may I borrow your pencil for a second?" (Joshua nods his head.)

FIGURE 4.4   (continued)

(The teacher approaches another student and speaks in a flat but polite tone of voice): "Alice, yesterday I gave you cuts at recess to play wall ball, but not today. Sorry."

(The teacher approaches another child and speaks in a gentle, but firm voice): "I'm sorry, Bobby, I would loan you my ponoil, but the last time you didn't return it."

Teacher: Now I'll show you what it looks like when you don't speak kindly to others. (Teacher approaches Bobby again and speaks in a harsh and loud tone): "I'm sorry, Bobby, I would loan you my pencil, but the last time you didn't return it."

(The teacher approaches another child and speaks in a flat, cold, abrupt tone): "What are you looking at? Do I owe you money or something?"

(The teacher approaches another student and asks in a harsh, gritting tone): "Where's my pencil?"

(The teacher speaks to the entire group): "Okay, I want you to watch and tell me if I'm speaking kindly to others or not." (The teacher approaches Joshua and speaks in a kind tone): "Where's my pencil?"

(The teacher presents several other positive and negative examples and asks students, "Am I speaking kindly to others?" Students respond by answering yes or no.)

Delivering Instruction

The two features of delivering instruction most associated with problem social behaviors during instruction are (1) the pace of instruction, and (2) the opportunities for responding. If the pace of instruction is either too fast or too slow, students may become distracted and frustrated, which may set the stage for behavior problems. The appropriate pace of instruction depends on the nature of the tasks and the learner, but in general, the pace of instruction should be brisk. In the case of complex tasks, the pace of instruction may need to be slowed, especially when tasks involve multiple steps and complex student responses. If the tasks are strictly verbal (e.g., a verbal chain such as days of the week, months of the year, mathematics facts), then the pace should be fairly brisk.

Students should also have ample opportunities to respond during instruction. When students are responding, the teacher has a basic measure of the student's engagement in the lesson. If students are not given an opportunity to respond, then the stage may be set for problem behaviors to occur.

AFTER INSTRUCTION: REFLECTING AND ADJUSTING INSTRUCTIONAL CLASSROOM MANAGEMENT

The final phase of the Instructional Classroom Management approach is that of reflecting upon the instruction after it is completed. In addition, the After Instruction phase should be the time for adjusting the instruction for the next Before Instruction phase. The After Instruction phase includes the features listed as follows, but stated in question form.

After Instruction Phase

Reflecting on Instruction
1. How do you feel about the lesson?

Assessing the Instruction
2. Were students able to perform the task at an appropriate criterion level?
3. Were there any serious or persistent behavior management problems?

Modifying the Instruction
4. Is there a pattern to student academic errors?
5. Are behavior problems associated with specific task dimensions?
6. Was the instruction motivating for students?
7. Did the lesson accommodate students' individual differences?

Reflecting on Instruction

After instruction, the teacher must take time to reflect on the lesson. The question for the teacher to answer is rather straightforward: "How do I feel about the lesson?" Obviously, this question requires teachers to make a subjective judgment about their performance. As such, the reflection can take many different forms. It can be focused on a specific task dimension, or it can be general in its focus but not targeted on a particular feature of the instructional session. The primary purpose of this exercise is to provide teachers with an opportunity to examine their feelings about the instructional session.

Assessing the Instruction

One of the most important considerations in the After Instruction phase is that of assessing the instruction based on student performance in the During Instruction phase. Specifically, the teacher must determine the answers to a series of questions. For example, "Were students able to perform the task at an appropriate criterion level?" The answer to this question is important because if students aren't able to reach the target criterion level, which is set by the teacher for the specified task, then the task may be too difficult, or the criterion inappropriate. Students' failure to reach criterion level performance may set the stage for problem behaviors. At first the problems may be minor ones, but any sustained failure to reach criterion level over time will take its toll on students (and teachers) and create potential management problems. Moreover, if students aren't reaching criterion level performance, then it's unlikely that they are accomplishing the objectives of the lesson.

Another important consideration is that of identifying any serious or persistent behavior problems that occur during instruction. Identifying these problems, however, only represents the first step of this process. In order to remediate the problems, it is also important to determine the degree to which the problems are associated with specific instructional task requirements. This requires an analysis of task dimensions and student responses. The strategies to address the persistent behavior problems are instructional ones (e.g., reteaching component skills, clarifying rules and expectations, preteaching), and punishment should be used only as a last resort.

Modifying the Instruction

In order to modify instruction in an effective and efficient manner, it is important to determine if there is a pattern to students' academic errors. Similarly, it is important to determine, as noted earlier, whether any behavior problems were associated with specific task dimensions. The modification of task dimensions is not easy and will require continued teaching and testing to discern the task requirements that are causing problems for students.

Finally, as part of the after instruction routine, we recommend that teachers determine whether students' individual differences (e.g., race, culture, disability) have been accommodated during instruction. However, while we feel that teachers must be knowledgeable about and sensitive to students' racial, cultural, and linguistic differences, from our reading of the literature, we believe that there is no valid or reliable evidence that instructional adjustments should be made *solely* on the basis of a student's race or ethnic background. Teachers must consider the full array of instructional and management options when individualizing their instructional and management programs.

The following list provides the reader with factors to consider and five suggestions for modifying the instruction when individualizing Instructional Classroom Management procedures. While the suggestions in this list are but a few among many, they serve as a starting point for teachers to make appropriate instructional and management adjustments for students.

Managing for Individual Differences

Factors to Consider
- As demographics change in the United States, students with diverse cultural and linguistic backgrounds comprise an increasingly large segment of the school population.
- There is evidence of an interaction between the teacher's rate of reinforcement and the race, gender, or disability of the student.
- Evidence suggests that punishment procedures are used more frequently with students from diverse backgrounds and students with disabilities than with other students.

- Students with disabilities and students from low-income homes are at greater risk for dropping out of shcool.

Individualizing Strategies
- Use multiple assessment approaches (e.g., written, oral) to accomodate students with diverse cultural and linguistic backgrounds.
- Monitor the rates of reinforcement that are used for all students to insure equitability across all students (e.g., race, ethnicity, gender).
- Teach students how to be sensitive to students from diverse ethnic, cultural, and linguistic backgrounds.
- Always document how frequently punishment is used with students and the effects it has on both behavior and academic performance.
- Develop training/information packages for parents from diverse cultures about special programs (e.g., special education, gifted education) that are available at school.

SUMMARY

In this chapter, we proposed a three-phase framework for thinking about and planning instructional classroom management. The framework consists of Before, During, and After phases of instruction and allows the teacher to gauge the students' instruction and management needs in each phase. By relying on this temporal framework, the teacher will be able to respond to students' instructional classroom management needs in ways that link teaching and managing behavior before, during, and after instruction. Moreover, by attending to the requirements of each phase of instruction, the teacher sets the stage for a proactive approach to instruction.

CHAPTER ACTIVITIES

1. Using the five questions that guide the teacher's thinking about rules and expectations in the classroom presented in the chapter, discuss your expectations for your classroom for each of the questions.
2. Choose a content area (e.g., social studies, science) and develop a 45 minute lesson that would help eliminate behavior problems. For this lesson, provide the time allotments for each lesson segment along with a discussion of the specific teaching and learning activities.
3. List and discuss the major components of each of the three phases of instruction.

SUGGESTED READING

Kameenui, E., & Simmons, D. (1990). *Designing instructional strategies: The prevention of academic learning problems.* Columbus, OH: Merrill.

chapter 5

Instructional Classroom Management Assessment

INTRODUCTION

Assessment activities in classroom management include the information-gathering techniques that a teacher uses to document behavior problems and to determine their causes. An assessment plan is developed to organize assessment activities, systematize information gathering, and develop a mechanism for program refinement. Assessment in classroom management has at least two primary purposes: (1) to determine the causes of ongoing behavior problems so that the teacher can develop interventions immediately, and (2) to help the teacher refine the entire instructional program so that the probability of misbehavior is decreased.

For this chapter, we have designed an assessment model that includes procedures that teachers implement as part of their instructional program. Instructional Classroom Management assessment is not intended to provide comprehensive assessment information; rather, it enables the teacher to place assessment activities in the context of instruction so that instructional solutions to behavior and learning problems can be developed. Unlike other approaches, the assessment activities and questions we propose link assessment to instruction. Many teachers think of assessment in behavior management as an entirely separate activity from instruction. We believe this approach has a negative effect on developing successful behavior management programs.

WHY DEVELOP AN ASSESSMENT PLAN?

There are several important reasons for developing an assessment plan integral to the teaching program. First, a careful assessment of classroom organization, behavior management, and instructional design before instruction begins allows the teacher to develop a teaching program that actually decreases the potential of behavior problems. If assessment is completed carefully and systematically, it can be an effective tool for preventing classroom behavior and learning problems.

Second, if an assessment plan is in place, it is possible for the teacher to respond to a behavior problem humanely and effectively. Proper assessment will allow the teacher to collect information that will assist in the development of an instructional program that teaches students how to behave appropriately.

Assessment can aid the teacher in increasing the achievement of students while at the same time improving social behavior. Simply put, if a detailed assessment plan is in place, the teacher is more likely to make proper refinements in the teaching program.

In many assessment approaches, the teacher is taught to evaluate the behavior of the student only when he or she is disruptive. Consequently, the focus of assessment in behavior management is on only one dimension of the teaching equation—the learner. The teacher will usually employ assessment activities that document and identify student misconduct (e.g., rates of on-task behavior, frequency of talk-outs, and percentage of correct responses). In another approach, the teacher will use standardized instruments to determine the seriousness of a problem. These instruments, often developed in the form of a checklist, do not provide the teacher information to help determine causes of the behavior problems. This approach separates assessment from instruction and limits the usefulness of the information to the teacher.

The assessment model described in this chapter contains no dichotomy between teaching and assessment because both are integral to the teaching plan. This chapter introduces an assessment model that is tailored for instructional classroom management. We describe the features of the Instructional Classroom Management assessment model and the specific assessment activities for each of the different phases of instruction. The proposed model expands the focus of assessment to include instructional and noninstructional variables that may contribute to disruptive classroom behavior. The explicit purpose of this model is to provide a direct linkage between assessment and instructional activities. To achieve this goal, we describe procedures that allow for assessing the instructional task, the learner, the setting, and the curricular materials.

TRADITIONAL ASSESSMENT IN BEHAVIOR MANAGEMENT

Based on our analysis, it appears that most assessment models are used in one of two ways. First, many assessment activities are designed for a specific classroom management approach. For example, in assertive discipline, a series of teacher worksheets serves as the assessment tool for Canter's program. Teachers are asked to respond to a series of discipline-related questions such as, "For which students have you failed to set sufficiently firm consequences?"; "In general, how do you verbally respond to the student's behavior that you want?" (Canter & Canter 1976, p. 183).

Dreikurs's logical consequences also have an informal system of assessment built directly into the program. The teacher is directed to answer several key questions related to the refinement of the consequences for misbehavior (Duke & Meckel 1984). For example, the teacher might ask, "What is the goal of the student's disruptive behavior?" and "What are the logical consequences of the student's behavior?" These questions are obviously narrow in focus and do not guide the teacher to evaluate the entire teaching program systematically. In each of these assessment models, the evaluation questions do not provide teachers the necessary information to develop instructional solutions to behavior problems.

Another large group of assessment activities is derived from generic models not associated with specific classroom management programs. Within this group, the behavioral approach and the standardized testing approach are cited most frequently.

Kameenui and Simmons (1990) suggest that the purpose of norm-referenced assessment "is to determine a learner's degree of deviation from the norm group" (p. 24). Norm-referenced measures in behavior management present information on how a student is behaving relative to his or her peers, under standardized testing conditions. In general, these tests do not provide the teacher instructionally relevant information on how to manage students in the classroom.

Behavioral assessment focuses on the student's behavior. This will often yield information on the frequency of the behavior, the context in which the problem behavior surfaces, and the duration of the behavior. This information is important to consider when developing strategies to react to classroom management problems. However, in our opinion, behavioral measures are less helpful in providing the teacher information on the instructional aspects of a behavior problem.

Limitations of Assessment Models in Behavior Management

There are four significant limitations to several current assessment approaches in behavior management, which are the failure to (1) link assessment to instruction, (2) provide information that would allow the teacher to develop proactive classroom management procedures, (3) assess all phases of instruction, and (4) incorporate assessment activities within the normal teaching routine. Each of these limitations is discussed as follows.

Linking Assessment to Instruction.   First, most assessment models fail to link assessment activities to procedures for improving instructional programs. For example, when discussing how teachers should first implement assertive discipline, Canter states, ". . . it [discipline planning] involves periodically at the end of the day, week, etc., focusing your attention on any existing or potential problems you may have" (Canter & Canter 1976, p. 148). Interestingly, this recommendation focuses the assessment strictly on the student's behavior. No call is sounded for a detailed instructional assessment of the behavior problem. Canter's approach greatly limits the effectiveness of a teacher's assessment activities. If, for example, a teacher's first assessment activity in response to disruptive behavior is to count the off-task behaviors, then it is not possible for the teacher to link this assessment information to specific instructional solutions to the behavior problem. If classroom disruption is in part caused by the inadequacy of the instructional materials or teaching methods being used, then an assessment model must include activities that assess these areas. Traditional assessment models in behavior management fail to guide the teacher in ways that lead to development of instructional solutions to classroom behavior problems.

Developing Proactive Procedures. A second limitation is that many of the models do not provide teachers with information that will allow for proactive classroom management. Instead, teachers are instructed to implement assessment activities in response to classroom disruption. For example, in Assertive Discipline, the teacher is never directed to complete an assessment of the instructional environment and teaching materials. Rather, teachers are asked to evaluate how they respond to disruptive behavior. In this approach, there is no acknowledgment that behavior problems may be related to, or promoted by the teacher's instructional program. This, in our opinion, often fosters reactive solutions to classroom disruption. Because the assessment focus is on the behavior of the student, the teacher is generally not looking at ways to solve classroom management problems proactively. Without a thorough examination and assessment of the contribution that instruction makes to disruptive behavior, the teacher is not able to modify teaching procedures to maximize student learning.

Considering the Phases of Instruction. Another limitation of many assessment models is that the procedures are not *dynamic;* that is, they do not provide a flexible framework for assessment of behavior problems for each specific phase of instruction. Because the focus is rather narrow (e.g., keying only on the consequences of misbehavior as in the Dreikurs model), teachers are locked into a rigid model that may not have relevance to their particular classroom problems. Furthermore, assessment procedures are not differentiated for the Before, During, or After phases of instruction (Kameenui & Simmons 1990). In addition, most assessment models do not provide specific assessment activities tailored to the various phases of the 180-day school year. By not addressing the entire school year schedule, we assume that the same classroom management activities developed for the beginning of the year must then apply to the end of the year.

Incorporating Assessment into Teaching. Finally, most assessment models are designed so that evaluation activities are supplemental, not primary, to the teacher's instructional responsibilities. Because instruction is not usually linked to assessment, many teachers assume that assessment is to be completed only in response to behavior problems. Teachers are not trained to consider that behavior problems can be caused by weak instruction or poorly designed curriculum programs. Consequently, many teachers have not learned how to incorporate assessment activities within their normal instructional activities.

Given the problems just described, it is not surprising that most assessment models do not pose the correct assessment questions. Instructional classroom management considers the curriculum, the task, and the context in which the misbehavior occurs. The purpose of assessment in instructional classroom management is to gather information necessary for simultaneously improving the academic and social behavior of students.

FEATURES OF THE INSTRUCTIONAL CLASSROOM MANAGEMENT ASSESSMENT MODEL: LINKING ASSESSMENT, MANAGEMENT, AND INSTRUCTION

Before we describe the specific components of Instructional Classroom Management assessment, we need to discuss the features of the model briefly to help the reader understand the specific assessment activities. If the features of the assessment model are not consistent with the features of the instructional and behavioral model, then linking the teaching, management, and assessment models is premature. The Instructional Classroom Management assessment model provides for proactive assessment that is comprehensive and linked to the teaching plan. Each of these features is discussed as follows.

Proactive Assessment

The well-known aphorism states that an ounce of prevention is worth a pound of cure. Prevention in classroom management is possible with effective, proactive assessment procedures. One important feature of the Instructional Classroom Management assessment model is that it identifies instructional features a teacher should consider when attempting to determine the causes of misbehavior.

Comprehensive Assessment

To be effective, an assessment model must be comprehensive. The teacher must include assessment questions that sample activities that occur before, during, and after instruction. The assessment model must also reflect the structure of the instructional plan. Because the Instructional Classroom Management assessment model is comprehensive, as illustrated in Figure 5.1, the teacher is engaged in assessment activities throughout the school day, not as separate, isolated activities, but as part of the regular teaching routine. The teacher routinely evaluates the classroom organization, the behavior management strategies, and the adequacy of the instructional program as part of her teaching.

Assessment Linked to Instruction

A critical feature of the Instructional Classroom Management assessment model is that assessment activities are linked to instruction. The evaluation questions a teacher asks in each of the three phases of the model are tied directly to variables related to achievement and compliance. Once teachers have collected assessment data, the information can be used to make changes in the instructional program.

Instructional Classroom Management Assessment Model.   The language of most assessment models reflects the clear separation between instruction and assessment. Most assessment models in behavior management focus on control. There is little information on how to incorporate programs that teach students alternatives to misbehavior. The Instructional Classroom Management assessment model is qualitatively different. Rather than emphasizing control, this model focuses on developing instructional procedures to teach students appropriate classroom behavior. The foundation for developing teaching programs in behavior management is the assessment plan a teacher uses to make program adjustments. If the assessment plan focuses primarily upon the punitive aspects of behavior management, then the teacher's intervention program will reflect the same emphasis.

The Instructional Classroom Management assessment model is presented graphically in Figure 5.1. The multifaceted model is composed of three assessment phases:

FIGURE 5.1   Instructional classroom management assessment model

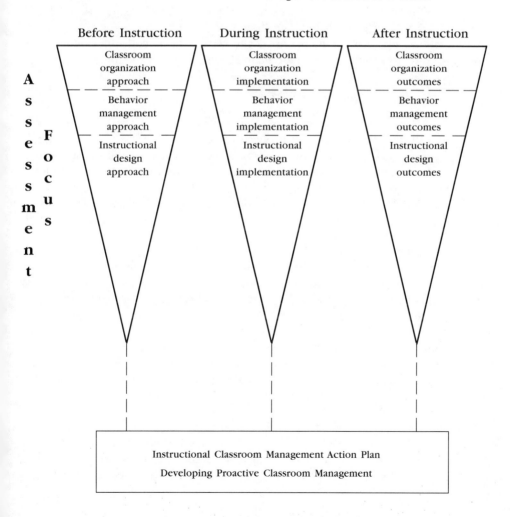

Before Instruction, During Instruction, and After Instruction. In addition, each phase employs a three-level assessment approach that examines class organization, behavior management, and instructional design. The triangles denote that initial assessment activities are completed with broad strokes, across all three phases. That is, broader questions that assess organization are asked first. Next, behavior management questions are posed. To complete the assessment plan, the teacher focuses on specific instructional design features related to classroom management. Finally, as Figure 5.1 shows, the information collected during assessment is ultimately converted into a plan for developing proactive modifications in the areas of classroom organization, behavior management, and instructional design.

ASSESSMENT BEFORE INSTRUCTION

The Before Instruction phase focuses primarily on preparing instructional activities that must be in place *before* the instruction is delivered. Assessment in this phase begins long before students enter the classroom by collecting information on classroom organization, behavior management, and instructional design.

Classroom Organization

In Figure 5.2, specific questions are posed for each level of assessment within each phase. In the Before Instruction phase, the questions are designed to prompt the teacher to examine his or her approach to classroom organization. We recommend that teachers ask and answer these questions well before students arrive in the classroom at the beginning of the school year.

   If adjustments are warranted, then the target feature needs to be revised. For example, the teacher may need to revise the amount of independent seatwork assigned or the criterion level of performance expected of students during independent seatwork or homework.

   An important part of the Instructional Classroom Management assessment model for each phase of assessment is the Evaluate/Revise/Reconsider (ERR) process. This process involves urging teachers to evaluate, revise, and reconsider their responses to each question. This three-step process allows for a systematic and organized approach to assessment. During the evaluation step, the teacher asks the eight assessment questions related to classroom organization. It is at this point that the teacher collects assessment information proactively to increase the probability of positive academic and behavioral outcomes in the classroom. The assessment questions cover activities in transition, instruction, and organization. To evaluate each question, the teacher need not engage in a formal and lengthy evaluation process. Instead, the teacher simply needs to target the particular feature (e.g., transition between classroom activities, assignment completion) and take stock of the situation by deciding if adjustments are required. For example, the teacher asks question number 2 (see Figure 5.2): Are students completing

Goal:	To evaluate, revise, and reconsider the general problems in the organization and administration of instruction
Phase:	Before Instruction
Focus:	Approach to classroom organization

Evaluate/Revise/Reconsider (ERR)

1. Does the classroom organization and structure allow for smooth transition between groups, classes, or activities?

2. Are students completing their assignments at a high criterion level of performance?

3. Are students happy, cooperative, and considerate of each other and the teacher?

4. Is adequate time allocated for instruction in critical academic areas?

5. Is the plan for organizing and managing the classroom proactive?

6. Is the physical arrangement of the class designed to facilitate optimal learning?

7. Do students receive clear and systematic feedback on their work and classroom/school behavior?

8. Have classroom routines been established to facilitate order?

FIGURE 5.2 Level 1: Classroom organization assessment

their assignments at a high criterion level of performance? If this is an area that needs attention, then the teacher revises the teaching plan to reflect the necessary change. The teacher may conclude that the number of independent worksheet assignments is too great and make the appropriate adjustment. This is accomplished during the revise step. Once a revision is completed, the teacher enters the reconsider step and evaluates the revision in the context of other changes made in the teaching and management plan. This is an important step because changes in one area of a teaching plan may require adjustments in another.

The teacher uses the three-step procedure (ERR) for each of the remaining assessment questions. For example, the teacher poses question 1: Does the classroom organization and structure allow for smooth transition between groups, classes, or activities? We recommend that the teacher consider the location of instructional groups and instructional materials to determine the likelihood of quick student transitions from one activity to another. If the room organization does not facilitate easy student movement and quick teacher preparation for each instructional group, then the classroom organization must be modified.

Behavior Management Approach

The second level in the Before Instruction phase (see Figure 5.3) focuses on the Behavior Management approach. As illustrated in Figure 5.1, the assessment focus becomes more narrow, and the assessment questions a teacher asks are related directly to issues in behavior management. Why does the teacher wait until after classroom organization has been evaluated before addressing behavior management? Classroom organization is concerned with the entire classroom or school environment and allows the teacher to cast a broad assessment net to address potential management and instructional problems. In contrast, the behavior management and instructional design strands of each phase are more narrow in scope.

The six assessment questions key the teacher to the following critical assessment areas: (1) the presence of classroom rules, (2) the use of reinforcement, (3) the process for responding to severe or chronic behavior problems, (4) data collection procedures, and (5) the role of punishment in the classroom.

There are three reasons for focusing on these areas before instruction. First, employing a mechanism to determine the appropriate use of reinforcement and punishment is critical if we conceptualize classroom management as basically a teaching endeavor. A management system will not work effectively over an entire academic year if classroom rules and reinforcement and punishment approaches are not appropriate. Second, we recommend that the teacher place emphasis on the mechanism for responding to serious and chronic behavior problems. If an effective process is not in place for managing this type of behavior, it is unlikely that the teacher can maintain a positive learning environment for all students in the class.

We also recommend that the teacher follow the three-step assessment process: Evaluate/Revise/Reconsider. The teacher first asks an assessment question (e.g., Is a delivery system in place for responding to serious behavior problems?), and if the answer suggests a revision in the teaching plan, the teacher makes the required adjustment. Finally, the teacher reconsiders the change in the context of other changes made for this assessment phase. For example, if the teacher determines that an adequate system is not in place for recording and documenting serious behavior problems, an adjustment must be made in the organization of the Behavior Management approach. By making this change before any serious behavior problems occur, the teacher proactively manages the classroom.

Goal: To evaluate, revise, and reconsider specific problems in the management plan of the classroom

Phase: Before Instruction

Focus: Approach to behavior management

Evaluate/Revise/Reconsider (ERR)

1. Are the classroom rules clear, established, and posted in the classroom?

2. Is a delivery system in place for praising, acknowledging, and rewarding students' academic accomplishments and social responsibilities?

3. Is a mechanism in place for responding to serious behavior problems?

4. Is a systematic process in place for recording and documenting behavior problems?

5. Is the punishment system designed primarily as a transition tool?

6. Are classroom routines clearly defined, established, and posted in the classroom?

FIGURE 5.3   Level II: Behavior management assessment

Instructional Design Approach

The final level of assessment in the Before Instruction phase (see Figure 5.4) requires that the teacher evaluate his or her approach to instructional design as part of the preinstructional activity. Included in this assessment are the evaluation of the type of instructional program to be used, the types of student responses to be required, and the teacher's role during the presentation of new content. A teacher cannot exert instructional control over students unless the curriculum approach is designed to facilitate clear and sound instruction.

The 14 assessment questions for this level are presented in Figure 5.4. We recommend that the teacher answer each question carefully to determine the extent to which the design of the instructional program will foster learning.

FIGURE 5.4 Level III: Instructional design assessment

Goal:	To evaluate, revise, and reconsider the specific features of instruction
Phase:	Before Instruction
Focus:	Approach to instructional design

Evaluate/Revise/Reconsider (ERR)

1. Is it necessary to add more examples of the target skill to the lesson?

2. Is it necessary to change the sequence of examples in the target lesson?

3. Will students require more practice examples of the new target skill?

4. Will students require a new schedule of instruction that involves sequencing easy, familiar task with the new, difficult and unfamiliar task?

5. Will students require highly prompted, teacher-directed guidance, which includes frequent reinforcement and mastery performance on progressively more difficult segments of the new skill?

6. Are instructional materials adequately designed to meet the needs of the lowest performing student?

7. What preskills are required of students in order for them to learn from the target lesson?

8. What is the required criterion level of mastery for the lesson? (e.g., Are students required to master x number of problems at 100 percent accuracy? 85 percent accuracy?)

9. Will students require guided instruction from the teacher during the first part or segment of the lesson?

10. Will students require a more time or less time to work on a new or difficult part of the lesson?

FIGURE 5.4 (continued)

11. Is it necessary to make the student response format easier? (oral-choice response before written-choice or production responses).

12. Will students be directed by the teacher during the target lesson in a large group, small group, or independently?

13. Does the target lesson involve *new* skills, operations, or strategies for the learner?

14. Are clearly defined procedures developed for teaching rules and routines?

We recommend that the teacher examine these assessment questions, especially when students are presented with new or more varied instructional content. In order to institute this level of assessment effectively, the teacher must look at the specific structure of classroom academic programs. For example, question 6, Are instructional materials adequately designed to meet the needs of the lowest-performing student?, requires that the teacher evaluate curriculum programs at a technical level. The teacher must evaluate the number of practice examples, the sequence of instructional examples, and the time scheduled for teaching the skill. Behavior problems are more likely to develop if the technical adequacy of a program is questionable.

ASSESSMENT DURING INSTRUCTION

The assessment plan for the During Instruction phase focuses on issues relevant to the teacher delivering instruction. As in the Before Instruction phase, these questions are related to the classroom organization, behavior management, and instructional design. However, in this phase, the focus of assessment is on implementing the instructional program. If the information in this phase is used correctly, the teacher can improve classroom behavior while also increasing students' academic performance. In the Instructional Classroom Management assessment model, classroom organization questions are asked first, followed by questions concerning implementation in behavior management and instructional design.

Implementation of Classroom Organization

In Figure 5.5, seven assessment questions about the implementation of classroom organization are presented. The teacher continues to follow the ERR system during this assessment phase to ensure that assessment activities will be

Goal:	To evaluate, revise, and reconsider specific problems in the behavior management plan for the classroom
Phase:	During Instruction
Focus:	Implementation of behavior management

Evaluate/Revise/Reconsider (ERR)

1. Do you review the rules?

2. Are students attending, following along and responding to the lesson?

3. Is the rate of reinforcement high, and is it delivered contingently?

4. Is punishment used too frequently to control inappropriate behavior?

5. Is the process for recording data simple and unobtrusive?

6. Are students interacting positively and enthusiastically to the lesson?

FIGURE 5.5   Level I: Classroom organizational assessment

administered in a systematic manner. The assessment information that is derived from these questions will help the teacher make ongoing adjustments in the teaching program if behavior problems exist in the classroom. The questions for this level are general and assess implementation issues in classroom organization. The focus is on how the teacher can facilitate effective organization while teaching.

We recommend that the teacher pose these questions early in the school year so that the teaching program can be adjusted accordingly. We also suggest that teachers ask these classroom organization questions frequently during instructional activities. In fact, even if behavior management problems are not evident, the teacher would be wise to collect assessment data periodically in this area. The answers to several of these questions may change as the school year progresses. For example, the answer to question 2, "Are students responding at a high rate and enthusiastic about the lesson?," can change to reflect students' placement in instructional programs. A student may be enthusiastic during one instructional unit but relatively unenthusiastic during another. The teacher can use this assessment information to adjust and fine-tune the classroom organization.

Implementation of Behavior Management

The next area of assessment in the During Instruction phase is in behavior management (see Figure 5.6). The teacher should ask six questions during assessment.

The six questions cover a wide range of activities in behavior management. If the answer to, "Do you review and reinforce the rules?" is "no" to either part, then the teacher must begin to review and systematically reinforce the stated rules. We have found that many behavior problems occur because the teacher does not review and reinforce those students who follow the classroom rules. A negative answer to any of the remaining questions also points to the need for significant changes in behavior management. The basis for potential behavior problems may be in low levels of student attention (question 2), low rates of teacher reinforcement (question 3), inappropriate use or high rates of punishment (question 4), and inappropriate data collection procedures (question 5). We also have found that insufficient student enthusiasm and involvement in the lesson can portend classroom disruption as well (question 6).

FIGURE 5.6   Level II: Behavior management assessment

Goal:	To evaluate, revise, and reconsider specific problems in the behavior management plan for the classroom
Phase:	During Instruction
Focus:	Implementation of behavior management

Evaluate/Revise/Reconsider (ERR)

1. Do you review and reinforce the rules?

2. Are students attending, following along, and responding to the lesson?

3. Is the rate of reinforcement high, and is it delivered contingently?

4. Is punishment used too frequently to control inappropriate behavior?

5. Is the process for recording data simple and unobtrusive?

6. Are students interacting positively and enthusiastically to the lesson?

Instructional Design Implementation

The final focus of assessment for the During Instruction phase (see Figure 5.7) is in the area of instructional design. How instructional materials are designed, the manner in which a teacher presents the content, and the sequence of teaching examples are a few of the variables that have great influence on student behavior.

The focus of the questions in the instructional design area is narrow and centers primarily on instructional variables. The 11 assessment questions incorporate three areas of concern: (1) teacher presentation techniques, (2) student responding, and (3) instructional content. For example, three questions relate to the teacher's presentation of material (e.g., question 1, pace of instruction; question 2, think time for students; question 5, amount of teacher involvement). If a teacher adequately presents material to the students, the students will likely follow classroom rules and perform more closely to the levels expected by the teacher. Research suggests that proper teacher presentation techniques positively influence the behavior of students and their academic performance (Kameenui & Simmons 1990).

The teacher is able to assess the quality of students' responses by answering question 3 (Are students meeting specified criteria?), question 7 (Is the student response form acceptable?), and question 10 (Are students following directions?). Disruptive behavior can be prompted by the type of responses students are asked to make. For example, if students are asked to write lengthy responses to questions when their writing skills are not sufficient, some students may respond by engaging in inappropriate behavior.

Five questions (4, 6, 8, 9, and 11) directly assess the instructional content of the lesson to determine if behavior problems are a result of the lesson structure. The teacher must determine the extent to which the content of the lesson should be modified to prevent or eliminate disruptive behavior. For example, if the teacher fails to provide students adequately with detailed corrections to errors during instruction (question 4), then social and academic problems may arise.

ASSESSMENT AFTER INSTRUCTION

In the Instructional Classroom Management assessment model, the final phase of assessment occurs after instruction is completed. This phase focuses on the outcomes of the instructional and management program. By following the three-phase cycle of assessment, the teacher ensures that the assessment plan will be continuous throughout the unit of instruction, which allows for ongoing modification of the instructional program.

Classroom Organization Assessment

As with the Before and During phases of assessment, After Instruction assessment begins with the teacher evaluating classroom organization. However, the focus of this phase is on *outcomes*. The six questions for this assessment component are presented in Figure 5.8.

Goal:	To evaluate, revise, and reconsider the specific features of instruction
Phase:	During Instruction
Focus:	Implementation of instructional design

Evaluate/Revise/Reconsider (ERR)

1. Does the pacing of instruction maintain student attention?

2. Are students given adequate think time?

3. Are students meeting the specified criterion level of performance?

4. Are the procedures for correcting academic errors effective and timely?

5. Is the amount of teacher direction and prompting adequate? Is it too much? too little?

6. Are the instructional examples clear and unambiguous?

7. Is the student response form acceptable or is it too difficult?

8. Is the lack of prerequisite knowledge and skills interfering with acquisition of new knowledge?

9. Are academic errors occurring at too high a rate?

10. Are students following the directions during independent learning activities?

11. Are rules and routines taught using effective instructional procedures?

FIGURE 5.7 Level III: Instructional design assessment

Goal:	To evaluate, revise, and reconsider the general problems in the organization and administration of instruction
Phase:	After Instruction
Focus:	Outcomes of classroom organization

Evaluate/Revise/Reconsider (ERR)

1. Did you accomplish the goals you set at the beginning of the lesson?

2. Is more instructional time required to meet learning objectives?

3. Does the plan for managing instructional transitions need to be revised?

4. Does the criterion level of performance need to be revised to match the learning objectives?

5. Do the instructional materials need to be adapted, modified, or replaced completely?

6. Do other classroom rules need to be identified and taught?

FIGURE 5.8 Level I: Classroom organization assessment

These questions are expansive and allow the teacher to get an idea of whether an adjustment in the organization of the program is necessary. These questions will require the teacher to be reflective about the results of the instructional program. For example, the teacher must ask if he or she accomplished the goals set at the beginning of the lesson. If the answer to this question is no, the teacher must reassess his or her instructional goals and perhaps the classroom design and structure.

Important to this assessment phase is the teacher's evaluation of the students' performance records. For example, the teacher should look at criterion-referenced tests that were administered during the instructional program. This can help determine those goals that have not been met and may provide some insight into why instructional expectations have not been fulfilled.

It is during this assessment phase that the teacher determines if instructional time was adequate to meet instructional goals. Increasing instructional time in difficult content areas may be a way to increase student performance. The plan for making transitions and adequacy of instructional materials are also assessed at this time. We recommend that outcomes in classroom organization be assessed at the completion of each instructional unit. This assessment does not demand excessive time, and the program adjustments made will be important for preventing and decreasing behavior problems and for improving the school performance of the students.

Behavior Management Assessment

The assessment of outcomes in behavior management is the next level of evaluation that the teacher completes. Five questions for assessment of this area are presented in Figure 5.9.

The teacher assesses the effects of reinforcement techniques, the classroom monitoring system, classroom rules, and punishment procedures. These assessment questions should be asked at the completion of each instructional unit. It should be emphasized here that even if the teacher has not encountered behavior problems, it is important to complete all assessment activities and answer all

FIGURE 5.9   Level II: Behavior management assessment

Goal:	To evaluate, revise, and reconsider specific problems in the behavior management plan of the classroom
Phase:	After Instruction
Focus:	Outcomes of behavior management

Evaluate/Revise/Reconsider (ERR)

1. Are the rules appropriate for the current learning objectives?

2. Is the reinforcement system effective?

3. Is the mechanism for managing serious behavior problems effective?

4. Is the student monitoring system effective?

5. Are the punishment procedures acceptable?

questions. It will then be easier for the teacher to make the transition from one instructional unit to the next effectively.

Instructional Design Assessment

The 11 questions for this final assessment are presented in Figure 5.10. This level of assessment will take more time to complete than the first two levels of this phase.

The 11 questions for this final assessment activity require the teacher to reflect on instructional design outcomes. For this phase of assessment, the teacher takes both a short-term and a long-term view of management and determines if adjustments are necessary to maintain the cooperation of the students for the course of the entire school year. The first five questions have a short-term focus and center on daily outcomes of the students. For example, in question 1, the teacher determines the role that instructional pacing plays in behavioral and academic outcomes. The teacher's attention is on either the outcomes from the daily lesson or the unit of instruction. Similarly, question 4 asks if the sequence or number of instructional examples needs adjustment so that student performance can be improved.

The last six questions focus on instructional design issues that are long term. These questions require the teacher to look beyond the daily lesson or unit of instruction. Question 6, for instance, requires the teacher to assess criterion levels of performance in relation to the target learning and behavioral objectives. In this case, the teacher must look beyond short-term objectives and focus instead on whether criterion levels of performance need adjustment to increase performance. Question 10 (Are the students transferring learned skills to new learning contexts?) and question 11 (Do procedures for teaching classroom rules and routines need to be modified?) are examples of long-term assessment questions. In this case, the teacher looks for evidence of transfer of learning or the potential for transfer. We recommend that all assessment questions for outcomes of instructional design be asked frequently throughout the school year.

Instructional Classroom Management
Assessment Checklist

Figure 5.11 presents a checklist of all features of the instructional classroom management assessment previously described. To utilize the checklist, teachers employ a three-point rating scale. The scoring mechanism is designed to allow the teacher to prioritize necessary teaching modifications quickly. For example, after a teacher completes the Before Instruction phase of assessment and answers each of the assessment questions for classroom organization, behavior management, and instructional design, she completes the appropriate sections of the checklist. If the teacher feels that the area being evaluated is not in need of change, then a 1 (Acceptable) is checked, indicating that no teaching modifications are needed. However, if the teacher finds teaching modifications

Goal:	To evaluate, revise, and reconsider the specific features of instruction
Phase:	After Instruction
Focus:	Outcomes of instructional design

Evaluate/Revise/Reconsider (ERR)

1. Does the pacing of instruction need to be adjusted?

2. Do students require more think time?

3. Are the procedures for correcting academic errors effective and appropriate?

4. Does the instructional lesson require more examples or a different sequence of examples?

5. Do prerequisite knowledge and skills need to be taught?

6. Does the criterion level of performance need to be increased in relation to the learning objectives?

7. Is more (or less) teacher direction and prompting required?

8. Are the student response forms appropriate?

9. Is the plan for teaching students to work independently effective?

10. Are students transferring learned skills (behavioral and academic) to new learning contexts?

11. Do procedures for teaching classroom rules and routines need to be modified?

FIGURE 5.10 Level III: Instructional design assessment

ASSESSMENT FOCUS   INSTRUCTIONAL PHASE

Classroom Organization

	BEFORE	DURING	AFTER

Teaching Modifications 1 2 3   1 2 3   1 2 3

BEFORE	DURING	AFTER
Transitions to Group ☐☐☐	Facilitating Transitions ☐☐☐	Are Goals Accomplished ☐☐☐
Completion of Assignments ☐☐☐	Student Responses ☐☐☐	More Teaching Needed ☐☐☐
Students' Attitudes ☐☐☐	Error Data Collected ☐☐☐	Transition Plan ☐☐☐
Allocated Instructional Time ☐☐☐	Monitoring Individual Work ☐☐☐	Criterion Level ☐☐☐
Proactive Management Style ☐☐☐	Student Arrangement ☐☐☐	Instructional Materials ☐☐☐
Classroom Arrangement ☐☐☐		
Feedback System ☐☐☐		

Behavior Management

BEFORE	DURING	AFTER

Teaching Modifications 1 2 3   1 2 3   1 2 3

BEFORE	DURING	AFTER
Classroom Rules ☐☐☐	Review Rules ☐☐☐	Revise Rules ☐☐☐
Reinforcement ☐☐☐	Are Students Attending ☐☐☐	Reinforcement System ☐☐☐
Severe Behavior Problems ☐☐☐	Rate of Reinforcement ☐☐☐	Serious Behavior Problems ☐☐☐
Data Collection ☐☐☐	Rate of Punishment ☐☐☐	Punishment System ☐☐☐
Punishment ☐☐☐	Data Collection Procedures ☐☐☐	Monitoring System ☐☐☐
	Student Interactions ☐☐☐	

Instructional Design

BEFORE	DURING	AFTER

Teaching Modifications 1 2 3   1 2 3   1 2 3

BEFORE	DURING	AFTER
Examples ☐☐☐	Appropriate Pace ☐☐☐	Pacing Adjustments ☐☐☐
Sequence ☐☐☐	Think Time ☐☐☐	Think Time ☐☐☐
Practice ☐☐☐	Criterion Peformance ☐☐☐	Criterion Level ☐☐☐
Instructional Schedule ☐☐☐	Error Corrections ☐☐☐	Error Correction ☐☐☐
Use of Prompts ☐☐☐	Teacher Direction ☐☐☐	Teacher Direction ☐☐☐
Instructional Materials ☐☐☐	Instructional Examples ☐☐☐	Student Response Form ☐☐☐
Criterion Levels ☐☐☐	Student Response Form ☐☐☐	Prerequisites ☐☐☐
Guided Instruction ☐☐☐	Prerequisite Skill ☐☐☐	Students' Independent
Time Adjustments ☐☐☐	Rate of Errors ☐☐☐	Work ☐☐☐
Student Response Form ☐☐☐	Do Students Follow	
Teacher Role ☐☐☐	Directions ☐☐☐	
Type of Target Skill ☐☐☐		
Type of Student Response ☐☐☐		

Rating System
1 = Acceptable
2 = Monitor
3 = Change

FIGURE 5.11 Classroom management action plan: Translating assessment data into management changes

necessary, then either 2 (Monitor) or 3 (Change) is marked. By checking either 2 or 3, the teacher immediately prioritizes his or her assessment activities. For example, if a teacher is evaluating the adequacy of classroom rules for the Before Instruction phase and decides that the rules need adjusting but not immediately, then 2 is checked in the appropriate box. This tells the teacher that modification of classroom rules should be completed after all priority changes (i.e., those indicated by checking 3) are made.

We recommend that a classroom teacher begin the school year with an assessment of the Before Instruction phase to determine if her approach to classroom organization, behavior management, and instructional design is conducive to effective instructional classroom management. Because a teacher's assessment plan should be tied to instruction, we also recommend that the formal evaluation of the Before Instruction phase be done periodically, whether there are behavior problems or not. Changes based on information collected for this phase will help the teacher keep her teaching program updated during the school year.

Assessment of the During Instruction phase focuses on the implementation of classroom organization, behavior management, and instructional design. Among the program components evaluated during this phase of instruction are students' attitudes, reinforcement systems, use of instructional prompts, type of student response, and mastery levels. We recommend that the teacher evaluate implementation once the instructional program is in place. It is important for the teacher to use the checklist throughout the year and not just in response to a behavior problem. Continuous use of assessment will allow for a proactive approach to classroom management.

Outcome measures are the focus of assessment activities during the After Instruction phase. During this assessment routine, the teacher evaluates outcomes in both behavioral and academic areas. As part of the assessment activities for this phase, the teacher evaluates the academic measures (e.g., tests, quizzes, worksheets) completed by students.

ADAPTING INSTRUCTIONAL CLASSROOM MANAGEMENT ASSESSMENT

An important feature of instructional classroom management assessment is that it can be easily adapted to the specific needs of teachers. We encourage teachers to modify the assessment procedures described in this chapter when necessary. As discussed earlier, the assessment model described in this chapter is not a comprehensive diagnostic tool. We recommend modifications in the following areas, so that instructional classroom management assessment procedures can be better adapted to the teacher's individual needs.

Add Assessment Questions When Necessary

The assessment questions we pose should not be considered exhaustive or comprehensive. Instead, they serve as a guide to the teacher when assessing the classroom for developing effective interventions and refining instructional programs. We encourage teachers to add their own assessment questions to any of the assessment phases to increase the suitability of the model.

Use with Individuals and Student Groups

We have developed instructional classroom management assessment so that it can be used with individual students or with groups. When the assessment activities are used with groups of students, we recommend that the teacher pay close attention to the lower-performing student in the group when determining the adequacy of classroom management and instructional procedures.

Combine with Other Assessment Procedures

We also recommend that teachers combine instructional classroom management assessment with other assessment activities if teachers are interested in collecting alternative assessment information. For example, instructional classroom management assessment can be used effectively in conjunction with functional assessment procedures (Gelfand & Hartman 1984), critical incidence log recordings (Sugai 1986) or with any type of curriculum-based assessment activities (Mercer & Mercer 1989).

SUMMARY

In this chapter, we presented a model for Instructional Classroom Management assessment. First, the features of the assessment model were identified and discussed. Next, assessment activities and questions were presented for the Before, During, and After phases of instruction. For each phase, a three-level assessment approach was provided that examined class organization, behavior management, and instructional design.

The chapter concluded with a discussion of how teachers can translate assessment information into an action plan for making management changes. A checklist was provided for teachers to summarize and organize assessment information.

CHAPTER ACTIVITIES

1. Discuss the limitations of traditional assessment models in classroom management.
2. Develop a set of five supplemental assessment questions for each level of the three phases of instruction.
3. Visit either a regular or special education classroom and assess the behavior of two students using the Instructional Classroom Management Assessment Checklist. Next, develop teaching and management modifications from the assessment data for each of the three phases of instruction (e.g., Before, During, After). Be very specific when you discuss your teaching and management modifications.

SUGGESTED READINGS

Jacobs, L. (1991). Assessment concerns: A study of cultural differences, teacher concepts, and inappropriate labeling. *Teacher Education and Special Education, 14,* 43–48.

Koorland, M. A., Monda, L. E., & Vail, C. O. (1988). Recording behavior with ease. *Teaching Exceptional Children, 21,* 59-61.

Shoemaker, B., & Lewin, L. (1993). Curriculum and assessment: Two sides of the same coin. *Educational Leadership, 50,* 55-57.

chapter 6

Reinforcement in Instructional Classroom Management

Chapter Overview

INTRODUCTION

Reinforcement of student performance is a major management activity. How rcinforcement techniques are used will, in large measure, determine the success of the instructional management program. When teachers are primarily positive in their interactions with students, the stage is set for increased academic achievement and improved student conduct. Teachers who fail to use reinforcement as part of their instructional routine or those who rely substantially on punishment to control the behavior of students will in the end create disruptive, underachieving, and resentful students.

In this chapter, we examine reinforcement within an instructional context by describing a comprehensive reinforcement plan. First, we present the details of how to organize reinforcement activities into a plan of action that is proactive and part of the regular instructional program. Next, we discuss reinforcement features and how teachers can link specific reinforcement activities to task dimensions.

WHY DOES REINFORCEMENT SOMETIMES FAIL?

If reinforcement is such a powerful teaching and management device, why isn't it always effective in controlling student behavior? The answer to this question is rarely straightforward because of the complexity of classroom instruction and schooling. However, an example of what often occurs in classrooms helps to illustrate the limitations of a conventional approach to behavior management.

EXAMPLE: REINFORCEMENT

Sam, a learning-disabled student, is frequently disruptive in his reading class. He refuses to complete assignments and follow directions, and he is often involved in arguments with other students. His outbursts often occur without any provocation or are initiated when the teacher, Mr. Barnbrook, hands out an assignment for Sam to complete. Because Mr. Barnbrook has been trained to use a variety of reinforcement techniques, he assiduously applies several of these techniques once a behavior problem occurs. For example, after Sam's outburst, Mr. Barnbrook praises other students for sitting quietly, and then he acknowledges Sam's effort when he does start to work. He even developed a point system to reinforce all students for completing written assignments. However, all of this is to no avail because Mr. Barnbrook still can't reliably control Sam's disruptive behavior.

Why was this an ineffective approach to reinforcement? One problem is that Mr. Barnbrook failed to establish a comprehensive instructional reinforcement plan that is linked to instruction and implemented at the very beginning of the school year. In such a plan, the teacher considers the instructional task when developing reinforcement procedures. Without an organized approach to reinforcement, the use of isolated reinforcement techniques is likely to be ineffective in the long term.

An instructional reinforcement plan allows the teacher to develop a positive learning environment for students by (a) aligning reinforcement with task dimensions, (b) coordinating the use of various reinforcement procedures, (c) using reinforcement procedures proactively, and (d) integrating instruction and reinforcement activities into a comprehensive plan. Mr. Barnbrook, however, used reinforcement in a reactive manner. That is, he used reinforcement techniques only in response to Sam's behavior problems. In fact, when Sam's behavior deteriorated further, Mr. Barnbrook quickly developed a point system; however, it was not coordinated with any other management or instructional strategies.

Because Mr. Barnbrook did not have an overall plan, he was not able to link reinforcement to instruction. More importantly, he had not conceptualized reinforcement as part of instruction. Instead, he treated reinforcement as a set of activities and actions separate from instruction. Furthermore, Mr. Barnbrook never considered how difficult assignments might have been instrumental in creating Sam's disruptive behavior. His failure to link his behavioral management program to instruction limited the power and reach of the reinforcement activities. Moreover, it limited Mr. Barnbrook's ability to influence Sam's academic and social behavior.

CONCEPTUALIZING REINFORCEMENT AS INSTRUCTION

It is important to define again what is meant by reinforcement. According to Rusch, Rose, and Greenwood (1988), positive reinforcement "refers to the process of presenting a stimulus as a consequence of a response that results in an increase in the probability that the behavior will increase in the future" (p. 217). Although technical, this definition consists of two critical elements necessary to the understanding of how reinforcement can be a vital part of instruction.

First, the goal of reinforcement is to increase a learner's behavior, not now, but in the future. As Kameenui and Simmons (1990) note, the teacher in effect is "behaving now for later." For all practical purposes, what the teacher does now can be viewed as a roll of the die. There is no guarantee that the teacher's immediate actions in response to a particular behavior will lead to increasing the learner's positive behavior in the future. In short, it is a game of chance and probabilities. Specifically, will the behavior occur in the absence of instruction, and will the stimulus chosen to reinforce the behavior actually work? This game of chance need not be so "chancy" or based solely on pure luck. If every teacher–student interaction represents a chance to increase the probability of the student winning in the game of learning, then what is required is to take advantage of every opportunity for reinforcement. Therefore, the most frequent opportunities available to the teacher for reinforcement are those involving instruction. Simply put, as teachers, we want to maximize the opportunities or chances to influence the learner's behavior in a positive and powerful way in the future; but in order to influence the future, we must act now and take advantage of every opportunity to shape the learner's behavior—these opportunities are primarily instructional.

The second important element of reinforcement is that it involves presenting a "stimulus as a consequence of a response" (Rusch, Rose, & Greenwood 1988, p. 217). The technical jargon conceals an important feature of reinforcement: A stimulus that serves as a reinforcer can be anything. It can be a beautiful flower or an ugly one, if it's presented as a good-natured joke in reference to some past experience. It can be simply a very small piece of colorless paper or it can be a fancy, smelly, perfumed sticker that makes sounds. What is important is not the stimulus itself, but the response that it follows and the effect the stimulus has on the response!

The problem with holding too closely to the definition of reinforcement provided by Rusch, Rose, and Greenwood (1988) is the impression that teachers must wait around for the learner to make responses in order for reinforcement to take place. In other words, the process of reinforcement is nothing more than "reacting" to the learner. The traditional reinforcement model looks something like this: The learner responds, and the teacher simply reacts with a "stimulus as a consequence of the response." In the reinforcement example involving Sam, we noted how Mr. Barnbrook set up his reinforcement plan as a reaction to Sam's misbehavior. As with most traditional reinforcement approaches, Mr. Barnbrook's plan was ineffective because it simply reacted to Sam's behavior and failed to create opportunities to teach Sam behaviors that could be reinforced.

What the traditional reinforcement approach fails to consider is the opportunities available to the teacher to create, stimulate, initiate, and in short, teach students to respond. Effective teaching naturally sets the occasion for reinforcement by leaving less to chance. If the teacher wants to reinforce students' appropriate behavior, such as talking politely to other students, then the teacher must ensure that this behavior occurs. This is accomplished by teaching the skill to students and then providing opportunities for students to practice it. If this is done, teachers will have increased opportunities for reinforcement. In the instructional reinforcement plan discussed in this chapter, the teacher initiates the process of reinforcement by creating opportunities for instruction and learning, which is in contrast to waiting around for the learner to respond at will, either positively or negatively. This model is one that is particularly important for teachers who work with students who have learning and behavior problems.

THE INSTRUCTIONAL REINFORCEMENT PLAN: ITS PURPOSE AND ROLE IN INSTRUCTIONAL CLASSROOM MANAGEMENT

Unlike many classroom management approaches that focus on a series of reinforcement techniques, our approach focuses on the development of an instructional reinforcement plan. In the following section, we present the features of our instructional reinforcement plan and describe how it is incorporated into daily teaching activities.

An Integrative Purpose

A major role of the instructional reinforcement plan is to integrate all reinforcement techniques and activities. The plan should help the teacher decide which reinforcement techniques to choose and how to integrate reinforcement with instruction. Often reinforcement activities are used without regard for developing a coherent strategy. Thus, teachers often have little patience with any technique that does not work immediately and will substitute a new reinforcement activity prematurely. For example, we have observed teachers who used a point system to increase the completion of assigned independent work, not unlike Mr. Barnbrook in the example presented earlier. If, however, the implementation of the point system fails to improve the student's performance, the teacher will often respond in one of two ways: (1) Either the reinforcer (e.g., the number of points for the completion of the assignment) will be increased to improve student motivation, or (2) the point system will be replaced with one that is more elaborate. In each of these cases, the teacher may communicate to students who are misbehaving that new and more intensive rewards are associated with inappropriate behavior. Obviously, this is not the lesson we want to teach students. The reinforcement plan should help teachers develop a management plan that maximizes the effective use of reinforcement as an instructional tool. For maximum benefit, the instructional reinforcement plan should set priorities for the use of reinforcement procedures, specify guidelines for modifying a reinforcement strategy, and describe how to choose a reinforcement strategy that will fit the academic task.

Increasing Academic Performance

A major purpose of the instructional reinforcement plan is to provide a system to increase the academic performance of all students, thereby increasing the teacher's opportunity to reinforce. One could ask, "Why isn't the main purpose of the reinforcement plan to eliminate classroom behavior problems?" In instructional classroom management, if the teacher provides instruction that meets the needs of every student, then the likelihood of behavior problems developing is dramatically decreased. Students who are performing at their potential tend not to be behavior problems. Conversely, if behavior problems do exist, it is likely that the teacher will need to modify the teaching plan. We recommend that the teacher use aggressive reinforcement procedures during regular teaching routines. The teacher should consider the learning task, the teaching context, and the history of the learner when developing a reinforcement strategy. For example, if a student with an attention deficit disorder is being taught sound-symbol relationships during decoding instruction, the teacher must use reinforcement procedures that increase the student's attention and participation, as well as correct responding.

Using Reinforcement for the School Year

Conventional reinforcement systems tend to employ the same activities at the beginning of the school year and at the end of the school year. Such an approach simply ignores the different instructional demands that teachers face at different times of the school year. For example, many of the tasks students are required to complete during the last three months of school are either familiar (e.g., introduced previously) or old (e.g., mastered). The reinforcers the teacher chooses during this time should be linked appropriately to the specific type of task that is being completed. Familiar and old tasks, as we will discuss later in this chapter, are best taught using less-intensive forms of reinforcement.

Reinforcement as Instruction

For teachers to be effective classroom managers, they must use reinforcement techniques to teach students the social and academic behaviors that will translate into improved performance levels. Quite simply, some students may not understand the classroom rules, know how to follow directions to complete assignments, or know how to cooperate with classmates and teachers. To provide students with these critical skills, the teacher must instruct students in behaviors that will increase academic performance and cooperation. For example, to prepare students to complete independent work activities, students should be taught how to (a) use resource materials in the classroom, (b) determine whether the work they have completed is accurate, (c) ask for assistance during independent activities, (d) check their own work, and (e) know what to do if they finish the independent work before the allocated time is completed.

REINFORCEMENT DIMENSIONS AND PROCEDURES

Before describing the melding of task dimensions with reinforcement, a knowledge of reinforcement is essential. This section describes the dimensions of reinforcement, which include: categories of reinforcers, frequency of reinforcement, the schedule of reinforcement, the intensity of reinforcement, and the structure of reinforcement.

Categories of Reinforcement

Like most who write about reinforcement, Sprick (1981) organized reinforcers into three categories: tangible, social, and activity. Table 6.1 presents an overview of each of these categories of reinforcers, including the advantages and disadvantages of each type. Immediately following the table, there is a discussion of how teachers can best use each category.

Tangible Reinforcers. Tangible reinforcers include any physical object that can be given to students as a reward for good behavior (Sprick 1981). Tangible reinforcers include food (edible) and other items (nonedible) that can be given to students contingent upon performance. Edible reinforcers that are often used are popcorn, raisins, crackers, cookies, and candy. Nonedible reinforcers include pens and pencils, small toys, books, award certificates, and so forth. Tangible reinforcers are used with students of all ages and ability levels.

This category of reinforcement combines two qualitatively different types of reinforcers: primary reinforcers and secondary reinforcers. Primary reinforcers, such as foods and liquids, are biologically important to human beings and are described as "natural, unlearned, and unconditioned" (Alberto & Troutman 1986 p. 197). In contrast, secondary reinforcers do not have biological importance to individuals and are used to replace primary reinforcers eventually. These reinforcers include social praise and tangible reinforcers (Alberto & Troutman 1986).

There are some advantages in using tangible reinforcers. Food reinforcers, in particular, can be effective when a teacher is working with low-performing primary or elementary students. If the teacher cannot quickly determine exactly what reinforcers will be effective with the student, edible reinforcers are likely to be an effective alternative. These reinforcers are particularly effective with young students who have learning and behavior problems. Tangible reinforcers are most effective when teachers are trying to teach entry-level skills to young, inattentive students. The use of tangible reinforcers should not be prolonged or

TABLE 6.1 Categories of Reinforcers

Reinforcer	Advantages	Disadvantages
Tangible	Easy to deliver Effective with low-performing students Effective with young students	Ethical issues Cost Disruptive
Social	Easy to deliver Useful in most settings Useful with most students	Obtrusive Disruptive
Activity	Powerful with many students Supplements instruction Acceptable to most teachers	Time consuming Disruptive Requires scheduling

extensive. Once the student has established a positive learning and behavior pattern, we recommend that the teacher switch to social or activity reinforcers.

Tangible reinforcers have several disadvantages when they are used in a school setting. Most teachers do not like to use tangible reinforcers in a systematic fashion because they equate these reinforcers with bribery. Some teachers feel it is not "right" for students to be paid off with "things." Another disadvantage of using tangible reinforcers is that even if they are effective, the results are often short lived. Finally, tangible reinforcers cost money, and teachers are usually required to purchase them.

Although tangible reinforcers have a limited role to play in classroom management, they can be an important tool, especially with low-performing students working on difficult tasks. We recommend that teachers use tangible reinforcers in a limited manner and primarily as an incentive to get unmotivated students started on difficult tasks.

Social Reinforcers.   Social reinforcers involve interactions between two or more people (Sprick 1981). If the student finds the attention from interactions rewarding, teacher–student interactions are likely to increase the occurrence of the behaviors they follow. The most common form of social reinforcer found in the classroom is teacher praise. Other examples of social reinforcers are pats on the back, use of positive facial expressions, and positive telephone calls home to the student or parent. Principals, teacher aides, parents, and classmates can also serve as effective social reinforcers.

There are many advantages to using social reinforcers in the classroom. First, these reinforcers are easy to use and they do not consume instructional time when delivered appropriately. Most elementary-age students and many older students find attention from the classroom teacher rewarding and are likely to work hard to receive this attention. In fact, it is doubtful that there are many students for which social reinforcers are not rewarding. An important advantage in using social reinforcers is that they can be easily tied to academic performance and effectively delivered in instructional situations. Social reinforcers are a versatile tool for use with either individual or groups of students, regardless of their ages.

Even though social reinforcers can be an effective tool, there are disadvantages associated with their use. For a handful of students, social reinforcers are simply not rewarding and are ineffective. In some cases, the excessive use of social reinforcers can interfere with the delivery of instruction, particularly with secondary students, or students who are very active and easily distracted. This can result in decreased student performance.

Social reinforcers are effective in all beginning instruction activities and play a major role in helping students generalize skills to new learning contexts. Social reinforcers should be utilized throughout the academic year. We also recommend that teachers use many forms of social reinforcement, particularly with lower-performing students. It is also important for teachers to combine handshakes, pats on the back, or hugs with verbal praise.

Activity Reinforcers. Activity reinforcers are defined as any activity that children might be allowed to do as a reward for appropriate behavior. There are two types of activity reinforcers: nonacademic and academic. Examples of non-academic reinforcers include using a tape recorder, listening to a record, playing a nonacademic board game, and so forth. Academic activities that serve as reinforcers are those that involve learning. Examples of these activity reinforcers include tutoring another student, practicing previously learned math skills, reviewing stories, reading to a student or teacher, and so forth.

There are several advantages in using activity reinforcers. First, these reinforcers can help the student develop mastery of difficult skills. If, for example, a student is allowed to practice previously learned math skills as a reward for completing assigned tasks, then the extra practice may help the student develop mastery of the practiced skills. Activity reinforcers greatly increase the opportunities for the teacher to reinforce students during learning activities. Another advantage of activity reinforcers is that they can be very helpful in altering the routine of the instructional unit. When students are allowed the opportunity to participate in activity reinforcers, the monotony of the instructional session is minimized significantly. For example, students with learning disabilities who have decoding problems require intensive instruction to learn sound-symbol relationships and sound blending. Careful placement of activity reinforcers is one method teachers can use to help students maintain enthusiasm during these reading tasks. Activity reinforcers can also provide an opportunity for the teacher to instruct students in how to work cooperatively with classmates.

One drawback with activity reinforcers is that teachers must have a specific period of time built into the instructional plan to accommodate these activities. If not used properly, activity reinforcers can prove disruptive and can detract substantially from the teacher's instructional program. Another drawback is that it can be very difficult to ease students back into the regular instructional schedule once they have been exposed to activity reinforcers.

For low-performing students who also exhibit behavior problems, we recommend that the teacher initially use nonacademic reinforcing activities. These students will respond more positively to nonacademic rewards. With more advanced students, however, we recommend that the teacher use academic activities as reinforcers. These reinforcers can be instrumental in increasing the achievement levels of these students.

Schedule of Reinforcement

The *schedule of reinforcement* refers to the frequency with which reinforcers are delivered in a particular environment (Rusch, Rose, & Greenwood 1988). Reinforcement frequency can be high, moderate, or low. When a response is followed continuously by reinforcement, it is called *continuous* reinforcement (Whaley & Malott 1971, p. 102). For this schedule, the teacher reinforces each correct academic response or target behavior. For example, in a beginning reading task, the teacher reinforces the student every time he or she identifies a correct letter-sound correspondence. Or, if the target behavior was to increase the frequency of polite statements made by a student, the teacher would reinforce each instance of this behavior. In less frequent schedules, the teacher reinforces the target behavior only occasionally. This is referred to as *intermittent* reinforcement (Whaley & Malott 1971).

The reinforcement schedule can affect the behavioral and academic performance of students. Regardless of the type of reinforcer used by the teacher, the frequency of reinforcement influences a student's behavior in profound ways. There are two rules that we recommend teachers follow when determining frequency of reinforcement. The first rule is to use reinforcement as often as necessary to achieve the lesson objectives. However, teachers should remember that frequent reinforcement is not always the most effective reinforcement. For example, if the teacher is maintaining high academic performance and student cooperation with relatively low rates of verbal praise, it does not make sense for the teacher to increase the use of praise.

The second rule is for teachers to consider the student's skill level when determining reinforcement frequency. If the student is poorly motivated and experiencing difficulty learning basic skills, then the teacher would be well advised to use a high frequency of reinforcers, at least during the initial teaching routine. However, regardless of the level of the student, we recommend that the teacher slowly and systematically decrease the frequency of reinforcement once the student begins to perform adequately. This is particularly important for teachers who work with students with disabilities. Teaching students to work for less reinforcement from the teacher is an important part of an effective transition program.

Intensity of Reinforcement

The intensity of reinforcement refers to the strength of the reinforcement, which can be measured in quantity or incentive value. Specifically, reinforcement intensity can be high (i.e., high in number or value), or low. We recommend that high-intensity reinforcement be used in difficult learning situations such as when students are first introduced to complex writing assignments or difficult math computations. When students are presented with previously mastered material, then the teacher can use less-intense forms of reinforcement (i.e., less in number or value). Periodically changing the intensity of reinforcement is an instructional technique that will improve the motivation of some low-performing students. We have found that changes in reinforcement intensity help to increase the attention of distractible students (Darch 1993).

One of our student teachers was working recently with a young special education student who was highly distractible and unmotivated during arithmetic. This student was being taught numeral identification (5 through 10) and counting from a number other than one (e.g., counting from 4 to 7). Both of these skills were important prerequisite skills for this student. During lessons, this student's performance was variable and he was distractible and unmotivated. To accommodate this student, the student teacher increased the intensity level of the reinforcement by being more enthusiastic in the delivery of verbal praise and by adding a pat on the back and a handshake for appropriate behavior. The positive changes in the student's performance were immediate and dramatic. As this example illustrates, if students are properly placed in academic programs, the reinforcement intensity can be useful for increasing performance.

Timing of Reinforcement

There are two basic times when students can receive reinforcement when working on academic activities. A teacher can either reinforce students when they are working on a series of activities, or when they complete an entire unit of instruction. Each method has a place in effective classroom management. Reinforcement during a series of academic tasks is best suited for use with students who are (a) low performing and need frequent support during learning activities, and (b) inattentive during the teaching of new concepts, skills, or operations. In each situation, the teacher should use frequent reinforcement to maintain the student's motivation and attention to the task. Reinforcement that is applied at the end of an instructional unit is best suited for students who are approaching or at a mastery level on a task. Also, reinforcement at the end of the unit is most appropriate for those students who are learning to generalize new skills.

Integrating Reinforcement and Instruction

The classroom will be organized more efficiently if reinforcement and instruction are integrated. Before we begin our discussion on how teachers can align reinforcement with the various task dimensions, a general discussion is presented on how to establish a relationship between reinforcement and instruction. We recommend that teachers follow the three steps presented as follows.

   Step 1: Before initiating instructional activities, develop a comprehensive list of potential academic and nonacademic reinforcers. Teachers should have a comprehensive list of social, activity, and tangible reinforcers. Because reinforcers are defined only by their effect upon behavior, it is possible for even learning activities to motivate students. Not all students will need to be managed with nonacademic tangible, social, or activity reinforcers. Teachers sometimes assume that only certain activities function as reinforcers. Because of the diverse backgrounds of students, their disparate learning abilities and their different reinforcement and learning histories, teachers must have at their disposal a diverse set of reinforcers to meet the individual needs of students. Verbal praise can only be considered a reinforcer if it increases the behavior it follows. To accommodate these differences among students, it is important to develop an extensive set of potential reinforcers as part of their instructional classroom management planning. We suggest using learning activities as reinforcers whenever students find them motivating. The advantage of using learning reinforcers is that the teacher can increase the amount of time the students are engaged in appropriate academic activities.

Step 2: Consider the type of activity when selecting a reinforcer. During the school day, students are generally engaged in one of three activities: (1) teacher-directed instruction, (2) independent academic activities, and (3) social activities (e.g., collaborative or cooperative groups). We recommend using the most powerful incentives during instructional activities. Because the potential for disruption is the greatest during instruction, students will need frequent encouragement. When students are engaged in social activities (e.g., recess, class parties), less-powerful reinforcers, such as praise, can maintain appropriate behavior.

Step 3: Restructure reinforcement as students become motivated and skillful. If the same reinforcer is used continuously during an instructional unit, the effectiveness of that reinforcer will decrease and have little impact on student performance. When planning what reinforcers to use during instruction, the time of the school year should be considered. For example, tangible reinforcers (e.g., tokens, candy), are best utilized at the beginning of the school year, preferably during the first two to three weeks, while less-obtrusive social reinforcers (e.g., eye contact from the teacher) are most effective from midyear to the end of the school year. Also, the schedule, intensity, and timing of reinforcement can be altered as the students' skill levels increase.

ALIGNING REINFORCEMENT AND TASK DIMENSIONS

At first, the melding of reinforcement with instruction requires a close analysis of instruction. Such an analysis is complex and often Byzantine because there are numerous dimensions of instruction to analyze and it is difficult to decide where to start. These dimensions include: time (e.g., Before, During, and After phases of instruction); task features (e.g., complexity of tasks, sequence of examples); knowledge form (e.g., concepts, rule relations, principles, cognitive strategies); student response forms (e.g., demands placed upon students to respond); time allocation (e.g., 15 minutes vs. three successive 40 minute periods of instruction); grouping structure (e.g., one-to-one, small group, large group, cooperative structure); and so forth (Kameenui & Simmons 1990).

We have already introduced the phases of instruction (e.g., Before, During, After) in chapter 4 as the temporal framework for thinking about and planning instruction. The phases imply that what the teacher does to preempt or respond to behavior problems is determined in part by the phase of instruction. The temporal framework serves as a prompt for the teacher to think proactively about classroom management.

In addition to the phases of instruction, another major consideration is task dimensions. By considering the various dimensions of a task within the context of instruction, the teacher should be in a better position to align reinforcement activities with instruction. More importantly, the teacher will be able to *create instructional opportunities for reinforcement* and use reinforcement in a powerful way to increase learning in the future. In the sections that follow, we discuss how teachers can align the task dimensions (e.g., task history, response form, task modality, task complexity, task schedule, and task variation), discussed in chapter 3, with the dimensions of reinforcement.

Task History and Reinforcement

An important task feature that teachers must consider when selecting a reinforcement strategy is task history (i.e., the extent to which a task has been taught in the past). The teacher must determine if the activity that has been assigned to the student is new, familiar, or old. Table 6.2 presents the alignment of task history with the specific reinforcement dimensions (e.g., category, frequency, time, and intensity).

Task history plays an important role in determining how to select and structure reinforcement during instruction. As noted in Table 6.2, new tasks, those that have not been previously introduced, require powerful, varied reinforcement. This is particularly true for low-performing students who need a considerable amount of support and encouragement when learning new, difficult material. During this kind of instruction, students are most vulnerable and distractible and become easily disruptive. For example, if a teacher is presenting a lesson on how to decode CVCe words (consonant–vowel–consonant plus "e," such as *time, game, hope*) for the first time to low-performing students, we recommend selecting reinforcers from each of the three categories (i.e., social, tangible, activity) and

TABLE 6.2   Alignment of task history and reinforcement

Task History	*Category/Frequency/Time/Intensity*
New	Social, tangible, activity High frequency Immediate High intensity
Familiar	Social Less frequent Immediate or delayed Low intensity
Old	Social Less frequent Delayed Low intensity

using the different reinforcers to reinforce difficult responses, such as the ability to decode small differences in words (e.g., *hope* vs. *hop*). In this example, the purpose of reinforcement is to help the student respond correctly and immediately. The emphasis is to increase learning and motivation by designing instruction that ensures the success of all students. Given the difficult nature of this reading skill, the teacher must select reinforcers that will maximize the student's attention and motivation.

Varied reinforcement can be effective. The teacher may initially decide to use stickers (tangible reinforcers) as reinforcement for high percentages of correct responding, and also follow the lesson with a reading game (activity reinforcer) so that students can practice reading CVCe words in a less formal context. By using a game activity as a supplement to the regular reading lesson, students are exposed to increased opportunities for learning and the teacher is presented with additional opportunities to reinforce students when they are reading CVCe words. The teacher would also include high-frequency verbal praise (social reinforcer) immediately following correct responses during the reading lesson and reading game. This intensive reinforcement approach will help to maintain student motivation during a predictably difficult learning task. Because many less able students approach new tasks reluctantly, proper reinforcement will help the teacher maintain instructional control during potentially disruptive learning activities.

Task Response Form and Reinforcement

Another important task feature for the teacher to consider when developing the reinforcement plan is the student response form. By considering the response form, the teacher is able to select instructional and reinforcement procedures appropriate for the task proactively. As we discussed in chapter 3, certain response forms are more demanding, and thus, more likely to cause learning problems and disruptive behavior. Table 6.3 presents the alignment of the three response forms with the dimensions of reinforcement.

Different response forms require differential reinforcement techniques. Tasks that require the student to generate Yes/No responses (e.g., TEACHER: Is the ball red? STUDENT: Yes.) are easier than production responses (e.g., TEACHER: Tell me about the ball. STUDENT: The ball is red). Teachers can predict what type of reinforcement will be necessary given the task's response form. Students with a history of learning and behavior problems are at risk for learning and behavior problems when the response form is demanding. For example, in many high school science classes, much of the work that is assigned to students is independent reading of textbooks. Once the reading has been completed, teachers often require students to write lengthy essays (e.g., production responses) based on the reading selection (Kameenui & Simmons 1990). During this independent writing time, students, particularly those with poor writing and organizational skills, become disruptive (Darch 1993).

TABLE 6.3   Alignment of response form and reinforcement

Task Response Form	Category/Frequency/Time/Intensity
Yes/No	Social Less frequent Delayed Low intensity
Choice	Social/activity Moderate frequency Immediate or delayed Moderate intensity
Production	Social, activity, tangible High frequency Immediate High intensity

EXAMPLE: A HIGH SCHOOL SCIENCE LESSON

After completing a reading assignment on ocean currents and how currents affect weather patterns, the teacher requires students to write an essay on the influence of the currents on the weather in the states that border the Pacific Ocean. During other similar assignments, several students became quite disruptive at the beginning of the writing period, causing problems for the entire class. The behavior problems started immediately after the writing activity was assigned. Many students were hesitant to begin the writing, and even when they did, they seemed confused about how to organize the material and their thoughts.

In this situation, the purpose of the reinforcement plan is to: (a) get students started quickly in writing the essay, (b) use the assigned reading passage as a basis for developing the essay, and (c) decrease the probability of disruptive behavior. Aligning the correct forms of reinforcement with the essay task may help accomplish these goals.

For example, first, the teacher might provide students with an outline designed to help them organize their essays. Once students start using the outline to organize their thoughts, the teacher can reinforce this prewriting activity. The teacher can follow up with intensive verbal praise for getting a topic sentence written and secondary information organized. It is important to note that the teacher uses the most powerful reinforcers to help students get started on the essay. By doing so, the probability that students will become disruptive at the beginning of the lesson decreases greatly. Next, the teacher maintains high-frequency verbal praise as the students continue working on the written assignment. In addition, whenever possible, the teacher provides corrective feedback to the lower-performing students. Follow-up reinforcers can also be utilized, such as displaying the completed essays in the classroom for students and visitors to read.

Task Modality and Reinforcement

The response mode required of the student is an important dimension for teachers of all grade levels and content areas to consider.

Teachers must consider the task modality when they are structuring their reinforcement program. As noted in Table 6.4, reinforcement is structured quite differently for written tasks than it is for oral tasks. It is much easier for most students to answer questions from the teacher verbally than it is to complete written assignments. Therefore, when students are completing written assignments, we recommend that reinforcement be high frequency, immediate, and of high intensity. Conversely, we recommend less-extensive reinforcement during oral and motor tasks because these tasks are easier to complete for most students and less-powerful reinforcement is necessary.

Many elementary teachers use flash cards to provide drill and practice for students who have experienced problems with mathematics facts (e.g., addition, multiplication). Once this drill is completed, these students are often given a timed test. Generally, students are asked to write the answers to the problems as quickly as they can for a specified period of time. During this type of activity, teachers report that some students become distracted and frustrated with their inability to write numbers quickly and legibly. These students often wind up disrupting the entire class.

TABLE 6.4   Alignment of task modality and reinforcement

Task Modality	Category/Frequency/Time/Intensity
Oral	Social Less frequent Delayed Low intensity
Motor	Social/activity Moderate frequency Immediate or delayed Moderate intensity
Written	Social, activity, tangible High frequency Immediate High intensity

When low-performing students are required to complete a written, timed test, the potential for off-task behavior is increased considerably. Written tasks are hard, and those that are timed are even more difficult for students. When teachers time a task that requires students to use a difficult response mode, it is also necessary to plan reinforcement carefully. The purpose of reinforcement for the math activity discussed above is to (a) reinforce the completion of small segments of work, (b) increase accuracy of math facts, and (c) increase the rate of problems completed. More specifically, we recommend that teachers break down the task into smaller segments and reinforce students when targeted problems are completed. We also recommend that the teacher stand in close proximity to the students and provide encouragement, as well as physical prompts (e.g., pats on the back) as they work math problems. The delivery of these reinforcers should be done frequently and enthusiastically throughout the lesson. If this reinforcement plan is implemented correctly, the teacher can expect improved performance on the math facts and fewer disruptive behaviors. Designing instruction in such a manner increases the opportunities for learning and reinforcement.

Task Complexity and Reinforcement

Task complexity is defined as the extent to which a learning activity has multiple steps, presents new concepts, or involves unfamiliar procedures. The more complex the task, the greater the chances are that the student will have learning and behavior problems. Teachers can help students avoid some of these difficulties by carefully aligning reinforcement with task dimensions. In Table 6.5, we provide the reader with a reinforcement plan for managing easy and hard tasks.

Teachers must not only consider a reinforcement strategy for hard tasks, but they must also determine a strategy for easy tasks. When easy tasks are taught, behavior problems are more likely to occur during review and expanded teaching activities. Students are likely to encounter problems with easy tasks when they are first being taught to generalize these skills to new learning contexts. Therefore, when students are working on easy tasks, one purpose of reinforcement is

TABLE 6.5 Alignment of Task Complexity and Reinforcement

Task Complexity	Category/Frequency/Time/Intensity
Easy	Social Less frequent Delayed Low intensity
Hard	Social, activity, tangible High frequency Immediately High intensity

to foster the transfer of skills. When teachers are developing instructional sequences for transfer, the schedule of reinforcement must be carefully crafted.

An example of spelling instruction is used to highlight the importance of aligning reinforcement with task complexity. Words that are phonetically regular, (e.g., *sat, bland*) are easier for students to learn than irregular words (e.g., *could, one*). However, when students are learning how to spell phonetically regular words, a difficult and important part of the instructional strategy is to teach students to spell these words in new situations (e.g., themes, tests) (Darch & Simpson 1990). Therefore, when teaching an easier task, the focus of the reinforcement program must include developing generalized spelling skills. In order to develop transfer, the teacher should provide periodic verbal praise whenever a student spells target words correctly in all written assignments. By doing so, the teacher increases systematically the likelihood that the students will spell correctly across a variety of learning situations. In this case, reinforcement helps the student to use spelling skills across a variety of tasks. The rule, "You only reinforce spelling skills during spelling class," simply doesn't make sense. Instead, correct spelling of phonetically regular words (i.e., an easy task) in difficult learning contexts should be reinforced whenever feasible. The teacher would use written feedback to students on the accuracy of their spelling in all written assignments. This delayed, low-intensity feedback is instrumental in developing transfer and improving students' motivation and learning.

Task Schedule and Reinforcement

Task schedule is another variable that teachers should consider when developing a reinforcement plan. The amount of time that it takes for a student to complete a task can be used to predict which activities will result in learning or behavioral problems. Table 6.6 provides a reinforcement plan for abbreviated (e.g., tasks scheduled for short periods) and extended (e.g., tasks scheduled for long periods) tasks. In general, abbreviated tasks will be easier for students to complete and are less likely to foster disruptive behavior. Extended tasks, however,

TABLE 6.6   Alignment of Task Schedule and Reinforcement

Task Schedule	Category/Frequency/Time/Intensity
Abbreviated	Social Less frequent or moderate frequency Delayed Low or moderate intensity
Extended	Social, activity, tangible High frequency Immediate High intensity

can be fraught with complications for both students and teachers. For students, the length of these tasks often produces fatigue and frustration because of their difficulty in managing and using time efficiently to complete activities. Proper alignment of reinforcement during an extended task assignment is a crucial element of an effective instructional reinforcement plan.

Teachers assign activities for independent work periods that are usually long enough to be considered as extended tasks, especially in high school classrooms. Studies that have investigated the organizational structure of classrooms (Kameenui & Simmons 1990) have documented using extended tasks during independent learning activities. It is interesting to note that some of the more significant classroom management problems occur during these independent learning times (Darch 1993). As noted in Table 6.6, we recommend that teachers use carefully planned reinforcement procedures when students are required to work on extended tasks.

During social studies classes, teachers will often structure the day's lesson so that students independently read a selection from their textbooks and complete a set of extensive worksheets. Consequently, students will often work on extended assignments independently for the entire class. How a teacher structures reinforcement will determine whether students will work effectively. First, the teacher should use a variety of reinforcers. For example, the teacher could use verbal praise to engage the students in the reading activity initially. While students are reading, the teacher should move among the students and ask specific comprehension questions. This will allow the teacher to (a) make sure students are comprehending the material and (b) increase the opportunities for reinforcement during the learning activity. To preempt behavior problems at the beginning of the lesson, the teacher should concentrate on checking the progress of low-performing students. The teacher should also reinforce students when they make the transition from one activity to the next. For example, when students move from an oral reading assignment to written work, the teacher should praise students immediately when they begin the new activity. Many students have difficulty starting a new task after completing another extended-learning activity. By using reinforcement proactively, students are much less likely to become disruptive at the beginning of these tasks.

Task Variation and Reinforcement

The alignment of reinforcement with varied and unvaried tasks is an important part of the reinforcement plan. Unvaried tasks are a series of tasks that are not changed during an instructional sequence. Many instructional programs are designed so that students are required to work a lengthy sequence of similar tasks. For example, in elementary math programs, students are typically given many problems of the same type to complete during a specified period of time. For many students, the successful completion of unvaried tasks is difficult to accomplish because there is little or no variety to the tasks either in content, response requirements, complexity, or topic, and they are perceived as boring or tedious.

Students who have difficulty staying on-task for sustained periods of time will find unvaried tasks a challenge to complete without becoming distracted or bored. In contrast, a varied task sequence is one that alternates easy and hard tasks in an instructional sequence. Table 6.7 describes the features associated with aligning reinforcement and task variation.

An example taken from a clinical setting may help to illustrate the importance that task variation has in instructional classroom management:

EXAMPLE: A LESSON IN SOUND–SYMBOL RELATIONSHIPS

A teacher implemented a lesson designed to teach sound–symbol relationships to a group of remedial readers. The teacher designed a 20 minute lesson in which the only learning activity was oral reading of individual sounds. The teacher would point to a letter and then require students as a group to say the sound. This activity continued for the entire 20 minute lesson. During the lesson, the students' behavior became increasingly disruptive. Specifically, students were not attending to the lesson, several engaged in verbal arguments, while other students refused to participate in the activity. In addition, the students were also not able to identify the letter sounds accurately.

When this teacher was discussing a lesson and teaching modification, he indicated that it might help to increase the frequency of reinforcement and the amount of time devoted to the activity by presenting more sounds to the students to increase their practice time. In essence, he wanted to take a rather lengthy lesson that presented a sequence of difficult, unvaried tasks, and make it even longer. Would the students perform better during the revised lesson? Probably not. Instead, an alternative strategy is to present a series of varied tasks (e.g., easy, hard). For example, reinforcement during the hard tasks would be of high frequency, delivered immediately, and would incorporate several different reinforcers to maintain student motivation. During the easy tasks, reinforcement

TABLE 6.7   Alignment of task variation and reinforcement

Task Variation	Category/Frequency/Time/Intensity
Varied	Social Less frequent or moderate frequency Delayed Low or moderate intensity
Unvaried	Social, activity, tangible High frequency Immediate High intensity

would be less intrusive and would be designed to build student confidence. By integrating the instruction and reinforcement in this way, the teacher can expect improved performance from students.

SUMMARY

This chapter began with a discussion of why reinforcement sometimes fails as an effective management tool and how teachers can conceptualize reinforcement as instruction. The instructional reinforcement plan was presented next. This plan helps teachers to integrate all reinforcement techniques and activities. The dimensions of reinforcement were also presented and included the categories, frequency, schedule, intensity, and structure of reinforcement. This chapter concluded with a discussion on how teachers can align reinforcement and task dimensions. Specific classroom examples were presented to highlight this discussion.

CHAPTER ACTIVITIES

1. For each of the three categories of reinforcement:
   (a) Provide a description of reinforcers of that type
   (b) List the advantages and disadvantages
   (c) Provide three examples of reinforcers
2. Discuss how a special education teacher can individualize his or her reinforcement program for students who are culturally and/or linguistically different.
3. Interview a teacher to determine how he or she attempts to align reinforcement and task dimensions. Compare the teacher's methods to align reinforcement and task dimensions with those that are discussed in the text.

SUGGESTED READINGS

Jones, V. F. (1986). *Comprehensive classroom management: Creating positive learning environments.* Boston: Allyn & Bacon.
Martin, D. S. (1987). Reducing ethnocentrism. *Teaching Exceptional Children, 20,* 5–8.
Pasternak, M. G. (1979). *Helping kids learn multi-cultural concepts: A handbook of strategies.* Champaign, IL: Research Press.

chapter 7

Punishment: A Transition Tool Only

INTRODUCTION

Punishment plays a significant role in instructional classroom management, but only as a transition tool. Punishment is used as a temporary and transitional intervention that enables the teacher to stop an inappropriate behavior and to reestablish instructional control so that instructional and reinforcement strategies can be continued. Teachers must have a complete understanding of what punishment is, the role it plays in classroom management, and how to implement different punishment strategies if they are to be effective with students who pose difficult management problems.

Punishment can mean different things to different people. However, punishment, more often than not, is associated with negative connotations. When people think of punishment, the harshest images usually come to mind. Most people assume that punishment is always severe. It is often difficult to accept that consequences delivered in a consistent, firm, and calm manner will be effective in decreasing the frequency of behavior problems. This negative interpretation of punishment is "far removed from the definition of punishment" (Kameenui & Simmons 1990, p. 481), and it is even further removed from the role that we have prescribed in instructional classroom management.

In the first part of this chapter, we define punishment and describe its role as a transition tool. Next, we discuss several misconceptions many professionals have about punishment and its use in the classroom. We also present a list of specific guidelines that teachers should follow when implementing punishment procedures. In the last section of this chapter, we list and discuss specific punishment strategies for use in instructional classroom management.

DEFINITION OF PUNISHMENT

Punishment is the application of an aversive consequence that weakens the future occurrence of the behavior that it follows (Rusch, Rose, & Greenwood 1988). Punishment is defined by its effect on behavior. It is a mistake, therefore, to assume automatically that certain consequences (e.g., verbal reprimand, sending a student to the office, requiring students to stay after school) will function automatically as punishers for all students. For example, a teacher may require a student to go to the principal's office as a consequence for fighting in class. However, unless this consequence decreases the frequency of fighting, sending the student to the principal's office is not punishment, at least not for this student. Madsen, et al. (1968) have shown that the use of a teacher's "sit down" commands actually increased the number of times students were out of their seats. In this case, the sit down command, which most people would assume to be an effective punisher, was not. Consequently, when teachers decide to use punishment strategies, it is important that the behavior to be decreased is monitored closely so that the effect of the consequence can be determined. When using punishment, teachers must ask, "Is the frequency of the behavior decreasing because of the consequence?" If it isn't, the consequence is not likely to be a punisher.

PUNISHMENT USED AS A TRANSITION TOOL

Punishment in instructional classroom management is used primarily as a transition tool. Figure 7.1, adapted from Kameenui and Simmons (1990), illustrates how punishment can serve as a temporary transition strategy. As noted in Figure 7.1, punishment serves as a bridge between the implementation of two stages of instructional strategies. In this conceptualization of punishment, it is used only after a comprehensive instructional program is designed and implemented and alternatives to punishment are considered when behavior problems first occur. If the behavior of a student suggests that punishment strategies are warranted, they are then applied, but only temporarily, and only as a transition to instruction. As punishment strategies are applied, we recommend that the teacher quickly assess the instructional program and make modifications in the areas that will help to establish instructional control. As soon as students are responding and cooperative, punishment should be withdrawn.

The advantages of punishment can only be achieved with short-term use. Punishment helps to eliminate behavior problems while also giving the teacher the time to modify the instructional program. This, in turn, gives the teacher greater opportunities for instruction and reinforcement. If a teacher uses punishment indiscriminately, over an extended period of time, the potential for abuse is greatly increased. For example, research shows that students with disabilities

FIGURE 7.1 Punishment: A transition tool

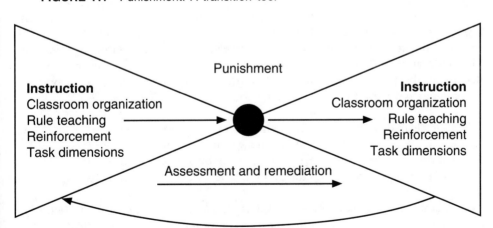

are sometimes victims of improper punishment procedures. Teachers who use punishment frequently usually focus on aversive procedures and rarely, if ever, consider instructional-program modification to be part of the intervention model. Conceptualizing punishment as a transition tool helps teachers to use primarily positive management strategies.

Alternatives to Punishment

Punishment has several disadvantages when used in the classroom. One disadvantage of punishment is that when it is used in the absence of reinforcement, it is not an instructional procedure; that is, it does not teach. It only stops the behavior (Sprick 1981). Teachers who use punishment as their primary intervention strategy do not teach students alternative forms of behavior. One other disadvantage is that using punishment frequently in the classroom can create a hostile learning environment for all the students in the classroom. When punishment is overused by a teacher, the students will spend a considerable amount of time figuring out ways to avoid punishment. Finally, punishment does not eliminate the desire of the student to engage in the misbehavior. Consequently, it is only an effective strategy while the threat of punishment is present.

Because of these disadvantages, before punishment is selected as an intervention strategy, we recommend that teachers consider using alternative strategies to decrease disruptive behavior. The alternative strategies we discuss are relatively easy to use and do not require lengthy implementation. The four strategies that we recommend are listed and discussed as follows.

Discuss the Problem with the Student.   As Sprick (1981) points out, it is possible that disruptive students are unaware that their behavior is a problem. This may be the case with young children who exhibit both learning and behavior problems. As the first alternative to punishment, we recommend that teachers discuss the problem behavior with the student during a neutral time. The best choice for discussing the problem with the student is during a time when the student is not engaged in a demanding and frustrating learning activity. By choosing a time when the student is relaxed and cooperative, it is more likely that he or she will listen attentively and constructively to the discussion of the problem. This alternative is most appropriate for mild forms of disruptive behavior. When discussing the problem with the student, the teacher should be sure to provide the student with the following information:

1. A clear description of the behavior in question
2. An example of the behavior and when it occurred in the class
3. A description of when the problem behavior seems to occur
4. An explanation of why the student's behavior is unacceptable

After talking with the student, the teacher should monitor the problem behavior and decide if another intervention strategy is required.

Reinforce the Behavior of Other Students.   Another alternative to using punishment is to reinforce the appropriate behavior of other students, especially in the presence of the behavior problem. Reinforcement that is provided to the students who are engaged in appropriate behavior should be delivered frequently and intensively. This method can be effective if the student learns that one way to earn the attention of the teacher is to follow classroom rules. This alternative is particularly effective if the student's behavior problem has been drawing considerable attention from the teacher and other students. Reinforcing appropriate behavior of other students is most effective if it is paired with ignoring the problem behavior. It should be noted that this strategy will not work quickly, and it is most appropriate to use with students who are not exhibiting severe forms of disruptive behavior.

Use Differential Reinforcement of Other Behavior.   Differential reinforcement of other behavior (DRO) is defined as "the contingent presentation of a reinforcer for any behavior more appropriate than the response to be reduced (Wolery, Bailey, & Sugai 1988, p. 384). For example, to decrease the frequency of a student's arguing with her classmates, the teacher would reinforce any appropriate interaction that this student had with others. By doing so, the teacher increases the frequency of the student's appropriate interactions while decreasing arguing. DRO is an attractive alternative to punishment because it emphasizes positive reinforcement.

Differential reinforcement of other behavior is not as effective and would have to be combined with other strategies if (a) the student is engaging in many types of disruptive behaviors, (b) the reinforcers that are maintaining the behavior are not controlled by the teacher, and (c) the reinforcers that are being used by the teacher are not as powerful as those that are maintaining the inappropriate behavior.

Ignore the Behavior Problem.   Ignoring is the process of withholding rewards (e.g., teacher attention) following a behavior that has been rewarded previously. For example, if a student frequently talks to another student during class, the teacher may react by saying, "Tonya, remember there is no talking during class. Please finish your work quietly." If this strategy does not decrease the student's talking, it is possible that the teacher's attention may actually encourage the student's behavior. In this example, ignoring the behavior may be a very effective strategy to decrease the student's talking.

One misconception about ignoring inappropriate behavior is that it is sometimes equated with tolerating and accepting the behavior problem. Some teachers feel that an ignoring strategy is too passive. We disagree with this notion. Ignoring inappropriate behavior can be effective if the teacher follows three implementation guidelines. First, the teacher must define the behavior that will be ignored. By doing so, the teacher can accurately monitor the frequency of the behavior to determine whether the ignoring strategy is effective. Second, the teacher must use the ignoring strategy consistently, each and every time the target behavior occurs. For example, if the teacher decides to ignore a student's persistent negative comments about himself or herself (e.g., "I'm no good at school and will never be able to finish this work."), it is important that the teacher ignore these comments every time they are made. If the teacher ignores these negative comments only on occasion (e.g., "Come on Sid, finish your work and stop stalling."), then the ignoring strategy will not be effective. In fact, if ignoring is applied incorrectly, the frequency of the student's negative comments will increase and strengthen over time. Third, for the ignoring strategy to be effective, the reinforcer for the disruptive behavior must be the teacher's attention. If the reinforcer for the behavior problem is something other than the teacher's attention, then ignoring the behavior will not be effective. Finally, ignoring is an appropriate alternative to punishment for behavior problems that occur infrequently and are not considered severe. Examples of these types of behaviors are minor rule violations, negative comments made by the student about school (e.g., "I hate reading class."), and other forms of inappropriate verbal behavior (e.g., talking during class). The ignoring strategy is also effective with mild problem behaviors that often occur at the beginning of the school year. For example, students who are taken from the regular classroom to special education or remedial programs will often, early in the academic year, make excuses for why they should not be required to go to the special class program. Teachers who carefully ignore these comments and reinforce successful work activity should be able to manage mild student complaints. The ignoring strategy can be effective with students of all ages and ability levels. Ignoring can be an effective strategy because these kinds of inappropriate behaviors are often used by the student to gain attention from other students or the teacher.

Modify the Instructional Program.   As Figure 7.1 indicates, it is possible to eliminate behavior problems with instructional methods and strategies that are designed to help the student become a more successful learner.

GUIDELINES FOR USING PUNISHMENT AS A TRANSITION TOOL

In order to use punishment correctly, as a transition strategy, it is important that teachers follow several administrative and implementation guidelines.

Administrative Guidelines

Develop a List of Punishment Strategies.   We recommend that teachers develop a list of punishment strategies at the beginning of the school year. In the latter part of this chapter, we present specific punishment strategies and list the advantages and disadvantages for each technique. Teachers should choose only those strategies they are comfortable using.

Inform Parents about Punishment Strategies. We recommend that teachers apprise parents of their overall management plan. This should include a list and explanation of punishment strategies. This can be accomplished by sending parents a letter at the beginning of the school year, or by an oral presentation at a school open-house. Informing parents of punishment strategies will ensure that they are not surprised by any disciplinary procedures used during the school year. Informing parents about the instructional program increases the likelihood that they will play an effective and positive role in their child's instructional program during the school year. For some strategies, such as time-out from positive reinforcement, it is advisable to obtain parental consent as well.

Inform Students about Punishment Strategies. At the beginning of the school year, punishment strategies should be discussed with the students. By doing so, students will not feel that a teacher is unfairly singling out individuals for punishment. This discussion will communicate to students that the teacher is organized and thoughtful in all aspects of the instructional program.

Implementation Guidelines

Use Punishment in Conjunction with Reinforcement. Punishment is most effective if it is used in conjunction with reinforcement. If punishment strategies are used in the absence of reinforcement, the long-term effects can be destructive. Punishment used in isolation will create a negative classroom, characterized by sullen and unhappy students, critical parents, and disillusioned, if not cynical, teachers. Punishment used by itself is not an instructional intervention because it does not teach students alternative responses.

Implement Punishment Strategies Calmly. The effectiveness of punishment is not increased by implementing these strategies aggressively and angrily. Rather, punishment strategies are most effective when they are implemented calmly and with as little emotion as possible. It is the consistency of the application of punishment that makes it effective. Teachers will be better able to apply punishment procedures more consistently if they are not angry. Also, if teachers are not calm when they punish, students may feel that the teacher has a personal vendetta against them. A calm presentation of punishment procedures makes it less likely that a student will think, "The reason I am getting punished is that the teacher does not like me."

Apply Strategy Consistently. Once a teacher decides upon using a punishment strategy, it is important for it to be applied consistently in the presence of the behavior problem. A punishment strategy will not be effective if a teacher applies the consequence only occasionally. Many students, particularly those that have more chronic forms of behavior problems, will not alter their behavior unless punishment is applied consistently over a period of time.

Withdraw Punishment Strategies As Soon As Possible.   We recommend that punishment be used as a transition tool. Once the behavior problem is under instructional control, it is important that teachers concentrate their efforts on developing instructional modifications and reinforcement.

PUNISHMENT STRATEGIES

There are four punishment procedures that we recommend teachers consider using for decreasing behavior problems after alternative procedures are attempted. The four punishment strategies we will discuss are *verbal reprimands, quiet-time, owing-time,* and *time-out* from positive reinforcement.

Verbal Reprimands

A verbal reprimand or warning signals students that if their inappropriate behavior continues, they will receive a specified consequence. Research evidence suggests that a teacher's verbal reprimands decrease the frequency of a limited number of behavior problems (Walker 1979), especially mild behavior problems. For example, reprimands can be an effective method to decrease students' inappropriate talking during study time. However, reprimands will not eliminate fighting. Also, reprimands are effective with only recent behavior problems. The teacher must use this strategy the first few times the student engages in the inappropriate behavior. This strategy will not be effective with persistent behavior problems. In fact, there is some research evidence that using verbal reprimands may actually increase the frequency of persistent behavior problems (Walker 1979).

We recommend that the teacher follow five specific implementation guidelines to decrease the behavior problems when using verbal reprimands.

When Reprimanding a Student, Tell the Student What Behavior Is Inappropriate and Why.   To make sure that the communication between the teacher and the student is unambiguous, it is important that the teacher tell the student what the problem behavior is and why it is a problem. For example, if a student is taking too much time and purposely stalling when moving from a reading group to another assigned activity, an incorrect verbal reprimand would be, "Antonio, let's go!" This reprimand may be clear to the teacher, but it may be ambiguous to the student. A more appropriate reprimand would be, "Antonio, it is taking you too long to get to your spelling group. You're wasting class time. If you waste more time, you will have to make it up after class!" This is a more appropriate reprimand because it gives the student more information and links a specific consequence to future rule violations.

Always Pair a Verbal Reprimand with a Consequence. When giving a student a verbal reprimand, always specify the consequences for continued rule violation. In the example we just presented, Antonio was told that if he continued to dawdle, he would have to make up the time after school. The reprimand should be consistently backed up with consequences that are effective in decreasing the behavior problem. If reprimands are not linked with the consistent delivery of consequences, the reprimands will not work.

When Delivering a Verbal Reprimand, Position Yourself Close to the Student and Speak in a Quiet but Firm Voice. Reprimands are less effective if the teacher is physically distant from the student. We have seen some teachers reprimand students from across the room. This approach is less effective than when the teacher calmly walks up to the student and delivers the reprimand. We are not suggesting that the teacher confront the student in a menacing and pejorative manner. However, by getting reasonably close to the student, the teacher is more likely to gain the student's attention when delivering the reprimand. Also, reprimands will be more effective if the teacher uses a calm, firm voice. Screaming the reprimand will render it ineffective because the student is less likely to hear the reprimand and more likely to hear the loud screaming.

Follow Verbal Reprimands with Reinforcement. We recommend that teachers be prepared to use reinforcement following verbal reprimands. After a student is reprimanded for a rule violation, it is important for the teacher to reinforce the student for following instructions as soon as possible. For example, if the teacher reprimands a student for talking during independent work time, the teacher must also reinforce that same student when he or she is working quietly. Verbal reprimands will not be effective unless the teacher also reinforces the student for appropriate behavior. Reinforcement will help teach the student alternative ways of behaving in the classroom.

Advantages of Verbal Reprimands

Reprimands Are Easy to Implement. Reprimands are one of the easiest punishment strategies to implement. They take little or no instructional time and do not require a considerable amount of planning.

Reprimands Require No Change in the Instructional Program. One significant advantage of reprimands is that teachers do not need to make adjustments to their instructional program. While reprimands are being used, teachers can continue their instructional program. In addition, reprimands can be effective in almost any instructional context, provided that the teacher is following the prescribed guidelines properly.

Reprimands Can Be Used with Students of All Ages and Ability Levels. Because reprimands can be effective in elementary and secondary school settings, it can be a versatile tool for teachers. However, reprimands are particularly effective with students who are not having academic problems and only exhibit mild behavior problems.

Disadvantages of Verbal Reprimands

Reprimands Are Not an Effective Long-Term Management Strategy. Teachers should not rely on reprimands as a primary management strategy to decrease behavior problems because they are not an effective long-term management tool.

It Is Possible for Reprimands to Become Reinforcers for Students. If teachers use reprimands exclusively without the application of reinforcement, it is possible that a verbal reprimand will serve as a reinforcer and actually strengthen and increase the frequency of the behavior problem. Some students find any attention from the teacher reinforcing, which is much more likely to happen if the teacher fails to link consequences with the verbal reprimand.

Reprimands Are Not Effective in Decreasing High-Frequency Behavior Problems or Problems That Have Occurred Persistently, over Time. Even when used properly, this technique is not a powerful punishment procedure. Reprimands will only be effective in decreasing very mild forms of inappropriate behavior. For behavior problems that occur frequently or are more severe, other punishment strategies are more appropriate. Consequently, verbal reprimands are not likely to be effective with students who have had a history of serious behavior problems.

Quiet-Time Strategy

Another punishment strategy to decrease the occurrence of behavior problems is the quiet-time strategy. In this intervention strategy, students are asked to stop all activities and, for a specified period of time, remain quiet. Once the teacher has reestablished control, the students are allowed to resume their assigned activities. This strategy is most successful in decreasing the frequency of mild forms of disruptive behavior in elementary age students (e.g., loud and boisterous behavior during group activities).

There are five steps a teacher should follow when implementing the quiet-time strategy.

Step 1: Require children to stop what they are doing immediately. For example, if the entire class is too noisy during the completion of an art project, the teacher can initiate quiet-time by stating, "I want everyone to stop what they are doing right now!" If some students continue to talk, the teacher should present the same statement again and wait for the students to become quiet.

Step 2: Require children to remain absolutely quiet. It is important that the teacher require students to be absolutely quiet. This means no talking, whispering, or questions by any students during the quiet-time. In some cases, depending on the nature of the inappropriate behavior, it may be appropriate to require the children to put their heads down on their desks. If students are in the halls or on the playground, require students to stand against the wall or away from potentially distracting activities or equipment, if possible. The quicker the teacher can establish silence, the more effective the strategy will be.

Step 3: Maintain quiet-time for one or two minutes. We recommend that the quiet-time period last no longer than two minutes. It would be difficult to require students to remain absolutely quiet for a longer period. In fact, requiring longer periods of quiet would make the procedure less effective.

Step 4: Have the students resume previous task. After the students have remained quiet for the prescribed time, the teacher then requires the students to continue working on the previous task. The teacher should praise the students who quickly get back to work. It is important that the teacher monitor all the students and make sure that everyone is working on the assigned activity. The teacher should not lecture or draw any attention to the quiet-time strategy. However, the teacher should remind students of the appropriate behavior for working on the assigned task.

Step 5: Use reinforcement to maintain appropriate behavior. Once all the students are working quietly, the teacher should systematically and immediately reinforce students positively for working quietly. It is important that the teacher not discuss the quiet-time incident with children at this time. However, the incident should be discussed at the end of the school day or at the beginning of the next school day. We recommend that preteaching and rule teaching be used at the very beginning of the next day's class or session regarding rules and the teacher's expectations related to the incident.

Advantages of Quiet-Time Strategy

It Is Effective with Groups of Students. The quiet-time strategy is designed for use during group activity, so it has many applications (e.g., recess, group learning time) in the elementary school setting. Because of the group focus, quiet-time is an efficient intervention strategy.

It Is Efficient to Implement. Because this strategy should not take more than two or three minutes to implement, it is efficient to use. In addition, the teacher is not required to make any adjustments in the teaching plan.

An Instructional Component Is Included. In the quiet-time strategy, students are not only punished for engaging in inappropriate behavior, but are provided instruction on how to comply with rules through the teacher's review of rules and reinforcement. Consequently, this strategy teaches students the classroom rules and how to engage in appropriate behavior.

Disadvantages of Quiet-Time Strategy

It Is Not Effective for Severe Disruptive Behavior. The effectiveness of the quiet-time strategy is limited to mild forms of disruptive behavior that occur infrequently. It is not an effective intervention strategy for more severe forms of disruptive behavior such as fighting, not following directions, and aggressive verbal behavior (e.g., "I don't have to finish my work if I don't want to."). For these types of inappropriate behaviors, punishment procedures that are designed to work with individuals are more appropriate (e.g., owing-time, time-out).

Using Quiet-Time Can Be Unfair to Some Students. Because the quiet-time strategy is typically implemented with groups of students, sometimes students who have not violated classroom rules are involved. It is possible that some students will be required to stop their work and remain quiet with the entire class even though they have not violated any rules. Because of this, we recommend that this strategy, as well as all punishment strategies, be used as transition tools only. Repeated violations of classroom rules require that teachers make substantial changes in their instructional programs.

Owing-Time Strategy

The third punishment strategy is owing-time. In this intervention, the student who is disruptive during organized class activities is required to "pay back" any instructional time that was wasted as a result of his or her disruptive behavior (Sprick 1981). The student is also required to complete all unfinished work. Requiring the student to owe time as a function of disruptive behavior is a versatile punishment strategy because it can be applied with students of all ages and ability levels. One reason we recommend this strategy is that instructional time is not lost. This is a significant issue for teachers working with low-performing students who can ill afford to miss instructional opportunities.

There are at least two types of situations when this punishment strategy should be used. First, when the problem behavior occurs frequently throughout the course of a day (e.g., talk outs, name calling, talking back to the teacher, fighting), the teacher records each incident and converts this number into a specified amount of time the student is required to "pay back." For inappropriate behavior that lasts longer than one minute (e.g., out-of-seat, late for class) the teacher converts the number of minutes that the inappropriate behavior lasted and requires the student to "pay back" an equal amount of time (Sprick 1981).

There are four steps to follow when using the owing-time strategy. This strategy is more intricate than the other punishment procedures we have discussed. Its success is contingent upon a well-developed and carefully implemented plan.

Step 1: Identify the behaviors/circumstances that will result in owing time. The first step that must be taken is to determine the types of behaviors that will result in the student owing time. The teacher should define precisely the behaviors that will result in owing time and those that will not. For example, if a teacher has had problems with a student talking back after an assignment is given, then examples of "talk backs" that will result in owing time must be identified and defined by the teacher. In this case, the teacher may decide to penalize any verbal behavior that challenges the assignment and the teacher's authority. Examples might include: (a) "I don't have to do the math problems if I don't want to," (b) "That assignment is unfair, it's too long, and I am not going to do it," and (c) "No way, I'm not going to do it." A list of acceptable comments should also be developed so that the teacher has a clear idea of what statements to penalize and what statements to accept. Acceptable statements could be any statement that expresses concern but does not challenge the teacher's authority. For example, this might include comments such as (a) "Do I have to complete all of these before I go home?" (b) "Boy, is that unfair!" and (c) "How come Sheneka doesn't have to do this work too?" In each of these statements, the student expressed irritation about the assignment, but never challenged the teacher's authority by stating explicitly that he or she was not going to complete the work.

Step 2: Discuss the situation with the offending student. Before the owing-time procedure is implemented, the teacher should discuss the problem behavior with the student. We recommend that the teacher use the same discussion strategies that we presented in the section, "Discuss the Problem with the Student," earlier in the chapter. The teacher should provide the student with clear examples of the problem behavior and discuss the problem during a neutral time.

Step 3: Determine how much time the student will owe. There are two procedures for determining the number of minutes that will be owed. When counting the number of misbehaviors (e.g., talk outs, fights, noncompliance), the teacher must first determine how many minutes the student will owe for each misbehavior. For situations where the inappropriate behavior occurs frequently, each rule violation should translate into at least one minute of owed time. For example, if a student engaged in ten talk-outs during an instructional session, the student would owe ten minutes. Sprick (1981) recommends the following guidelines for determining the number of minutes owed by the student.

Number of Misbehaviors	Number of Minutes Owed per Infraction
1–3	10
4–6	5
7–10	3
11+	1

According to this chart, if the student engages in four verbal arguments, he or she owes 20 minutes. The teacher should also consider more severe, low-frequency misbehaviors. It would be necessary to adjust the number of minutes owed to reflect the severity of the misbehavior.

If the duration of the misbehavior is being recorded (e.g., the number of minutes the student was late for class), we recommend that for each minute of rule infraction the student would owe an equal amount of time. If, for example, a student was seven minutes late for class, this student would owe the teacher seven minutes. Students should be informed about how the number of minutes to be owed is determined before this strategy is used.

Step 4: Identify when students will owe time. The next step is to determine the time of day when students will be required to pay back the time they owe. After-school, recess, or free-time periods are possible to consider. It is important that the student not miss any instructional time when paying back owed time. When students are paying back time, we recommend that the teacher require the students to sit quietly at their desks and complete any assignments that were missed as a result of their misbehavior. If the students do not have any specific assignments to complete, they should be required to read or study. We also suggest that the teacher not talk to the student during this time period. It is important that this session not become reinforcing for the students.

Advantages of Owing-Time Strategy

Owing-time Is Effective with Most Forms of Misbehavior.   Owing-time can be used to decrease the occurrence of most forms of disruptive behavior. However, this strategy is particularly effective in controlling severe forms of inappropriate behavior such as fighting and noncompliance. The versatility of this punishment procedure makes it appropriate for both elementary and secondary classrooms.

Owing-time Makes the Student Accountable.   Another advantage of this strategy is that students learn that they are responsible for completing their assignments and are accountable to make up any time that was wasted as a result of their misbehavior. Owing-time is an excellent method to decrease misbehavior in a way that teaches students responsibility. The teacher must be sure not to link academic work with punishment, however.

Disadvantages of Owing-Time Strategy

The Procedure Is Time Consuming for the Teacher.   Because the student must be monitored during the payback period, owing-time can take a significant amount of the teacher's time. Given the busy schedules of teachers, this is a significant issue and should be considered before this punishment strategy is selected.

Record Keeping Is Cumbersome.   Because this strategy requires the teacher to record and track the amount of time students owe, it adds to the teacher's workload. In addition, the record-keeping demands of the owing-time strategy may interfere with the teacher's activity schedule.

Consequences Are Delayed.   Another disadvantage of this strategy is that students receive delayed consequences. Usually, students pay back time long after they have violated classroom rules. Delayed consequences are less effective than consequences that are immediately delivered.

Time-Out from Positive Reinforcement

Time-out is a powerful punishment procedure that can be used to decrease the frequency of severe forms of misbehavior. There is a large body of research that has demonstrated that time-out can be effective with most types of behavior problems in elementary and secondary classrooms. Time-out from positive reinforcement is defined by Wolery, Bailey, and Sugai (1988) as "a procedure where, contingent upon a target behavior, the student experiences a period of time when less reinforcement is available" (p. 416).

There are two types of time-out procedures. In the first, nonexclusionary time-out, the student remains in the environment where the problem behavior occurred. For example, if a young student hits another student during a group project, a nonexclusionary time-out procedure would require the disruptive student to put his or her head down on the desk for a specified period of time. While the student has his or her head down, the teacher and other students do not attend to the student. Exclusionary time-out requires the student to be completely removed from the setting where the problem occurred. Sometimes a separate part of the classroom is used as the time-out setting or the student is placed in a separate room. This seclusion ensures that the student does not have access to any reinforcers from the original setting.

The procedure for using time-out from positive reinforcement is composed of six steps.

Step 1: Define the behaviors that will result in time-out being implemented. The teacher must first make a list of the behaviors that will result in time-out. Teachers should not only list the behaviors, but should include a detailed description of the behavior. This description is important for two reasons: (1) the description will help the teacher recognize the behavior to be punished with time-out; and (2) when the teacher discusses this procedure with the students, a detailed description of the inappropriate behaviors that will result in time-out can be presented. We recommend that the teacher only select the two or three most severe behaviors (e.g., fighting, refusal to follow critical classroom rules). Time-out will be a more effective strategy if it is used only for a limited number of inappropriate behaviors.

Step 2: Decide location of the time-out area. In nonexclusionary time-out, the student does not leave the instructional setting when the procedure is implemented. We recommend that the teacher have the student place his or her head on their desk for time-out from positive reinforcement. It is important during nonexclusionary time-out that the teacher have control over the classroom so that other students do not interact with the student who is in time-out. To accomplish this, the teacher must reinforce students for working and not attending to the disciplined student.

For exclusionary time-out, the teacher must find a location, preferably outside the classroom, where the student will go for the duration of the procedure. We recommend that teachers select an area that is visible so that the student can be monitored during the time-out procedure. The time-out area may also be placed in a part of the classroom where the student will not have contact with other students.

Step 3: Implement time-out procedure calmly. When directing the student to the time-out area, it is essential for the teacher to be calm and without emotion. The teacher should draw as little attention as possible to the student. By implementing time-out calmly, it is unlikely that the student will find the time-out procedure reinforcing. When telling the student to go to the time-out area, the teacher should specify the inappropriate behavior and the consequence. For example, if a student hits another student, the teacher should implement exclusionary time-out by stating: "Jim, hitting others is not allowed in this room. You have to go to the time-out area." In this example, Jim is told what behavior is unacceptable and that he is going to the time-out area. The teacher should be sure not to present this direction in such a way as to suggest that going to the time-out area is negotiable. For example, the teacher should not say to Jim, "I would like you to go to the time-out area." This statement, in our opinion, suggests to the student that going to time-out may be optional.

Step 4: Determine the length of the time-out period. When students are directed to the time-out area, the teacher should track the time with either a stop watch or a kitchen timer. We recommend that the amount of time that a student spend in the time-out area be no longer than three minutes. Time-out periods that exceed two or three minutes are not necessarily more effective. Students should be told when they enter the time-out area that they must remain quiet for the entire three minutes. If the student leaves the time-out area or engages in any other disruptive behavior during the three minute period, the teacher should reset the timer and the time-out period should begin again. The cycle should continue until the student has remained quiet in the time-out area for the designated three minutes.

Step 5: Require the student to make up any work missed during time-out. It is important that students be required to make up any work that is missed during the time-out period. It is possible that time-out could become reinforcing if students learn that missing classes will get them out of completing assignments.

Step 6: When the student is out of the time-out area, reinforce appropriate behavior. When the student is out of the time-out area and working with the rest of the class, the teacher should immediately reinforce the student for engaging in appropriate behavior. For time-out to work effectively, it is important that the teacher not discuss the time-out incident with the student. The teacher should quickly reinforce the student for getting back to work quietly and completing assigned work. In addition, the student must be shown that the teacher harbors no grudge and that the "slate is wiped clean."

Advantages of Time-Out

Time-Out from Positive Reinforcement Can Be a Powerful Transitional Tool. If used properly, time-out is a powerful transition tool for decreasing the frequency of difficult behavior problems. Time-out is an effective punishment strategy that can be used to decrease serious behavior problems while students are taught to behave appropriately.

Time-Out Is a Versatile Punishment Procedure. Time-out can be effective with students of all age levels and implemented in most instructional settings. In addition, time-out can be an effective strategy to use with low-performing students.

Disadvantages of Time-Out

Loss of Instructional Time. One limitation of using time-out is that the student loses instructional time while he or she is placed in time-out. This is a significant limitation when used with low-performing students. Limiting the learning opportunities for low-performing students can contribute to their falling further behind their peers.

Time-Out Is a Complex Procedure to Implement. The possibility that teachers will fail to implement the time-out strategy correctly is great. Teachers must have a complete understanding of the time-out strategy before it is used in the classroom.

Time-Out Is Easy to Abuse. Time-out is a procedure that can be easily abused because it is easy to kick a disruptive student out of class. It must be monitored closely and used only under careful supervision.

Punishment Strategies and the Continuum of Complexity

Before using any of the punishment strategies discussed in this chapter, teachers should consider the "costs," which include the legal and ethical considerations, of each strategy before making a selection. In Figure 7.2, we present a model that illustrates the relationship between specific punishment strategies and their degree of complexity. The punishment procedures that are lower on the continuum are easier to implement and have fewer administrative, ethical, and instructional costs associated with their use. The quiet-time strategy is easier to use than is exclusionary time-out. For example, before teachers use time-out, the principal needs to give approval and parents should be informed. In addition, the legal and ethical concerns are much greater with time-out than with the quiet-time procedure or any other punishment strategies because the student is

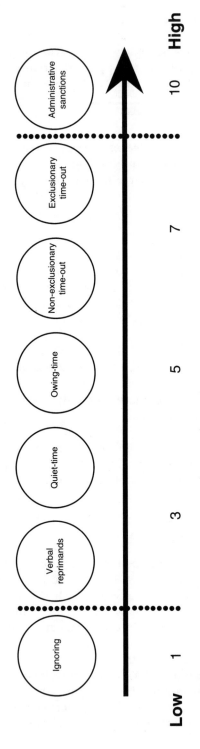

FIGURE 7.2 Punishment and the continuum of complexity

excluded from instruction in the classroom context. In general, punishment strategies that are higher on the continuum result in loss of instructional time. We recommend that teachers first use the punishment strategies that are lower on the punishment continuum before using strategies that are more complex.

SUMMARY

In this chapter, we discussed how punishment serves as a transition tool in instructional classroom management. We also recommended that teachers consider using five alternative strategies before selecting punishment. Administrative and implementation guidelines for using punishment strategies were also presented. Four punishment strategies to decrease inappropriate behavior were discussed. The punishment strategies presented were verbal reprimands, quiet-time, owing-time, and time-out from positive reinforcement. For each of these strategies, the specific steps for implementation were presented along with their advantages and disadvantages.

CHAPTER ACTIVITIES

1. Discuss how the authors suggest using punishment as a transition tool.
2. Identify and discuss the five alternatives to punishment described in this chapter.
3. For each of the following punishment strategies, provide (a) a definition and description, (b) the steps recommended for implementation, and (c) the advantages and disadvantages of using the strategy.
   • Ignoring
   • Verbal reprimand
   • Quiet-time
   • Owing-time
   • Nonexclusionary time-out
   • Exclusionary time-out
   • Administrative sanctions

SUGGESTED READINGS

Bartlet, L. (1989). Disciplining handicapped students: Legal issues in light of *Honig* v. *Doe. Exceptional Children, 55,* 357–366.

Rosenberg, M. S. (1986). Maximizing the effectiveness of structured classroom management programs: Implementing rule-review procedures with disruptive and distractible students. *Behavior Disorders, 11,* 239–248.

Sabatino, D. A. (1987). Preventative discipline as a practice in special education. *Teaching Exceptional Children, 19,* 8–11.

Skiba, R., & Raison, J. (1990). Relationship between the use of time-out and academic achievement. *Exceptional Children, 57,* 36–46.

chapter 8

Instructional Classroom Management: The 180-Day Plan

INTRODUCTION

Managing behavior always occurs within the context of time. Too often, however, the management of social and academic behavior is considered in either immediate terms (e.g., "How do I stop this behavior right now?"), or future terms (e.g., "What management strategies will stop the problem behaviors from occurring in the future?"). The typical approach is to conceptualize management strategies for specific problems and apply the strategy until the problem either decreases or increases, at which time we try another strategy or cease trying altogether. There is often no overall plan that directs the teacher's choice of management strategies over the course of the entire school year.

If we think about behavior management in instructional terms, then we must think about management of behavior in terms similar to those we use to teach a cognitive skill, operation, or strategy. Like academic learning, classroom management and the teaching of social behavior take place in phases. When someone learns an academic skill, such as story grammar strategies for comprehending narrative stories, the initial learning takes time and requires teacher assistance, practice, and feedback. The teacher supports the student's independent application of the story grammar strategy over time. During the initial phases of instruction, the teacher provides the environmental support in the form of direct instruction, modeling, and frequent feedback and guidance. After the initial phase of acquisition, the learner requires less teacher support and direction. During this "scaffolded" instruction, the learner attempts to apply the strategy independently of the teacher, who offers support at strategic points during strategy application or when necessary. Eventually, the learner reaches a state of full independence, the strategy is mastered, and instructional support is not necessary.

Instructional classroom management must be conceptualized in similar "phases." Like instruction, managing behavior takes place over a full school year, about 180 school days. Therefore, an Instructional Classroom Management plan must be conceptualized as a 180-day process that begins at least a few days before the first day of school and ends after the last day of school. Later in the chapter, we offer a rationale for starting before school and stopping one day after school ends. For now, a 180-day Instructional Classroom Management plan provides the teacher with a general blueprint for managing the classroom for the entire school year.

The development of a 180-day plan encourages teachers to think about the entire school year, not only the first two weeks of school or the long winter months. More importantly, the 180-day plan allows teachers to plan strategically and confidently for a full year of school, helping them anticipate periods of potential crisis (e.g., before holidays) and be proactive about managing problem behaviors. The 180-day plan also acknowledges certain realities of teaching and managing behavior. Behavior management is easier at the beginning of the school year than at the end. The reasons are obvious: (a) Teachers and students are energized by the new school year; (b) students are likely to be calm before the novelty of the new school year wears off; (c) teaching and learning fatigue are minimal at the beginning of a school year; and (d) at the beginning of the school year, students have yet to "test" the boundaries of acceptable and unacceptable behavior.

One problem with developing management plans concerned primarily with the beginning of the school year is that students are typically compliant. It is easy for teachers to develop management plans and strategies that fail to acknowledge management problems that may surface during the long winter months or at the end of the school year. By conceptualizing behavior management within the context of a 180-day plan, all periods of the school year are given full and equal consideration. A 180-day plan serves as a general blueprint of the strategies that are likely to be effective and necessary at different times during the year. The plan acknowledges the covariation between the time of the year, students' behaviors, teachers' behaviors and expectations, and students' academic and social performance. Teachers are likely to respond to inappropriate behavior differently in February than in September.

PHASES OF THE 180-DAY PLAN

The 180-day plan consists of three phases, each one composed of three months of the school year. The first phase consists of the first three months of school, the second phase, the winter months (December, January, February), and the third phase, the last three months of the school year. Each phase represents a unique set of conditions associated with designing and implementing a proactive instructional management plan. The instructional management plan for the first phase or first three months of the school year will be fundamentally different from the plan for the last three months of the school year. The first phase of the 180-day plan parallels the acquisition skills phase of learning because the primary objective is to "teach" students how to behave in the classroom and school contexts. The third phase of the 180-day plan parallels the maintenance and transfer phase of academic learning because the primary objective is the learner's retention of rules and expectations and the transfer of learning to new and untaught contexts.

One word of caution in thinking about and developing a 180-day plan: A well-developed plan does not involve making adjustments in objectives within a phase or across phases because of the mere passage of time. Instructional management changes and adjustments should be based on students meeting performance criteria established by the teacher.

Phase 1: The Fall Months

The primary focus of the first phase of the 180-day plan is to teach students appropriate classroom behavior. The first phase of the 180-day management plan is designed to organize instruction so that students are taught the rules and routines. Figure 8.1 presents a blueprint that specifies the management strategies the teacher will use for each week of the first three months of the school year. In the beginning of the school year, the classroom management plan is almost exclusively an instructional one. The primary role of the teacher is to teach students what behaviors are acceptable and unacceptable.

First Month (September).   The thrust of the first month of the management plan is instructional. The teacher carefully instructs students in appropriate classroom behaviors, and nothing is left to chance. As seen in Figure 8.1, we recommend that teachers invest time in organizing the classroom so that opportunities for disruptive behavior are decreased. Assessment plays a prominent role in this phase of the 180-day management plan. Through assessment, the teacher identifies the students' academic and social skill needs. The major management activity for the first month is to teach these skills. As discussed in earlier chapters, the teacher instructs students to follow all classroom rules and routines. These

First Month/September

	Week 1	Week 2	Week 3	Week 4
Organization				
Assessment				
Teach rules				
Preteaching				
R^+ rules				
Instruction				

Second Month/October

	Week 1	Week 2	Week 3	Week 4
Review rules				
Preteaching				
Organization				
General R^+				
Instruction				
Ignoring				

Third Month/November

	Week 1	Week 2	Week 3	Week 4
Preteaching				
R^+ academics				
Instruction				
Ignoring				
High criterion				
Monitoring				

R^+: Positive reinforcement

FIGURE 8.1 Management plan (phase 1): Fall months

behaviors are established through instruction and strengthened through reinforcement. By teaching students appropriate behaviors, the opportunities for the teacher to reinforce students are increased dramatically. In this part of the management plan, the teacher teaches students the behaviors that will allow them to succeed throughout the school year.

Second Month (October).   The focus of the second month of the management plan shifts slightly from teaching new skills to reinforcing and strengthening previously taught skills. This is not to say that teachers do not continue to teach students appropriate behavior when necessary. However, a significant amount of the teacher's time is spent helping students establish appropriate behavior patterns. As shown in Figure 8.1, we recommend that teachers review classroom rules and preteach behaviors that students continue to find difficult. For example, if students are still not making quick and quiet transitions from one instructional group to another, we recommend that preteaching continue through this phase of the management plan. Students with learning and behavior problems will require extensive preteaching and a review of all classroom rules and routines.

In the second month, there is a slight shift in the teacher's reinforcement strategy. Rather than reinforcing students when they comply with specific classroom rules, we recommend that teachers reinforce other appropriate behaviors as well. For example, when students are working independently, the teacher should reinforce the accurate completion of the assignment rather than working quietly. This shift in reinforcement is subtle, but important. The teacher is carefully and systematically teaching students that if they follow rules (e.g., working quietly) their performance will improve. The intent is to help students understand the relation between effort and performance.

If it is necessary to establish instructional control by using punishment strategies, we recommend that teachers select strategies that are the easiest to implement. For example, it would be inappropriate for the teacher to use exclusionary time-out at this time in the school year. Rather, we recommend that teachers use ignoring, and that they combine activity and social reinforcers to teach students appropriate behavior. By using this approach, the teacher is more likely to continue to emphasize instruction as the primary management tool. This positive emphasis will help the classroom continue to be a healthy learning environment.

Third Month (November).   The teacher continues to reteach appropriate behavior by demonstrating, reinforcing, and practicing what is expected during the third month of the management plan. If there are students who are still not consistently following classroom rules, the teachers should upgrade instructional procedures and increase the amount of time that students have to practice these skills. Instruction is still the key management strategy in this part of the plan. However, the majority of the teacher's effort should be geared toward reinforcing academic performance of the students.

Linking the instructional program to the management program is a primary goal during this component of the management program. To help accomplish this goal, we recommend that the teacher use reinforcement strategies to acknowledge the improved academic performance of the students. During this part of the management plan, students must begin to understand that every effort is being made to help them succeed in school. Students learn that the expectations are in both academics and behavior. Even for very young students, the teacher must emphasize improved academic performance through reinforcement. If the teacher has in place a properly designed instructional program, then all students should achieve success that is reinforced.

During November, we recommend that the teacher begin to increase the criteria of acceptable performance. Students should no longer be reinforced each time they comply with a classroom rule or complete an assignment. Instead, students should earn reinforcement for complying with rules for longer periods of time or in difficult learning contexts. In no way, however, does this suggest that students exhibiting behavior problems be excluded from reinforcement opportunities. As we have stated throughout this text, the teacher must continually modify the instructional program so that each student is successful.

Monitoring student performance plays a significant role in this part of the management program. Monitoring is particularly important because of the increased emphasis on the reinforcement of academic performance. The teacher must carefully monitor the behavior of the students to determine which academic and behavioral skills need to be taught. For low-performing students, monitoring provides the teacher with information to upgrade the instructional and management programs. Without careful monitoring, teachers may not be able to design an instructional and management program to meet the needs of all students.

Phase 2: The Winter Months

The focus of Phase 2 of the 180-day management plan is to develop a mastery of behavioral skills and academic competencies so that students can become independent learners. The three months that make up this phase (December, January, and February), represent the time frame when students must develop fluency with the behaviors they were taught during the beginning of the academic year. The primary tools that teachers use during this time are instruction, scheduling of instruction, and reinforcement. During these months, however, the instructional emphasis begins to switch to teaching students to be independent, self-directed workers. Students are no longer reinforced each time they follow a classroom rule. Instead, the students begin to learn that the teacher's expectations have changed over the course of the last several months. During this phase, the students play a significant role in monitoring their own behavior. As Kameenui and Simmons (1990) state, "The assumption at this point is that children are fully aware of the teacher's expectations and need few reminders. Children, in effect, have mastered the skills of how to behave in the school environment, and the teacher shifts the responsibility of management to the students" (p. 479).

Fourth Month (December).   December, the first month of Phase 2, is charac-terized by instructional procedures that initially foster mastery and maintenance of appropriate classroom and school behavior. To accomplish this, the teacher begins to restructure the instructional program so that students are required to work independently. In this phase of the management plan, the teacher plays a less prominent role in directing learning and social activities. The teacher's pri-mary focus is to teach and reinforce instances of independent and self-reliant behavior (see Figure 8.2). This is an important shift in instructional emphasis, for as students grow older, they are expected to develop independent work skills. Most programs do not teach students these skills directly. Instead, students are expected to develop independence naturally. The structure of the 180-day plan in instructional classroom management emphasizes teaching students to become independent learners.

The structure of the reinforcement program also changes during December. Skills that have been previously taught (e.g., old, familiar tasks) are reinforced less frequently, if at all. Instead, new behavioral and academic skills that are performed at a high criterion level are the focus of the reinforcement program. During this time, students are heavily reinforced for attempting to perform in ways that enable them to become more independent. For example, a student who is extraordinarily shy is reinforced for any spontaneous attempt he or she makes to meet other students. This behavior is reinforced with powerful reinforcers.

The role of punishment changes during this phase of the management pro-gram. As seen in Figure 8.2, we recommend that the quiet-time and owing-time strategies be used when necessary. Behavior problems present during this phase require more powerful interventions. By this time in the academic year, the assumption is that students understand what the teacher's expectations are in the classroom. Behavior problems that continue to occur in December need to be stopped with powerful strategies. The quiet-time and owing-time strategies are appropriate choices at this point.

Fifth Month (January).   In most settings, students return to school in January from their holiday vacation. They return energized and ready to tackle the remainder of the school year. For some students, however, returning after a long vacation is difficult. These students have forgotten classroom expectations and school rules. Just as some students will not retain certain academic content (e.g., multiplication facts) after vacation, others may forget the classroom rules. A significant part of the management plan for the month of January is to rein-troduce classroom rules and routines while helping students regain mastery of academic content.

We recommend that teachers reintroduce rules by reteaching students how to comply with the teacher's expectations. Teachers should model rule-following behavior and provide students with time to practice the rules. Rule teaching continues until all students are consistently following rules. The amount of time required for students to relearn rules will vary, but for most students it will be

Fourth Month/December

	Week 1	Week 2	Week 3	Week 4
Instruction				
Maintenance				
Change R^+				
P—Ig/OT				
High criterion				
Self-evaluation				

Fifth Month/January

	Week 1	Week 2	Week 3	Week 4
Review				
Reinforcement				
P—Ig/OT				
High criterion				
Self-evaluation				
Instruction				
Teacher R^+				

Sixth Month/February

	Week 1	Week 2	Week 3	Week 4
Reinforcement				
P—Ig/OT				
High criterion				
Self-evaluation				
Instruction				
Teacher R^+				

R^+: Positive reinforcement

P: Punishment (Ig = Ignoring; OT = Owing-time)

FIGURE 8.2   Management plan (phase 2): Winter months

short, no more than a few days. Once rules are retaught, the teacher should periodically prompt students to follow rules and provide practice throughout the month. Reintroducing classroom rules is not a step backward for the teacher or students, for in the long term, this proactive strategy will enable the teacher to teach students more advanced social and academic skills in the months that follow.

Once students have regained mastery of classroom rules and routines, the focus of the instructional program shifts to maintenance of the social and academic skills that were taught during the first three months of the school year. During this phase, the teacher primarily reinforces instances when students demonstrate independent behavior. When behavior problems occur, it is important that teachers implement a consistent plan to decrease the frequency of the behaviors. As shown in Figure 8.2, we recommend that the teacher use quiet-time and owing-time strategies in response to disruptive behaviors. These strategies are powerful if applied consistently and will be effective in controlling most behavior problems that occur during this phase of the school year.

There is no more demanding job than teaching. It becomes increasingly demanding during the winter months. As February approaches, many teachers begin to feel the stress of the academic year. As Sprick (1981) points out, no matter how much time a teacher spends preparing for the school day, there is always more to do. The management of behavior problems adds to the stress and frustration of many teachers. The physical and mental fatigue associated with the implementation of active teaching and management techniques often becomes apparent during this time. We recommend, as part of the teaching schedule, that teachers build in reinforcers for themselves.

Sixth Month (February). February marks the halfway point of the academic year. The management plan for February has two purposes: (1) management activities are designed to maintain previously learned behavioral skills and foster the student's independence; and (2) management activities in February are designed to prepare students for the final phase of the school year, the spring months. The teacher's first task is to ensure that students have developed mastery of behavioral skills so that they will be able to demonstrate these skills in new learning contexts. The teacher's second task for this month is to make sure that all students have the prerequisite skills for the learning demands of the third phase of the academic year.

Figure 8.2 presents the specific teaching strategies that are emphasized during February. Reinforcement and instruction continue to play a prominent role in the management plan. As in all phases of the 180-day management plan, we recommend that teachers continue to focus their efforts on teaching students new social skills while also helping them develop mastery on previously taught competencies. Even though students have had several months to learn and practice classroom rules and routines, some students will engage in disruptive behavior periodically.

Teachers can decrease the frequency of behavior problems during this phase by reviewing classroom expectations with students at least once a week. After this review, the teacher consistently reinforces appropriate behavior. This may seem indulgent, and some may ask, "Why should a teacher have to remind students of school and classroom expectations this far into the school year?" The reason is that commercial academic programs are designed to present the most difficult learning tasks at this time in the school year. The academic skills taught in this phase are complex, and it is assumed that the student is performing at mastery level on all prerequisite skills. As a consequence, students are at greater risk for learning difficulties. As we have indicated throughout this text, learning difficulties put students at risk for behavior problems. When students must struggle with difficult material that is new to them, they often become disruptive. Periodic review of classroom expectations helps to maintain appropriate student behavior, even in the context of difficult learning tasks.

We also recommend that teachers continue to teach students to be independent in the classroom. One feature of commercial academic programs is that by February, students are required to work independently on difficult learning activities. Many commercial programs reduce the teacher's role to that of monitoring student performance. Direct teaching of skills is not emphasized in this phase of the academic year. Even young students are expected to be much more self-directed at this point in the year. Therefore, it is important that teachers help students make the transition to independence by carefully structuring tasks and using reinforcement to increase the frequency of successful independent behavior.

Phase 3: The Spring Months

March ushers in the final three months of the management plan (see Figure 8.3). The variety of school activities that are scheduled for students during these months is considerable. Schools schedule field trips, plan special events within the classroom, and organize schoolwide assemblies during this time of the year. Many students, particularly low-performing students, have difficulty participating in these events without becoming disruptive. In fact, it is not unusual for teachers to exclude some students from participation in these activities because of potential behavior problems. Teachers can decrease the probability that students will become disruptive during these activities by preteaching expected behaviors before students participate in specific events.

Seventh Month (March).   The focus of the management plan during March should be on teaching students appropriate behavior for special events and activities. The instructional program is expanded to teach students appropriate behavior for different settings. During this month, the teacher should list the scheduled field trips, special classroom learning activities, and schoolwide programs. In addition, the teacher should schedule time to instruct students on the expected behaviors in these different settings. For example, if the teacher has scheduled a field trip to the post office, he or she should first introduce the activities that will occur on the field trip (e.g., bus ride, tour of the post office, lunch). For each separate activity, we recommend that teachers identify the

Seventh Month/March

	Week 1	Week 2	Week 3	Week 4
Expanded instruction				
Reinforcement				
Self-monitoring				
Independence				
P—OT/TO				
Teacher R$^+$				

Eighth Month/April

	Week 1	Week 2	Week 3	Week 4
Expanded instruction				
Reinforcement				
P—OT/TO				
Independence				
Transfer				

Ninth Month/May

	Week 1	Week 2	Week 3	Week 4
Expanded instruction				
Reinforcement				
Self-monitoring				
Independence				
Transfer				
Evaluation				

R$^+$: Positive reinforcement

P: Punishment (OT = Owing-time; TO = Time-out)

FIGURE 8.3 Management plan (phase 3): Spring months

expected behaviors for the students. If students are going to ride the bus to the post office, the teacher should explain and demonstrate appropriate bus behavior, as well as appropriate behavior for the post office.

During the teaching and practice sessions, the teacher should use powerful reinforcers to expedite learning, and, during the trip, the teacher should use high-frequency verbal praise for those students who are following rules. Afterward, the teacher should review the trip with the students and discuss what they learned.

Eighth Month (April). The focus of the management plan for April is similar to the March plan. We recommend that teachers continue to teach students appropriate behavior for new contexts. In addition, students should be reinforced when they demonstrate independent learning skills and social behavior. It is important for teachers to provide students with opportunities to be independent, with minimal teacher guidance.

Ninth Month (May). The end of the academic year is in sight, and students aren't taught many new skills at this time in the year. We recommend that teachers evaluate students' performance throughout the year and provide students with more practice on academic and social skills that have yet to be mastered. We suggest that 10–15 minutes per day be dedicated to review activities. Teachers can begin to consider ways to improve their management plan for the upcoming year by recording ideas while the year is still fresh in mind.

SUMMARY

A 180-day classroom management plan was presented in this chapter. Activities for classroom management in a 180-day plan of three phases were also discussed. In Phase 1, the fall months, we offered strategies for initially teaching students appropriate behavior. The focus of Phase 2, the winter months, was on strategies to help students maintain previously taught behaviors. Phase 3 introduced procedures for teaching students to transfer behavioral skills to new contexts independently.

CHAPTER ACTIVITIES

1. List and discuss the major classroom management activities for each month of Phase 1 of the 180-Day Plan.
2. List and discuss the major classroom management activities for each month of Phase 2 of the 180-Day Plan.
3. List and discuss the major classroom management activities for each month of Phase 3 of the 180-Day Plan.

SUGGESTED READING

Sprick, R. (1985). *Discipline in the secondary classroom: A problem-by-problem survival guide.* West Nyack, NY: The Center for Applied Research in Education.

chapter 9

Managing Persistent Behavior Problems: Strategies and Examples

INTRODUCTION

Nothing tests the effectiveness of an instructional program more than persistent behavior problems. When chronic behavior problems plague a classroom, students and teachers alike gain little from the instructional process. How these problems are managed will determine how successful teachers are at meeting their professional objectives for the academic year. In order to manage persistent behavior problems effectively and humanely, teachers must have a predetermined plan for altering the instructional task, modifying the learning context, and using reinforcement and punishment. In essence, the teacher must have multiple options because persistent behavior problems are complex problems. No one approach is effective for every situation. For some types of problems, the task must be changed; for others, the learning context or the amount of reinforcement must be adjusted. Unfortunately, most teachers have no such plans.

Colvin and Sugai (1988) have described how teachers are typically punitive in their responses to persistent behavior problems: "If the student fails to terminate this troublesome social behavior, the typical approach is to escalate the level of negative consequences, usually in the form of detention, suspension, and expulsion" (p. 341). What characterizes the approach that Colvin and Sugai describe is that it is not instructional, nor is it positive. It is understandable why this punitive, noninstructional approach is often taken, however. Attempting to manage persistent behavior problems is a fatiguing and troubling experience for teachers. The emotional drain caused by students who are always challenging school rules can quickly wear a teacher down. Even if teachers are initially successful in curbing chronic behavior problems, the exclusive use of punitive methods is destructive to the teaching mission. In the same vein, teachers who use spur-of-the-moment strategies will often find that persistent behavior problems will worsen.

In this chapter, we discuss a model and specific strategies for managing persistent behavior problems. We conclude this chapter with the presentation of a series of vignettes that provide specific examples of how to make adjustments to manage persistent behavior problems more effectively.

A MODEL FOR MANAGING PERSISTENT BEHAVIOR PROBLEMS

Figure 9.1 presents a model for managing persistent behavior problems. This model emphasizes developing instructional modifications to the teaching program. The guiding principle of this model is that *teachers must first exhaust all instructional remedies when responding to persistent behavior problems.* If this approach does not result in successful management of the problem, we recommend more-extensive program modifications and the use of punishment strategies.

As a first step in managing persistent behavior problems, we recommend that teachers complete a quick assessment of classroom organization and the instructional context. This assessment can be done quickly, yet effectively. After assessment, we also recommend that the teacher consider making adjustments in the organization of the program as well as changes in the learning task. Reinforcement strategies should be evaluated to determine whether adjustments are needed to increase program effectiveness. The final step of the model is the implementation of other teaching and management strategies that a teacher can use to eliminate persistent behavior problems. These strategies include

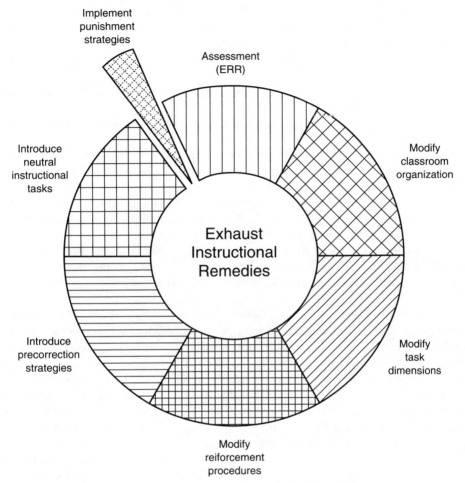

FIGURE 9.1 Model for managing persistent behavior problems

precorrection, developing neutral instructional tasks, and lastly, the implementation of punishment procedures. But it should be noted, punishment is implemented only after exhausting *all* instructional remedies.

Assessment

In the presence of persistent behavior problems, the purpose of assessment is to provide the teacher quickly with information on how best to modify the teaching program so that the student's behavior can be brought under instructional control. We suggest that teachers use a modified form of the assessment plan presented in chapter 5 as a guide to determine the potential causes of persistent behavior problems. The ERR strategy is the basis for these assessment activities. The teacher should reassess all aspects of the instructional program (e.g., classroom organization, reinforcement procedures) to determine what factors are maintaining the persistent behavior problems. We recommend that the teacher ask the following eight questions:

1. Are persistent behavior problems being fostered by the organization of the classroom?
2. Are the problem behaviors specific to a particular person or more than one person?
3. Are the problem behaviors specific to a particular time of day? setting?
4. Are the problem behaviors specific to a particular instructional task? response form? problem type? and so forth.
5. Are the problem behaviors specific to a particular sequence of events?
6. Do the problem behaviors usually surface during instructional activities?
7. Are certain types of reinforcers or reinforcement schedules more effective than others in managing the persistent behavior problem?
8. What punishment procedures have been effective in the past in decreasing the occurrence of disruptive behavior?

These questions provide the teacher with an informal procedure to evaluate key aspects of the instructional program. For example, question 1 asks the teacher to determine whether the classroom organization should be modified. The teacher should reconsider the procedures for transitions between groups, the adequacy of the classroom rules, as well as the teaching schedule. Many persistent behavior problems are related to difficulty in these areas. Questions 2 and 3 focus on the setting. These questions help the teacher to determine whether the problem occurs in the presence of more than one person and whether it is related to a particular time of the day. Questions 4, 5, and 6 require that the teacher look at the instructional tasks, while question 7 evaluates the reinforcement program and question 8 focuses on the identification of effective punishment procedures. By answering these questions, the teacher will be able to develop an appropriate instructional response to persistent behavior problems.

Modification of Task Dimensions

Persistent behavior problems, like any disruptive behavior, can be caused by improper task structure and selection. One indication that improper task structure is contributing to chronic behavior problems is if the student becomes disruptive at the same time a new task is introduced. The evidence for this is even stronger if the student was performing adequately on similar instructional tasks.

If students have completed previously introduced tasks without exhibiting learning or behavioral problems, it is possible that the new task is too difficult. Many low-performing students exhibit chronic behavior problems when new learning tasks are presented. The task may require prerequisite skills that the student has yet to master, or the structure of the task (i.e., multiple steps) may be too complex for the student. The student's frustration during instruction may be fueling the disruptive behavior.

As discussed in chapter 6, one method to decrease the persistent behavior problems is to adjust the task requirements. For example, if the persistent behavior problem occurs in the context of teaching complex multiplication (e.g., 23 × 19), the teacher should withdraw the original task and reintroduce several of the critical prerequisite skills (e.g., multiplication facts, how to carry from the ones to the tens column). Each of these prerequisite component skills should be reintroduced and taught to mastery before complex multiplication is reintroduced to the student. Because the student should perform more successfully on these component tasks, the teacher should also have more opportunities for reinforcement. By increasing success, it is less likely that the student will continue to be disruptive. Once the student is again working on complex multiplication, the teacher can modify the response modality. For example, rather than have students write answers independently, the teacher should have the student complete several problems orally, with teacher guidance. Once the teacher is convinced that the student can indeed complete the task, then the student should be required to complete the problems independently and in the original response form.

Modification of Reinforcement

The purpose of reinforcement in the management of persistent behavior problems is to help the student perform successfully in an appropriate learning activity as quickly as possible. Once adjustments have been made in the task, and the student has been presented with the new learning activity, reinforcement procedures are used to keep the student responding and to decrease the probability that behavior problems will recur. One method is to replace the current reinforcer with one that is more powerful. For example, rather than using social reinforcers, the teacher would use tangible reinforcers in response to persistent behavior problems. In addition, the teacher can increase the frequency of reinforcement if the current schedule seems inadequate. Because the student should perform more successfully in the new learning activity, the teacher is provided with an excellent opportunity to increase the frequency and intensity of the reinforcement program, which in turn increases the student's confidence and establishes positive instructional control.

We recommend that the teacher increase the intensity of the reinforcer early in the learning activity so that the student begins working with as much support as possible. Many persistent behavior problems occur at the beginning of a new unit of instruction. We also recommend that the teacher reinforce the student on increases in *academic performance,* however incremental. This helps to keep the focus in the classroom on academic activities. For example, if the persistent behavior problem typically occurred during oral reading of stories, then the teacher should use an intensified reinforcement approach when the student is working on skills that are prerequisite to oral reading (e.g., sound–symbol relationships).

Strategic Use of Precorrection Strategies

Precorrection is a valuable technique for reducing the occurrence of persistent behavior problems. Precorrection is a primary method teachers can use to reduce proactively the occurrence of persistent behavior problems. We recommend that teachers design and implement precorrection interventions after they have reevaluated their classroom organization, task dimensions, teaching structures, and reinforcement procedures. If persistent problems continue, teachers should follow a six-step procedure to implement precorrection strategies (Colvin & Sugai 1988).

Step 1: Determine the context that elicits persistent behavior problem. First, the teacher identifies the specific context in which the persistent behavior problem is most likely to occur. For this step, the teacher attempts to determine if there is a relationship between certain classroom activities and the occurrence of persistent behavior problems. The goal is for the teacher to ascertain if there are classroom variables that serve to elicit the disruptive behavior. A teacher must observe the students' behavior carefully to determine a functional relationship between contextual variables and disruptive behavior.

Step 2: Communicate the expected behaviors to the student. Once the learning context that precedes persistent behavior problems is identified, the teacher determines the behavior that is expected from the student. To do this the teacher asks, "What is the appropriate behavior that is incompatible with the persistent behavior problem?" The behavior requirements are then discussed with the student to ensure that the student understands the teacher's expectations. It is important that the teacher explain the behavior requirements to the student, using clear and understandable terms (e.g., "Eric, if you have a question, you have to raise your hand and wait to be called on."). If the student does not understand the expected behaviors, then the precorrection strategy will not be successful. We recommend that the behaviors that are discussed with the student be functional replacements for the persistent behavior problem. For example, the student understands that he or she can receive attention from the teacher by quietly completing assignments rather than talking to classmates.

Step 3: Modify learning context. The purpose of this step in the precorrection strategy is to change the task requirements and the student response form so it is more likely that the student will perform as expected and it is less probable that the student will become disruptive. For example, if a student is frequently disruptive during math class, it may be necessary to preteach the student the difficult parts of the lesson individually before the entire lesson is presented to the student. By preteaching the student difficult material in a simplified context (i.e., one-to-one learning context) and by allowing the student to practice the most difficult material with extensive teacher guidance, it may help the student perform more successfully when he or she is placed in the group. This preteaching will help to decrease the likelihood that this student will become disruptive during group math lessons.

Step 4: Provide practice on the expected behaviors. Even after the teacher discusses the expected behavior with the student, it is likely that the inappropriate behavior will continue. Although discussing the appropriate behavior with the student is a necessary step in the precorrection strategy, it is not sufficient to eliminate persistent problem behaviors. The next step in the precorrection strategy is to provide students with specific training on the expected behavior before they enter the original context. For example, if the behavior problem occurs during oral reading activities, the teacher should have the student practice the expected behaviors just before oral reading group. If a student tends to interrupt other students while they are reading out loud, the teacher should practice with the student on following along while others read and raising his or her hand to make a comment during an oral reading session. This behavioral rehearsal can last four or five minutes and continue each day until there is improvement in the student's behavior.

Step 5: Strongly reinforce the expected behaviors. When teaching students to replace inappropriate behavior with an acceptable alternative behavior, it is important that teachers use powerful reinforcement procedures. As Colvin and Sugai (1988) state: ". . . the new behavior will be in competition with the old inappropriate behavior which has been reinforced intermittently over time. Therefore, to replace this behavior, strong reinforcement must be provided for the expected or replacement behaviors" (p. 12). We recommend that the teacher reread chapter 6, "Reinforcement in Instructional Classroom Management," to gather ideas on how to increase the power of their reinforcement procedures. No matter how a teacher decides to increase the power of reinforcement, it is important to use reinforcers early and frequently to help decrease the likelihood that disruptive behavior will reoccur.

Step 6: Prompting expected behaviors. Teachers should expect to use extensive prompting procedures to elicit appropriate behavior during the early stages of learning. Once placed back into the original learning context, students will have a tendency to fall back into old and inappropriate ways of behaving. Teachers will have to provide the student with assistance for behaving in new ways in old contexts. Colvin and Sugai (1988) suggest a prompting strategy that has two parts. First, they recommend that the teacher reinforce any occurrence of the expected behavior immediately and intensively. Next, they suggest that the teacher periodically remind students about the expected behaviors. This reminder should occur throughout the lesson. For example, if the expected behavior is hand raising (as opposed to students calling out answers), the teacher could say, "Class, I'm going to ask you to discuss several important industries in the state of Oregon. Remember to raise your hand if you can discuss the industries that I am going to name."

Strategic Use of Neutral Tasks

A strategy to decrease the frequency of persistent behavior problems is to introduce neutral learning tasks in the place of an activity that is fostering disruptive behavior. Neutral learning activities are those that are not related to the current instructional activity and are moderately easy for the student to complete. As we have discussed, for some students, certain learning activities may prompt many types of disruptive behavior. Persistent behavior problems are frequently linked to difficult learning tasks. Once these high-risk learning activities are identified, the teacher is in a position to have a set of neutral learning activities readily available to use when disruptive behavior occurs. The purpose of introducing neutral tasks is to provide the student with an activity that is not associated with frustration and increase the opportunity for the teacher to establish instructional control.

For example, if a second-grade student becomes verbally noncompliant (e.g., "You can't make me do these problems and I won't do them no matter what you do!"), rather then attempting to "force" the student to comply with the assignment, the teacher could alter the sequence of instructional tasks by introducing an activity that the student is likely to complete. This approach defuses the situation and increases the probability that the student will participate in a learning activity. What follows is an example of using neutral tasks. It is important to note that neutral tasks are used as a temporary intervention and in conjunction with the other management strategies.

EXAMPLE: USING NEUTRAL TASKS

TEACHER: Yolanda, I want you to read the list of words that is on the board. First, I want you to sound out each word and then I want you to say the word quickly. Get ready. [*The teacher points to the first word in the list.*]

STUDENT: [*The student sounds out the word* mast.] Mmmaaassst.

TEACHER: Say the word quickly.

STUDENT: Mast.

TEACHER: Good. Look at the next word. [*Teacher points to the word* with.] Get ready to sound it out. [*The teacher points to the word* with.] [*At this point, the student becomes inattentive and starts to talk to another student who happens to be sitting nearby. The student disregards the teacher's request to read the list of words.*]

TEACHER: [*The teacher presents a neutral learning task, an activity that she knows that the student can complete successfully.*] Yolanda, listen, I want you to count by 5's to 25, OK? Listen, count by 5's to 25. Get ready. Count.

STUDENT: After a brief pause, the student counts by 5's to 25.

In this example, the teacher presents a counting activity as a neutral task. The student is more likely to comply with the command to count by 5's because she has been successful completing this type of task before. The teacher should present another counting task before reintroducing the original reading task. If the student responds appropriately, the teacher should reinforce her good work. The reinforcement should be completed intensively and frequently. An example of a sequence of neutral activities and new learning tasks is presented in Table 9.1.

In this sequence, neutral tasks are presented once disruptive behavior occurs. As noted in Table 9.1, three neutral tasks are presented, each lasting only one minute or less. Once the disruptive behavior is eliminated, the original learning task is reintroduced (reading words from the board). It is important to note that when reading is reintroduced, the student only has to read for approximately one minute. Immediately following that, another counting activity is presented followed by the reading task for two minutes.

Strategic Use of Punishment Strategies

As Figure 9.1 illustrates, punishment strategies are used only after the teacher has exhausted all instructional interventions. In addition, punishment is used only after careful assessment is completed and students are taught appropriate alternative behaviors. However, punishment plays a significant role in managing persistent behavior. If used properly, punishment will help the teacher regain instructional control while making further modifications in instruction. We recommend that teachers follow three steps when implementing punishment procedures to decrease persistent behavior problems.

Step 1: Is punishment used correctly? If punishment is currently being used, the teacher should evaluate the procedure to make sure it is implemented correctly. It is important for the teacher to determine whether the procedure has been implemented using the guidelines we outlined in chapter 7. For example, if verbal reprimands are used to decrease talk-outs, the teacher should use reprimands consistently. Also, for reprimands to be effective, the teacher must tell the student what the consequence will be for talking-out.

TABLE 9.1   Task sequence for responding to persistent problems

Task Sequence and Description	Task Level	Time
Reads words from board	new	3 minutes
Becomes noncompliant		
Counts by 5's	mastered	30 seconds
Counts by 2's	mastered	30 seconds
Reads words on board	new	1 minute
Counts by 10's	mastered	1 minute
Reads words on board	new	2 minutes

Step 2: Select another punishment strategy. The most powerful option that a teacher has to eliminate persistent behavior problems is to substitute the current punishment strategy with one that is more powerful. For example, if the owing-time strategy has been used to eliminate the fighting of a student and it has been ineffective, we recommend that the teacher select either non-exclusionary or exclusionary time-out. As another example, if verbal reprimands are not decreasing the out-of-seat behavior of elementary-grade students, a more powerful strategy should be selected (e.g., quiet-time, owing-time).

Step 3: Give the new punishment strategy time to work. It sometimes takes a considerable amount of time to eliminate persistent behavior problems completely. For example, if owing-time has been selected to decrease the occurrence of coming late to class, it may take a week or two before the student consistently arrives on time.

MANAGING PERSISTENT BEHAVIOR PROBLEMS: FOUR EXAMPLES

In this section, four examples that are illustrative of the types of persistent behavior problems teachers often face are presented. Each example is followed by an analysis that describes potential causes of the behavior problems and concludes with a discussion of several instructional strategies that can be used to eliminate persistent behavior problems.

EXAMPLE: PERSISTENT PROBLEM 1

SETTING: Regular third-grade classroom of 32 children

CONTEXT: Small-group reading instruction

TIME: Friday morning, 8:30 A.M.

PHASE: Winter (January)

ACTIVITY: Individual oral reading in basal readers

Mr. Coddens is listening to Jewel read. Sitting next to Jewel is Andy, who is following along with his finger and paying attention to every word that Jewel is reading. While reading, Jewel makes a decoding error and before he has a chance to correct his error, Andy tells Jewel the correct word. Jewel does not like the fact that Andy corrected his reading mistake and starts an argument with Andy, telling him to mind his own business. An argument ensues. This problem has occurred for several weeks and is escalating in frequency and intensity. For example, this is the third time this week that Andy has corrected Jewel's reading and is the second time that an argument has developed. Mr. Coddens has ignored Andy and Jewel's arguments in the past, but today he tells Andy to leave the room and go into the hall until he can behave himself. Andy stays in the hallway until the reading class is completed.

Instructional Analysis of the Problem

The problem that Mr. Coddens faces is not an unusual one; instead, it's fairly representative of the kinds of problems that surface in the day-to-day routine of instruction, especially during January when the long winter season is unfolding. In this case, the problem is the result of three general management responses.

1. **Failure to specify and teach rules *before* instruction.**
   Mr. Coddens failed to clarify what the rules and expectations were for student correction of errors during oral reading. This ambiguity resulted in Andy correcting Jewel's reading errors, which is contrary to what Mr. Coddens wants to happen.
2. **Failure to understand and implement a punishment procedure.**
   Mr. Coddens chose to ignore Andy's corrections the first two times they occurred but decided to attend to Andy's correcting of Jewel on the third occasion. In a sense, Mr. Coddens gave up on his punishment procedure and attended to the problem when it was most intense.
3. **Inappropriate use of punishment procedure.** Mr. Coddens's response was his use of exclusionary time-out. The use of time-out appeared excessive for a problem that Mr. Coddens initially decided could be ignored.

Instructional Strategies for Prevention

By applying an instructional classroom management approach, Mr. Coddens could have avoided the problem. The following strategies could have been implemented:

1. **Identify and teach rules and instructional routines.** Develop and teach a rule for responding to errors during oral reading. The following rule could be used: "When you're following along and you hear an error, raise your hand quietly. Do not yell out by saying, 'Andy made an error. Andy made an error.' Instead, raise your hand (teacher demonstrates by raising his hand) quietly and keep your eyes on the reading. Let's practice following that rule." The teacher would demonstrate the rule and role play with students by demonstrating positive and negative examples of following the rule.
2. **Determine if task requirements are clear and appropriate.** There are two sets of task requirements in this situation. For the reader, the task requires the oral reading of words in the basal passage. It is important to determine if the oral reading task is too difficult or too easy. If the task is too difficult, then oral reading errors will abound and the reader will be greatly frustrated. If the task is too easy, the reader may become sloppy from an eagerness to rush through the reading. For students required to follow along, the task requirement is to follow along by pointing at each word and raising a hand when an

error is noted. The motor response form may be difficult for some learners to coordinate and execute, and an easier response form may be required, such as requiring students to circle the word that was misread. The teacher would then stop at the end of each sentence and ask students to identify any errors that the reader made.

3. **Utilize a precorrection strategy before instruction.** In order to prevent the problem, the teacher should employ a precorrection strategy in which the teacher reviews the rules and expectations for responding to errors during oral reading *before* the oral reading group is called. Because of the history of the problem between Jewel and Andy, the precorrection strategy would have prepared Andy for the oral reading lesson because the correct way to respond to Jewel's reading errors would have been reviewed. This precorrection procedure could be easily conducted immediately prior to the oral reading lesson and would require less than a minute or so of instruction.

4. **If necessary, change the task requirements.** In some cases, it may be necessary to change the task requirements. In this particular situation, the teacher is requiring students to focus on something negative; that is, oral reading errors. If the history between Jewel and Andy is such that a negative cycle of interactions is being maintained, then it may be necessary to change the context of their interactions. Specifically, instead of requiring Andy to note the oral reading errors that Jewel makes, the teacher would require Andy to note the most difficult word that Jewel read correctly. The change in the task requirements now reinforces both Andy and Jewel.

EXAMPLE: PERSISTENT PROBLEM 2

SETTING: Regular seventh-grade classroom of 25 students
CONTEXT: Hallways
TIME: Friday morning, 11:00 A.M.
PHASE: Fall (October)
ACTIVITY: Transition from one class to the next

Ms. Titus's seventh-grade English class ends at 11:00 A.M. at which time a bell rings. Ms. Titus always gives her students about five minutes before the bell to prepare for the end of class. During this time, students collect their materials, put things away, and, unfortunately, mostly talk and argue. By the time the bell rings, most of the students are overly boisterous and are arguing. When the noise and disruption start to get out of hand, Ms. Titus verbally reprimands the students. The students usually respond to the bell by running into the hall to continue their talking and arguing. Ms. Titus uses the time between classes to prepare for her next class. The five minutes between classes is difficult for Mrs. Titus and the rest of the faculty as students are usually noisy, uncooperative, and disruptive. Several of Ms. Titus's students are often late to the next class because of the chaos in the halls. When students are late, the teacher usually tells the students not to be late again. Ms. Titus's students are considered the worst offenders at the 11:00 A.M. break. The situation has gotten so disruptive that the principal met with Ms. Titus and asked that she eliminate the hallway disruption. Prior to the meeting, Ms. Titus had spoken with her class several times about the problems they were creating in the hallway and told them to "stop acting like a bunch of third-graders." Ms. Titus even required several students to stay after school for disruptive hallway behavior. However, up to this point in time, none of these interventions has eliminated the persistent disruptive behavior in the hallways.

Instructional Analysis of the Problem

Many junior and senior high schools face the problem of disruptive hallways between classes. This management problem is often persistent and escalates as the school year progresses. Casual approaches to the management of this problem will almost always be ineffective. The problem is the result of three instructional/management decisions made by Ms. Titus and the school principal.

1. **Failure to structure the last five minutes of the class and failure to teach transition behavior in the hallways.** One of Ms. Titus's critical mistakes was how she has organized the last five minutes of the class. As the example illustrates, students were already disruptive before they left the classroom. The disruptive behavior was allowed to escalate once the students were in the hallways going to the next class. In addition, students were running from the classroom immediately after hearing the bell. Ms. Titus should have established better instructional control by requiring students to wait for her to dismiss them. This simple strategy would facilitate instructional control and order during the initial stages of transition. It is easier to prevent disruptive behavior than it is to stop it once it is a problem.

2. **Failure to articulate clearly to the students the expected behavior in the hallways.** The feedback students received was erratic and reactive. Students were never provided with a clear explanation of what was expected of them when they passed from class to class. Neither Ms. Titus nor the principal provided clear and consistent rules for behaving in the hallways. In fact, when students were fooling around in the hallway and late for class, there was no consistent reprimand made by Ms. Titus or any other teacher.

3. **Use of reactive approaches to management.** The entire management system that was put into place was reactive and punitive. Ms. Titus failed to provide consistent reinforcement when students behaved properly in the hallway. In addition, there was no schoolwide discipline

plan for all teachers to discuss with students so that their response to the disruptive behavior would be consistent throughout the school. (See chapter 10 for a complete discussion of a schoolwide management plan.)

Instructional Strategies for Prevention

This problem would have been avoided if Ms. Titus had instituted a proactive management strategy in her classroom and if the principal had instituted a schoolwide plan for monitoring the hallways between classes.

1. **Structure the last five minutes of class.** One of the major problems that contributed to the unruly behavior was that the students in Ms. Titus's class were disruptive *before* they left Ms. Titus's class. One strategy for preventing the hallway problem is to use the last five minutes for some activity that can be better managed. The goal of this activity would be to make sure that all the students were following classroom rules at the bell. It would then be much easier for Ms. Titus to ensure that her students would leave her room and enter the hallway quietly.

2. **Identify specific rules for behavior in the hallways and have students practice transition behavior.** Ms. Titus should discuss with her students the problems that they are causing in the hallways between classes. Next, she should identify a list of behaviors that are acceptable in the hallways and a list of behaviors that are not acceptable. These behaviors should be presented clearly enough so that students know what is appropriate behavior. Once this list is completed, Ms. Titus should use class time and have students practice passing from class to class. This practice session should be continued until all students complete the activity appropriately.

3. **Use a precorrection strategy immediately preceding the end of each class.** Once students have had an opportunity to practice passing classes, Ms. Titus should use part of the last five minutes of the class to review what is expected of them when they are in the hall. She should be very specific about the behaviors that are acceptable while passing classes (e.g., quiet talking) and those behaviors that are unacceptable (e.g., running, pushing, shoving). Also, Ms. Titus should present clearly articulated consequences for disruptive behavior and for arriving late to the next class. This precorrection strategy can be completed in less than a minute and should be implemented each day until students begin to follow the established rules. Ms. Titus should periodically represent the precorrection strategy, about once a week, so that students do not fall back into bad habits.

4. **Monitor behavior closely and increase reinforcement for following rules.** Two important aspects of the program for managing hallway

behavior are to monitor the behavior of the students while they are passing classes and to deliver reinforcement as they improve their performance. For example, unless the hallway behavior is monitored, reinforcement that is contingent on performance can't be reliably delivered. Ms. Titus should expect to leave her classroom during the 11:00 A.M. break and to monitor her students as best she can. In addition, other teachers must be willing to take positions in the hallway to help monitor students. This strategy would help guard against the escalation of disruptive behavior. There also needs to be established a method for teachers to increase the level and intensity of reinforcement for students for following the rules while going from one class to the next. In fact, Ms. Titus should start the reinforcement process as soon as she dismisses students and they are leaving the classroom. She should praise those students who walk to the door in a quiet and orderly fashion. This strategy will help to prevent disruptive behavior early in the transition process and make management easier. To accomplish this in the most efficient manner, it would be helpful if Ms. Titus positioned herself at the door before students were dismissed so that she could easily monitor their behavior within the classroom and in the hallways. This would help increase the frequency with which she praises students for following the rules. This reinforcement strategy should be used each day and should become part of her instructional routine.

5. **Establish consistent use of discipline procedures.** Ms. Titus, along with the other teachers in the school should institute specific consequences for hallway misbehavior. In chapter 10, we provide the details of how to conceptualize and implement schoolwide discipline policies.

EXAMPLE: PERSISTENT PROBLEM 3

SETTING: Resource room for students with mild learning/behavior problems
CONTEXT: Spelling class, eight students
TIME: Monday morning, 9:00 A.M.
PHASE: Fall (October)
ACTIVITY: Students are completing independent spelling exercises

Juan is a fifth-grader who has been receiving special education services in a resource room for students with mild learning and behavior problems. Juan has academic problems in reading—he has severe decoding problems (i.e., he still has difficulty sounding out phonetically regular words). His performance is lowest and his behavior is most unmanageable during spelling. Ms. Wang, his resource room teacher, organized her spelling lesson so that students would practice writing the assigned spelling words each day (usually four new words per day) and would complete spelling exercises from a spelling book that is used in the regular fifth-grade classroom.

Ms. Wang, as part of her management routine, allows students to go to a free-time area and choose an activity once they have completed their work. This routine is followed daily except on Friday when students are required to take a spelling test in the regular classroom. During a typical spelling class, Juan does not pay attention to directions and, consequently, rarely finishes his assignment. He also wanders around the room aimlessly when other students are going to the free-time area, and he picks fights with other students.

Juan's parents have him under the care of a pediatrician who placed Juan on Ritalin to control his aggressive behavior and his hyperactivity. In fact, Ms. Wang had recommended to Juan's parents that he be placed on medication to control his social and academic behavior. Ms. Wang has several classroom-based strategies to respond to Juan's inappropriate behaviors. She attempts to control his attention and daydreaming by ignoring him during these times. During ignoring, Ms. Wang will not call on Juan or attend to his inactivity. Once Juan is attending to his spelling work, she tries to get him involved in the lesson by calling on him to answer a question. To manage his wandering behavior, Ms. Wang reprimands Juan when he gets out of his seat without permission (e.g., "Juan, get back to your desk. You know the rules!"). When Juan gets into a fight, which is usually when he is wandering around the room, Ms. Wang will sometimes have him stay after school for 30 minutes. Ms. Wang spends this 30 minutes discussing with Juan why it is important to get along with other students and not fight. During these discussions, Juan is responsive to Ms. Wang's concern. However, Ms. Wang is discouraged by Juan's continuing problems in class. Ms. Wang is not sure what to do next.

Instructional Analysis of the Problem

The persistent problems that are described in this example—inattention, failure to follow rules, and fighting—are typical behaviors of many students who are placed in instructional programs that are too difficult and in classrooms with loosely defined rules. When students engage in several persistent behavior problems, the teacher should: (a) establish a plan to control the behavior that is most disruptive and potentially destructive, in Juan's case, fighting; (b) determine the sources of the disruptive behavior by assessing the instructional context quickly; and (c) modify the instructional program accordingly so that in the future there will be fewer problems. In spite of the fact that Juan presents multiple problems, Ms. Wang must consider instructional solutions for managing his learning and behavior problems effectively.

1. **Failure to place Juan in the appropriate spelling activity and to provide appropriate instructional support.** A likely cause of Juan's inattention during spelling is that the tasks that he is assigned are too difficult. Requiring students to copy and to memorize four new spelling words per day is a daunting task for low-performing students. In

addition, Juan's reading problems should have alerted Ms. Wang that Juan needed spelling instruction that teaches him to spell phonetically regular words first. Also, Ms. Wang's decision to ignore his inattentiveness is inappropriate because it is likely that other, more powerful reinforcers (e.g., getting out of the assignment, other students attending to his inattentive behavior) are maintaining his inappropriate behavior. Also, many students who are inattentive are often unaware that they are daydreaming and not tracking the lesson. In Juan's case, ignoring does not provide instruction in how to attend to the spelling lesson.

2. **Failure to monitor student behavior consistently and planfully.** Ms. Wang has organized her classroom to allow students to get out of their seats without permission when they complete their spelling assignments. She rarely monitors the work of all the students to make sure everyone is following this rule. Consequently, Juan is receiving mixed messages. He is learning that you don't have to follow the rules because the teacher does not monitor student behavior.

3. **Failure to provide clear expectations about rules and routines during the spelling session.** Because students are not taught spelling skills and are not monitored carefully when they are practicing these skills independently, students' interactions in the classroom often occur randomly. In these situations, Juan, who often acts impulsively, will sometimes start a fight with another student.

4. **Failure to manage Juan's fighting proactively and to provide specific and consistent consequences for this behavior.** Ms. Wang has not dealt consistently with Juan's frequent fighting. Although she has a consequence in place (30 minutes after school), it has been used only infrequently and not immediately. Thus far, Juan is learning that he can create a major disruption with few consequences. Because Juan is poorly equipped to perform in the spelling class, he is probably insecure during this class. Often, the cause of fighting in students is insecurity. Inconsistent use of punishment is almost always ineffective with difficult students like Juan. In addition, Ms. Wang should not use the after-school time as a therapy session because it will likely reinforce Juan's fighting.

Instructional Strategies for Prevention

The problems described in this example are typical of the problems teachers have with students who are performing well below grade level in several areas. For example, in Juan's case, the fact that Juan's spelling problems are related to his reading problem should not be ignored. Nothing good can happen when a student like Juan is placed in a lesson where he or she does not have the skills to compete and learn. It is no mystery, then, that Juan's behavior reaches crisis levels in spelling class. An outline of one approach to manage Juan's persistent behavior problems is provided as follows.

1. **Develop plan to control Juan's fighting.** Ms. Wang should choose a punishment strategy to eliminate Juan's fighting immediately. The owing-time strategy or time-out from positive reinforcement would be acceptable and necessary alternatives to her present approach. It is critical that all the students in the class are told of the consequences for fighting and that a consequence is administered *each* time a fight occurs. In addition, Ms. Wang should reorganize her spelling session (discussed as follows) so that she can increase her positive interactions with Juan. Increasing the reinforcement frequency is as important as using the punishment strategy consistently.

2. **Place students appropriately and reorganize the spelling lesson to increase success of students.** The spelling session, as it is presently organized, is not conducive to successful learning. Once Ms. Wang places the students in the proper level of the spelling program, she should break the 45 minute lesson into four parts: (1) group instruction on critical spelling skills (15 minutes); (2) independent written spelling assignment that is carefully monitored by Ms. Wang (15 minutes); (3) a structured group activity where written assignments are checked orally by the teacher (10 minutes); (4) a brief quiz on information presented that day (5 minutes). This lesson structure allows for increased positive interactions, increases teacher feedback to the student and most importantly, it improves the quality of spelling instruction.

3. **Structure teaching activities to increase Juan's attention.** Once Juan and the other students are placed into the spelling program appropriately, Juan can be taught how to increase his attention to the task. Ms. Wang should choose a time to teach Juan how to attend to an easy or neutral task. The challenge of increasing his attention to task demands should *not* be done on spelling because it is a difficult skill for Juan. Instead, a neutral task should be used. For example, Ms. Wang could use a math task that is easy for Juan, such as numeral identification or skip counting. As Juan responds to the task, Ms. Wang should reinforce him for *attending*. He would have to be taught how to (1) manage his time, (2) complete sections of a task before moving on, and (3) monitor his progress through the activity. In addition, Ms. Wang should choose a powerful reinforcer for Juan for attending to his work. Finally, Juan should be held accountable to complete all spelling activities.

EXAMPLE: PERSISTENT PROBLEM 4

SETTING: Elementary school
CONTEXT: All unmonitored areas (e.g., hallways, playground, bathrooms)
TIME: Throughout the entire day
PHASE: Spring (April)
ACTIVITY: All unmonitored activities (e.g., hallways, free-time, boarding buses)

A day does not go by without the occurrence of fights, arguments, and general disruptive behavior in an unsupervised area in Monroe Elementary School. The locations where fighting occurs most frequently are the hallways, the restrooms, and the area where students are waiting to board the school buses at the end of the day. There is no standard school policy for teachers to use when handling these problems. Every teacher handles student disputes in unsupervised areas differently. For example, after breaking up a fight, one teacher might verbally reprimand the students, another might require that the students come in after school, while others may have the offending students report to the office to see the principal. Simply, each teacher chooses a consequence for these disruptions on the spur-of-the-moment. The frequency of fighting and other forms of disruptive behavior have increased consistently throughout the year at Monroe Elementary School.

Instructional Analysis of the Problem

The problem at Monroe Elementary School is one that occurs frequently in schools that do not have a coordinated policy and approach for monitoring and managing the behavior of students in all areas of the school. The situation at Monroe is consistent with that in many schools where each teacher handles fighting and other forms of disruptive behavior differently. In this section, we identify three problems with how the persistent fighting at Monroe Elementary School is currently managed.

1. **Inadequate monitoring of unsupervised areas in the school.** Persistent fighting and disruptions at Monroe occurred most frequently in unsupervised areas. The lack of supervision promoted inconsistent management of disruptive behavior. Although every area in the building can't be monitored at all times, it is clear from the description of the problem that certain areas (e.g., hallways, bathrooms) elicited most of the problems and required immediate adult supervision.

2. **Lack of consequences for disruptive behavior.** Because of the lack of consistent monitoring, many of the incidents of disruptive behavior were not handled by the faculty. Discipline procedures were not administered quickly and fairly at Monroe School. The students learned that if they fought in unsupervised areas, they would not be "caught."

3. **Failure to establish a schoolwide management program for Monroe Elementary School.** The most significant shortcoming of the faculty's response to fighting and disruptive behavior at Monroe School was the lack of a schoolwide discipline policy. The absence of a school policy fostered inconsistent management of unsupervised areas of the school.

Instructional Strategies for Prevention

A schoolwide policy would provide a coordinated approach for managing students in all areas in the school. An effective policy would define the types of behaviors that are prohibited at the school, would provide a plan for the faculty on how unsupervised areas of the school will be monitored, and would establish a set of consequences for fighting and other forms of disruptive behavior. This policy would also have a component that included parents in the management of students who display more severe forms of disruptive behavior. Chapter 10, "Schoolwide Discipline Policies," provides a complete discussion on how to establish procedures for managing the behavior of students throughout the school, including (a) the details of how a school can develop a mission statement, (b) the policies for consistent discipline of students, and (c) the roles that teachers, parents, and principals have in a schoolwide management program.

SUMMARY

In this chapter, we presented a model for teachers to use when designing proactive management approaches for persistent behavior problems. The model provides procedures for the assessment of persistent behavior problems, as well as ideas for modifying classroom organization, evaluating task dimensions, and reinforcing positive student performance. We also presented as part of this model specific procedures for implementing precorrection strategies, presenting neutral tasks, and using punishment procedures. This model will help teachers organize their instructional management approach to persistent behavior problems.

We concluded this chapter with the presentation of four examples of persistent behavior problems. For each problem, an instructional analysis of the problem was first introduced followed by the presentation of instructional strategies for prevention.

CHAPTER ACTIVITIES

1. Discuss the model for managing persistent behavior problems that was presented in this chapter. Be sure to list each component of the model and discuss the role each plays in managing persistent behavior problems.

2. Ask a teacher to describe a persistent behavior problem that he or she is having in the classroom. From this description, list and discuss the instructional strategies that would be used to prevent this type of behavior problem.

3. Following the format used in this chapter, develop an example of a persistent behavior problem. Include a complete description of the problem, an instructional analysis, and a list of instructional strategies for prevention. Have other students develop their own instructional analysis and instructional strategies for prevention for your persistent behavior problem.

SUGGESTED READINGS

Engelmann, S., & Colvin, G. (1983). *Generalized compliance training: A direct instruction program for managing severe behavior problems.* Austin, TX: Pro-Ed.

Sprick R. (1981). *The solution book: A guide to classroom discipline.* Chicago: Science Research Associates.

chapter 10

Schoolwide Discipline Policies: An Instructional Classroom Management Approach

Randall S. Sprick
Teaching Strategies, Inc.

INTRODUCTION

Discipline in schools used to be simpler. It was not too long ago that schools used suspension and expulsion as the primary discipline tactic. If a student misbehaved too severely or too often, we simply got rid of that student. A discipline policy that mainly emphasized a school's response to severe misbehavior was adequate when the main discipline tactic involved excluding any student whose behavior was not perfectly compliant. Many schools have reflected this approach in the written discipline policy or student code of conduct. The policy or code mainly presents information on severe infractions and how the school may use suspension or expulsion for these serious offenses. However, now that most schools are trying to reach every student more effectively, the traditional approaches to discipline need to be reexamined.

While informing students and parents about the consequences for severe infractions is still important, particularly in a secondary school, it is no longer adequate. Providing notice to parents and students does little to insure a consistent philosophy of discipline and it in no way provides for a variety of positive reinforcement, awards, and incentives. Discipline policies that are limited to consequences provide students with no information on the goals or directions toward which they are expected to strive. Most punitive policies provide staff no information on procedures for classroom management, no information on increasing student motivation, and no information on how to supervise students in common areas of the school, such as halls or the playground.

To respond effectively to schoolwide discipline issues, the staff, students, and parents need written information to increase the likelihood that discipline will be reasonably consistent and fair, and that positive procedures will be used to reduce the likelihood of student misconduct. Given the limitations to traditional policies, we propose a much broader alternative—the development of a staff manual related to the issues of discipline, motivation, and classroom management. A broad-based staff manual can accomplish a number of important things. First, it can specify a common philosophy of how the staff is expected to treat children. Second, it can increase the consistency with which adults within a school implement a policy. Third, it can give staff information on precise expectations for supervision of schoolwide areas. Fourth, it can specify how students will be taught expectations for appropriate behaviors in every school environment.

The development of a manual of this type must involve staff actively in all stages of the process. Staff members must see that they have had a voice in determining the policies and procedures that they must now carry out. Students and parents should also be allowed to have input in the final development of the school's policies and procedures relative to motivation and discipline.

The remainder of this chapter will examine the process for developing a comprehensive discipline policy, and then sample features of an effective discipline manual for staff will be suggested.

DESIGNING A STAFF MANUAL

Developing an effective school discipline policy that guides staff and students is a time-consuming and potentially difficult process. The remainder of this chapter will outline one way a school staff could develop a policy. Although other development processes may be equally effective, the sequence presented in this chapter has been effective at many schools.

The most important variable in the process of developing a policy that will be implemented appropriately and consistently by the staff is the active involvement of the staff in the development of the policy. Staff ownership of the procedures is critical. If some staff feel that the policy is being "shoved down their throats," those staff members will actively or passively undermine the new procedures. Because the staff are the people who need to implement the procedures outlined in the policy, they need to have a voice in shaping them.

One of the best ways to involve staff in the process is to divide the process into small steps and then have staff sign up to be on a committee to complete one part of the process. One committee should be assigned the responsibility of guiding the entire process. This group might be called the "Discipline Committee" or the "Responsibility Team." Each of the other staff committees would be responsible for drafting a particular section of the manual. The advantage of this approach is that when the policy is completed, every staff person will have participated in the design. The disadvantages are that such a process is time consuming and some staff may resent having to serve on a committee. However, the advantages of total staff involvement usually outweigh the disadvantages, and every effort should be made to include the entire faculty in some aspect of designing the policy. What follows is a sequence of steps a staff might implement.

Step 1: Achieve consensus that revising the current policies is a worthwhile endeavor.

Step 2: Identify schoolwide areas that are supervised by paraprofessionals or by rotating duty schedules of teachers. Areas or topics may include cafeteria, playgrounds or other outside areas, restrooms, assemblies, and so on.

Step 3: Establish a committee for each of the common areas and establish a discipline committee that will be responsible for writing a draft of the major part of the policy. The discipline committee will be responsible for developing a first draft of the policies and procedures that are pervasive and consistent regardless of the specific location.

Step 4: Establish a time line that each committee feels they can meet to accomplish Step 5.

Step 5: Each committee will be given a sample policy. The committee will then write a proposed policy, which can be based on the sample policy provided or drafted entirely from scratch.

Step 6: Each committee will present its proposed policy to the entire staff, who will be given an opportunity to make suggestions and provide feedback to the committee.

Step 7: The committee will rewrite the proposed policy to incorporate as many of the suggested revisions as possible.

Step 8: The discipline committee will compile the work of each committee and draft a proposed letter to students and a separate letter to parents describing the policies.

Step 9: The discipline committee will arrange to involve parents and students in giving input on some parts of the policies.

Parents and students should be allowed to have input in at least some portion of the policy. Parents should be invited to respond to a draft copy of the policy and procedures before anything is adopted for the school. Students should also be encouraged to provide input in the development stages. Student involvement is especially important at the secondary level. Because this is mainly a staff manual, the involvement of parents and students may come after staff has begun the process. Although parents should be able to participate in any part of the process, their involvement in some aspects of the policy, such as the role of teacher assistants, may be less critical than other parts, such as the school's philosophy.

Step 10: Based on input from staff, parents, and students, the discipline committee will prepare a proposed draft of the final policy. Staff will have one more chance to provide input.

Step 11: Staff will be given training in implementing the new policies. Special emphasis will be placed on training students in the revised expectations for their behavior.

FEATURES OF AN EFFECTIVE POLICY

Although the exact form of each school's staff manual will be different, we recommend organizing the material into five major sections. The first section includes a mission statement, philosophy, and goals. The second section describes the role of students and the role of parents. This section should include a copy of a letter to students and a letter to parents describing the expectations for student behavior and parental support. The third section of the manual describes the role of the principal, teachers, paraprofessionals, and other adults who work with students. The fourth section describes all schoolwide programs for reinforcing desirable behavior and any schoolwide programs for implementing consequences for infractions. The fifth and final section should include a document for each of the common areas of the school, such as the playground, halls, assemblies, and so on. Each of these documents should outline expectations for staff.

Section 1: Mission, Philosophy, and Goals

An effective policy includes the school's mission statement, a statement of philosophy regarding discipline, and a specification of goals that all people in the school are expected to strive to achieve. The mission statement should guide the development and implementation of all aspects of the policy. If a school does not have a mission statement, it needs one. A mission statement is necessary so that as the staff manual is developed, each section can be evaluated as to whether or not it helps to support the school's mission. If a given section does not support the mission, it should be modified.

A section on the staff's philosophy of discipline and motivation should specify some general principles that the staff agrees are important features of school discipline. A motto and goals can be a useful part of this section of the manual. Staff should determine what is required for success in the school. Specifically, three to six behaviors, attitudes, or traits that the staff considers most important for success should be identified. These goals should be stated in such a way that they apply to everyone in the school—not just students. If the staff decides it is appropriate, a motto can be an effective way to summarize the goals into a statement that is easy for students to memorize.

Below is a sample of this first section of a staff manual. These materials are taken from *Foundations: Establishing Positive Discipline Policies,* developed by Sprick, Sprick, and Garrison (1993). This in-service training material provides step-by-step information guidance in how to involve the entire staff in the development of a staff handbook for teaching students to behave responsibly.

Please note that Lincoln Elementary is not a real school and the samples included in this chapter are a composite of several schools that have developed a staff handbook for discipline and motivation.

Lincoln Elementary

Mission Statement

We the staff of Lincoln School are committed to providing our students with the behavioral and academic skills required to reason, communicate and live with dignity in a literate society. This means providing all our students with instruction that will allow them to reach their fullest potential.

Staff Philosophy of Discipline and Motivation

Every person in Lincoln Elementary School is expected to treat every other person with dignity and respect. Staff and students will all work together to help every person in the school reach their fullest potential. Any behavior or action which helps someone grow and mature will be encouraged. Any behavior or action which interferes with another person's growth or a student's own growth will not be tolerated. Students will be encouraged to remember the phrase, "**Do Your Best and Help the Rest.**" Should problems occur, the student will be asked to look at her own behavior and asked if she is following this motto.

When every person in a school is doing his best, the school becomes an exciting and warm place where every person is learning new things every single day.

Goals

Everyone in the school is encouraged to actively work on the following goals:

1. Always try.
2. Do your best.
3. Cooperate with other people and treat them with respect.
4. Manage yourself.
5. Respect the rights and property of others.

Section 2: The Role of Students and Parents

In this section, information should be provided on what the staff views as the student's role in discipline and what the staff views as the parent's role in discipline. Obviously, there should be congruence between these sections and the school's mission, philosophy, and goals. This section should also include copies of the letters to parents and students. For schools that have a student handbook, this information might be included within that handbook. Below is a sample of the sections from a staff manual that addresses the role of the students and the role of the parents.

Role of Students*

IN THE CLASSROOM: Students will follow the teacher's classroom rules. Because every teacher teaches differently, each teacher will communicate precisely how students are expected to behave in each activity. Consequences for misbehavior in the classroom are at the discretion of the teacher and are outlined under The Teacher's Role in Discipline. When students are trying their best, this effort will be acknowledged by the teacher.

IN THE HALLS, CAFETERIA, OUTSIDE AREAS, ON BUSES: Students will behave in a way that respects the physical safety and the emotional security of themselves and others. Therefore, no students will be allowed to run in the halls, engage in teasing, or to behave in any manner that might harm another person. Specific guidelines and consequences for halls, outdoor areas, cafeteria, and buses are included in another section.

SEVERE MISBEHAVIOR: Three categories of severe misbehavior warrant the involvement of the principal at the first infraction. These categories include anything illegal, anything physically dangerous, and insubordination—the direct refusal to comply with a direction given by an adult. Severe misbehavior may result in isolation, parental conferences, in-school suspension, out-of-school suspension, contact of the legal authorities, or other severe consequences.

Letter to Students on Discipline Policies

Dear Lincoln Elementary Students:

You are very special to us. We want you to be happy at school and to learn all that you possibly can. Your success is very important. We have identified five goals for your school behavior that will help everyone be successful.

Goal One—Always Try

The best way to learn something new is practice until you can do it. If someone is unwilling to try, they can not practice. When you first try to do something it is often difficult, but if you keep trying it gets easier and easier.

*Note: For middle school and high school students, more detailed information on specific misbehaviors and the corresponding consequences may be included in a student handbook.

Goal Two—Do Your Best
Examples include being on time, being prepared, and completing assignments to the best of your ability.

Goal Three—Cooperate with Other People
Cooperation includes being polite, treating people with respect, accepting differences between people, dealing with disagreements through STP (Stop, Think, Plan), and encouraging others to do their best.

Goal Four—Manage Yourself
All through your life you must decide how you will act. Therefore, we expect you to do what is right whether anyone is watching you or not. This is called "managing yourself." Walking, not running, in the hallways when your teacher isn't watching is also managing yourself. It isn't always easy, especially if someone else is not managing himself properly. It is important to remember that you are in charge of yourself and you can do what is right!

Goal Five—Respect the Rights and Property of Others
Everyone in this school must know that they are safe from harm. Any behavior that could hurt someone can not be allowed. Examples of respecting property include caring for our beautiful school, play equipment, the personal property of classmates and staff, and returning lost items to the lost and found.

The adults at Lincoln Elementary will help you achieve success at school. We will do this by helping you solve problems and protecting your right to learn.

Enjoy a good year!

The Parent's Role in Discipline

Parents are encouraged to participate in the education of their children. Without the cooperation and support of parents the school cannot effectively help a student reach his or her fullest potential. The major role of parents in discipline is to continually show the child that they are interested and supportive of how their child is doing in school. When the child sees that mom and dad are actively interested in whether or not he is doing his best, the student is given a real incentive to strive for excellence. Parents will be informed when their children are working to reach their fullest potential.

Parents may be asked periodically to support the teacher in helping the child to learn a particular skill such as independence, or remembering homework, or how to take responsibility for her own behavior, or how to handle anger in a mature way. If parents are asked to help teach a skill of this type, the school staff will provide specific information on different ways to accomplish this goal.

If there is a severe or recurring problem, parents will be asked to help the school staff teach the student an alternative set of behaviors. In such a case, everyone must recognize that the goal is to help the child learn to get along in the school environment so the child can be successful when going on to middle school and high school. By working together, parents and staff can help the student learn behaviors that will increase his chances of success.

Sample Letter to Parents Regarding Discipline Policies

This letter is to be sent home with children at the beginning of the school year. By September 20, any parents who have not returned the letter with a signature will be sent another copy via U.S. Mail. Any parents that have not returned a signed copy by October 1, will be contacted by the school social worker who will make an appointment to go over the information with the parent.

Dear Parents:

We want your child to be happy and successful at school. We believe that you, as parents, play an important role in helping your child achieve the Lincoln student goals.

We believe that your major role in school discipline is to continually show interest in and support for your child at school. The child's knowledge that parents are actively interested and supportive of the school program almost always reduces school discipline problems.

Please share with your child's teacher any helpful information about your child. This information can help the teacher deal with any special needs your child might have. We believe that communication between parents, students, and teachers is critical in teaching correct behavior.

We want your child to meet the five goals that we have set at Lincoln School. YOU play a key role in your child's success. Please review and discuss the five goals and school rules with your child. Post them in a place where your child will see them often.

We believe in a fair and consistent code of discipline and good classroom management. Our goal is an environment where courtesy and kindness prevail and where there is respect for differences of other people, customs, and cultures. We will treat children with courtesy and respect. When problems arise, we will work positively to find solutions. We will hold students accountable. We believe each student has the final responsibility for the consequences of his/her own behavior.

If your child exhibits unacceptable behavior at school, you may be asked to help us teach the child an alternative set of behaviors. You may be asked to conference with us and/or support us in selecting appropriate consequences to modify the behavior.

If you want more information on our philosophy of motivation and discipline, or information on student rights and responsibilities, please contact the principal at _____ .

Sincerely,
The Lincoln Staff

Please return this section to school:
We read and understand the Goals and Rules for Lincoln Elementary School.

_____	_____
Student Signature	Date
_____	_____
Parent/Guardian Signature	Date

Section 3: The Role of Staff in Discipline

This section of the manual is potentially the most difficult section to develop, but it is also very important. This section outlines the way in which staff will interact with students. It defines how adults treat students and how adults implement strategies for discipline and motivation. For example, if the staff agrees to implement an instructional management approach to discipline as outlined in this text, a summary of the approach should be given in the section on the teacher's role. In addition, this section should begin with statements about how all adults will interact with students. Separate sections should be developed for each of the distinct job roles of the school, including the administrator(s), teachers, counselor, psychologist, noncertificated personnel, and any other people who have a direct role in discipline and motivation issues.

The following sample specifies the role of a discipline committee that meets on a regular basis. If a school has a teacher assistance team that meets to assist in developing plans for students with behavioral problems, those procedures should be written up and included as part of this manual. The following pages show a sample of this section. Please note that the section for the teaching staff is based predominantly on the principles outlined in this text.

The Role of Staff in Discipline

Every staff person contributes to making Lincoln Elementary a friendly, inviting school environment. We set the tone. If we are calm, encouraging, and supportive, students will be more likely to want to put forth their best effort. The two most important procedures are to provide positive feedback to students when they are meeting expectations and to provide calm, consistent reprimands or consequences when students are not meeting expectations.

If every staff member follows the procedures recommended in this manual, we will achieve consistency of discipline. Without consistency, we can not expect students to learn to behave appropriately. For example, if only some of the adults will stop students who run in the halls, students will continue to run to see if they can get away with it. However, if every staff person stops someone who runs, in time, running in the hall will cease to be a problem. Each staff person is expected to implement the procedures defined in this staff manual.

Severe Misbehavior:

Most misbehavior will be dealt with by discussion or with mild consequences. For example, a student seen running in the hall will be required to go back and walk. However, there are three categories of misbehavior that will result in the student being immediately sent to the office, parents being notified, and perhaps other consequences. These three categories include any physically dangerous behavior (assault, fighting, and so on), any illegal act, and open disrespect of a staff member or insubordinate behavior. Everyone must recognize that dangerous behavior and disrespect will not be tolerated.

In the event that a staff member observes a behavior that is dangerous, illegal, or flagrantly insubordinate, the student or students should be immediately taken to the office. If students are fighting, inform them to stop. Take no action that could put yourself in physical danger. Send a student to get assistance if necessary.

If the student refuses to accompany you, inform the student that if he chooses to refuse to accompany you, he will just be making the problem worse. Make no attempt to physically take the student to the office. Inform the office of the behavior, the refusal to accompany you, and the student's name. If you do not know the student's name and she will not tell you, discuss this with the principal at your earliest convenience. There is an excellent chance that the principal knows this student already and will be able to identify the student from your description. Although following through with the above procedures may require more effort than just letting the student get away with the infraction, students must see that dangerous, illegal, and insubordinate acts will not be tolerated.

Student in Crisis:

If a staff member has any knowledge of a student in crisis or suspects the student might be in crisis, action should be taken immediately. Below is a possible list of potential crisis situations and the appropriate staff person with whom to discuss the problem.

Neglect: School nurse and principal

Poor hygiene: School nurse

Improper medication: School nurse

Physical or sexual abuse: School nurse and principal

Drug involvement: School nurse and principal

Depression: School counselor

Threat of suicide: School counselor and principal

The Classroom Teacher's Role in Discipline

The classroom teacher is the center of our school responsibility and discipline policy. Teachers will continually emphasize to both students and parents the importance of, "Be responsible. Do your best and help the rest." Teachers will focus on teaching and encouraging responsible behavior, rather than trying to "control" irresponsible behavior. This will be accomplished by helping students see how their behavior relates to our schoolwide guidelines emphasizing responsibility, trying, doing one's best, cooperating with others, and treating everyone with respect.

1. Three basic principles of behavior management will be implemented by all teachers.
   a. At the beginning of the new school year, and as necessary through the school year, students will be taught how to behave responsibly in each type of classroom activity.
   b. Teachers will strive to interact frequently with each student when the student is behaving appropriately.

c. When misbehavior does occur, teachers will calmly and consistently implement mild classroom consequences. The focus of interactions with each student will continue to be primarily positive with a ratio of at least three positive interactions to every correction required.

Though these principles will guide teachers in their classroom management, each teacher, each student, and each situation is unique. Specific procedures to be used will be at the discretion of the teacher and will be based on student needs, the situation, and the principles described above.

2. When chronic misbehavior occurs, staff will work collaboratively to assist a student in learning to behave responsibly. At Lincoln Elementary, staff acknowledges that teachers do not cause chronic misbehaviors, but may provide a student's best hope for learning to be more successful.

As we implement our basic classroom management procedures, we know that the great majority of our students will strive to meet our expectations for responsibility and self-discipline. However, we also know that no single set of procedures will work to help every student develop the behavioral skills and attitudes needed to be successful in school. Therefore, we will design a series of interventions for any students who have not been motivated by our schoolwide procedures. As we adapt our procedures, the focus will remain positive, while recognizing a continuing need for calm and consistent consequences. (See the sample sequence below.)

We also recognize that some students will present an extreme challenge. We therefore urge our teachers to keep the following concepts in mind:

a. No one is expected to have all the answers.

b. We live in a culture where an adequate education is critical to success. Therefore, we will make every effort to teach students to be successful in the school environment.

c. The Lincoln staff works collaboratively. Prior to feeling frustration, teachers are encouraged to seek assistance from other teachers, specialists, from the principal, the Intervention Planning Team or the Foundation Team.

d. Referral to special education will be made when improvement cannot be made in the regular program through the collaborative efforts of staff.

Sample Sequence*

The following sequence demonstrates the types of plans we will develop for students with chronic misbehavior. The sequence shows how a plan may evolve over a period of four to five months, with more energy devoted to encouraging success than into punishing failure.

Sample sequence: Encouraging a student who engages in chronic misbehavior to assume greater responsibility.

*Note: This is a sample sequence, designed to demonstrate how a series of interventions can be set up with energies directed into proactive, positive interventions, rather than into reactive-punitive interventions. Within this basic approach, the teacher has tremendous latitude for professional judgment in setting up a series of interventions to help a student with a recurrent behavioral problem.

a. Discuss the problem with the student, helping the student to see how his specific actions can be changed to reflect the school motto, "Be responsible. Do your best and help the rest." The goal of this discussion will be to clarify how the student can take control of his behavior. Suggestions will be clear and direct.

b. Set up an in-class time-out as a mild consequence.

c. Catch the student doing something right and provide positive feedback.

d. Set written goals with the student.

e. Encourage other staff members to interact positively with the student.

f. Call the parents when problems occur.

g. Diagnose whether the student is capable of being academically successful. If not, arrange for a peer tutor.

h. Call parents on days when improvement takes place.

i. Supply intermittent reinforcers when the student improves.

j. Change the time-out consequence to time owed off recess.

k. Give the student responsibilities in the classroom.

l. Ask for assistance from the Intervention Planning Team.

m. Arrange for a conference with the parents and the student to discuss future goals for behavior long-term expectations.

n. Set up an individual reinforcement system.

o. Work on improving self-image through positive self-talk.

p. Send the student to the principal for encouragement when improvement occurs.

q. Prearrange for the student to be isolated in the time-out room for short periods after each misbehavior.

r. Arrange for the school counselor to work with the student on relaxation and anger management.

s. Pair the student with an adult mentor who will meet with the student once a week.

t. If the student's behavior hasn't improved, ask for an observation from a school administrator, school psychologist, or other staff members who might collaborate.

u. Consider referral to special education for evaluation.

3. Each teacher will have a classroom discipline and responsibility plan on file in the office. (See samples in Figures 10.1 and 10.2.)

The Principal's Role in Discipline

The role of the principal in discipline is threefold. First, the principal should work with the discipline committee to help monitor, revise, and update the discipline policies and procedures. The principal will be responsible for making sure that the discipline committee meets on a regular basis and will guide the staff through the yearly review and updating of this manual.

The second role of the principal in discipline is to help staff implement classroom management and school management techniques. In this capacity, the principal will use this manual to train any new staff in the appropriate procedures. The principal will also provide staff members with positive feedback for following this manual. Given the massive amount of information in this manual, staff

Teacher _____

RULES AND EXPECTATIONS

1. _____   4. _____

2. _____   5. _____

3. _____   6. _____

POSSIBLE CONSEQUENCE FOR INFRACTIONS

Verbal reminder

Positive practice

Time-out desk (in classroom)

Contact parent

Time-out room (room 7)

Principal (dangerous, illegal, insubordination)

REINFORCEMENT PROCEDURES

Class

Individual

MONITORING

TEACHING RESPONSIBILITIES

FIGURE 10.1   Classroom discipline plan

members will make errors and interpret the suggested procedures differently. In either case, the principal will privately discuss the issue with the appropriate staff person.

The third role of the principal is to assist staff with handling severe misbehavior such as physically dangerous situations, illegal acts, flagrant disrespect of adult authority, and any chronic and recurring problems. In doing so, the principal will implement isolation, parental conferences, in-school suspension, out-of-school suspension, contact the appropriate authorities, or other severe consequences. The principal will ensure that all discipline procedures are in line with legal and ethical considerations. It is the responsibility of the principal to follow due process safeguards. Special due process considerations may need to be developed for students with disabilities (Leone 1985).

Teacher: _Miss Jackson_

RULES AND EXPECTATIONS

1. _Be responsible._
2. _Always try._
3. _Do your best._

4. _Cooperate with others._
5. _Treat everyone with dignity and respect._
6. _Be kind._

POSSIBLE CONSEQUENCE FOR INFRACTIONS

Verbal reminder

Positive practice

Heads down—think about behavior

Discuss better choices and fill out form with teacher

Time-out desk (in classroom)

Contact parent

Time-out room (room 7)

Principal (dangerous, illegal, insubordination)

REINFORCEMENT PROCEDURES

Class

*Points for best "team" behavior and weekly award.
Verbal praise.
Occasional free time for appropriate choices.*

Individual

*Verbal acknowledgement.
Intermittent awards and prizes for reaching goal.*

MONITORING

*Walk around room in proximity to behavior problems.
Hand on shoulder to warn and show support, and eye contact and smile.*

TEACHING RESPONSIBILITIES

*Provide support. Teach expectations for each activity.
Assist students in making responsible choices.
Use consistency in praise and consequences. Follow through on problems.*

FIGURE 10.2 Classroom discipline plan (sample)

It is not possible for the office staff to accept discipline referrals for minor problems. If minor problems are referred to the office, students soon learn that being referred to the office is "no big deal." To maintain potential effectiveness of office referrals, they must be used only for severe or recurrent problems.

Records will be kept by the principal and office staff on all office referrals. These records will be compiled and shared with the discipline committee at least four times a year. Using these records, the discipline committee and the administrative staff will determine if there is a need to revise the written policies within this manual or if there is a need for further staff development to encourage greater consistency on the part of staff in implementing the current policy.

The Role of the Nurse, Counselor, and School Psychologist

The nurse is currently assigned to Lincoln 50% of the time and is in the school every morning. If a student is suspected of being ill or hurt, he should be sent to the nurse. If the nurse is not available, the principal will make the decision whether the parents should be contacted and the student sent home. The nurse is also available to consult with staff on students suspected of drug involvement, a child who is depressed or makes threats of suicide, child abuse or neglect, children with hygiene or nutrition problems, and so on.

The counselor is currently assigned to Lincoln school for three days each week—Monday, Tuesday, and Thursday. The counselor will teach classes, with the schedule to be negotiated with each grade level. These classes will cover topics such as self-esteem, conflict resolution, and social skills training. The counselor will meet with individual students who need individual counseling services, with the schedule to be worked out with classroom teachers. Note: The counselor's office is not the place to send students for misbehavior. If a staff member feels a student could benefit from counseling, that staff member should discuss the situation with the counselor to determine if it is possible or necessary to provide counseling services. The counselor is also available to consult with staff on topics such as students with behavioral problems, students suspected of drug involvement, a child who is depressed or makes threats of suicide, child abuse or neglect, teacher stress, and so on.

The school psychologist is assigned to Lincoln one day per week—Tuesday. The role of the psychologist is to assess all students referred to special education. In addition, the psychologist is available to consult with staff on interventions for students with behavior problems and/or learning problems.

The Role of Teacher Assistants, Playground Supervisors, Custodial Staff, Office Staff, and Cafeteria Staff

Every staff person in the school contributes equally to implementing the discipline policy and procedures. Students should treat all adults with respect and all adults have the right to implement consequences for infractions of rules in common areas. This is true for aides, secretaries, bus drivers and any other job roles. All staff people are expected to interact with students in a friendly, respectful manner. Each staff person should fully understand all sections of this manual directly related to their job role. For example, playground supervisors must fully understand the information on playground procedures outlined in this manual. Staff members must understand that they not only have a right, but have a duty, to intervene with any misbehavior observed in a common area such as the halls, restrooms, or playground—by following the mild procedures recommended in this manual.

The Role of the Discipline Committee

The discipline committee will consist of the principal, two primary teachers, two intermediate teachers, a playground supervisor, and a representative from special education or student support services. The role of the discipline committee is fourfold:

1. To manage the development and the on-going implementation of this manual.
2. To review the records of discipline referrals to the office and to use this information to make recommendations to staff regarding changes in policy and/or staff development activities.
3. To conduct a yearly review of staff, student, and parental satisfaction of the current discipline policies by administering a "Satisfaction Survey." This information will be used to revise the policy and guide staff development activities. (Note: *The Foundations: Establishing Positive Discipline Policies* program includes sample surveys and other tools for evaluating the effectiveness of current policies and procedures.)
4. To arrange staffings on individual students with chronic behavior problems or upon request for a staffing from a staff member.

The discipline committee will meet regularly for approximately one hour every two weeks. Members of the discipline committee will be free from their turn at bus duty supervision to compensate for the time spent with discipline committee duties.

Section 4: Schoolwide Programs for Reinforcement and Consequences

Because this is a staff manual, staff should have written information on how and when to use any schoolwide programs and procedures. For example, if the school has a program of awards for behavior that are announced at a monthly assembly, staff should be given information on what criteria are used to pick students for these awards. If the school has an after-school detention room, to which teachers can send students as a consequence for misbehavior, the operation and use of the room should be explained in this section. One way to develop this section is to think about a new teacher to the building, and to try to explain all the procedures and programs for encouraging responsible behavior and correcting misbehavior so that new staff members will be able to use the programs.

The following is a sample of this type of section and includes both positive and punitive or corrective programs. The positive programs include (a) positive interactions and positive feedback, (b) students targeted for special attention,

(c) use of a "Goal Achieved" book that is kept in the office, (d) use of a "Homework Room" as an invitational place where children can complete their work, and (e) use of a "Guidance Assistance Center" where children can get special attention and assistance. In this sample, the only schoolwide punitive or corrective programs are (a) after-school detention, which is used for mild, but chronic, misbehavior and (b) office referral, which is used for severe infractions.

Positive Interactions and Positive Feedback

The most important means of reinforcement will be the minute-by-minute interactions that occur between staff and students. Staff will strive to interact with students in a friendly, supportive manner at all times. Staff will attempt to interact with each child three times more frequently when the child is engaged in positive behavior than when the child is engaged in negative behavior.

These positive interactions will consist of greeting students, talking to students, making eye contact, smiling, and using overt praise. When implementing praise, staff will attempt to provide students with specific information about what behaviors are contributing to success (e.g., "Alicia, you have been very responsible about remembering to hand in your homework on the day it is due").

Students Targeted for Special Attention

Occasionally, a student exhibits so much misbehavior that it is difficult for the classroom teacher to maintain ratios of three positive interactions to every negative. When this becomes evident, it is the responsibility of the teacher to discuss this information with the principal. One of the interventions the principal and the teacher may decide to implement is to inform the rest of the staff about the student, and to request staff to interact positively with this student. If every adult who sees this student in the halls, playground, and cafeteria were to say "Hello" and to give the student a few seconds of attention, the student would receive lots of positive attention. The hope is that by providing lots of positive attention, the student will have less need to misbehave to get attention and recognition.

Goal Achieved! Book and Certificates of Merit

The principal will keep the Goal Achieved! book in the office. Any staff member can refer a student to the office because of a positive behavior. Students should be sent to the office during the last five minutes of the school day. The staff member who is sending the student should fill out the Certificate of Merit and send this with the student. The principal will have each student put his/her name in the book. In addition, the principal will sign the Certificate of Merit and return it to the student to share with his/her parents. The principal will reinforce and congratulate students for effort to strive to meet the school motto and the goals.

Homework Room

The Homework Room is a service provided by the school for students and teachers. The room is open and supervised from 7:00 A.M. to 7:45 A.M., during both lunch periods, and after school from 2:45 P.M. to 4:00 P.M. Students are free to use this room whenever they feel they need extra assistance in catching up on their work. This room is supervised and the supervisor is available to help students who need assistance. Student peer tutors have been trained to provide additional assistance.

This room is *not* to be used for a punishment. When a student is beginning to get behind in her work, a teacher should encourage the student to make use of the homework room. If a student becomes seriously behind, a teacher may wish to make arrangements with the student's parents to assign the student to go to the homework room after school until the work is caught up.

Teachers should discuss the availability of the homework room and invite students to participate. The homework room should not be used as a threat to hang over students' heads.

Guidance Assistance Center

The Guidance Assistance Center is a warm, accepting, and orderly place where someone is always available to listen and positively encourage students. The center utilizes paraprofessionals who have been trained in interpersonal communication skills.

The center is not intended to be a detention facility or an alternative classroom. It is to be used as a reward, not to punish students. In addition, it is not a clinical treatment center or professional counseling center. The center is used primarily for at-risk students to reinforce them for success and to provide an environment where students can be taught social skills they might need.

One of the activities that takes place is small-group instruction in social skills. The paraprofessional runs small groups of two to eight students with scripted social skills lessons. A student may be placed in one of these groups by a counselor, the assistant principal, or the student study team. Teachers who feel they have a student who could benefit from one of these groups should discuss the student with a member of the counseling staff.

Teachers wishing to reward student achievement may send a student to the center. The center has a variety of positive reinforcers that a student could be awarded.

After-School Detention

Teachers and administrators may assign a student to serve in after-school detention. The detention room is supervised from 2:45 P.M. until 4:15 P.M. A student may be assigned a 45 minute or a 90 minute detention. During the detention period, students may be assigned a specific task by the classroom teacher. If the teacher wants the student working on a specific task, the teacher must put a memo in the detention room supervisor's box by 2:40 P.M. on the day of the detention. If no specific task has been communicated to the detention supervisor, she will allow the student to work on any task brought with him or her. Unless a specific task has been assigned, no effort will be made to monitor the quality or quantity of student work during the detention period.

The goal of the detention period is to bore the student. Consequently, students will not be allowed to talk to each other. The detention supervisor will monitor to see that students are working on tasks. If they have no task to work on, the detention supervisor has a file of worksheets and exercises that will be assigned to the student.

Records will be kept and periodically analyzed by the assistant principal and the Discipline Committee to determine if detention is working or if modifications might be necessary.

Office Referral for Severe Misbehavior

Office referral should only be used for extremely severe infractions. The staff has worked together and has defined three categories of behavior that are considered severe. These include physically dangerous behavior, illegal acts, and the absolute refusal to comply with an instruction given by an adult. Other, less severe forms of misbehavior should be handled in the place where the infraction occurred.

When using office referral, send the student to the office immediately and fill out the office referral form as soon as possible. If the student refuses to go to the office, call the principal or designee for assistance.

Section 5: Expectations and Procedures for Common Areas

One very important reason for developing a staff handbook for discipline and motivation is to increase staff consistency in common areas such as the playground, halls, cafeteria, assemblies, and so forth. For each of these environments, staff should specify their expectations for students. In addition, the expectations for staff should be developed. The information included in these documents can be used to increase staff consistency when supervising these environments. The following is a sample of the document for hall behavior.

Halls

Goal:
The halls and breezeways will be a safe and quiet environment where people interact with courtesy and respect.

Rules and Expectations:

1. When moving from one place to another, students will move safely through the hallways.
2. With 500 people in the halls at the same time, there is going to be noise. However, each individual should try to keep the noise down. Use a normal speaking voice. If you want to talk to someone down the hall, go to them rather than shouting at them.
3. During class time, you must have a signed pass to be in the halls.
4. Treat everyone with respect.
5. If an adult asks to speak with you, stop and talk with that person.

6. If an adult requests that you correct a behavior, do what the adult asks you.
7. No student should be in the halls prior to 8:15 unless escorted by an adult.
8. Students should go directly home after dismissal from class.

Consequences for Infractions

When a student misbehaves in the hall the student's classroom teacher is expected to correct the student and apply consequences if necessary. If the student's classroom teacher is not present, any staff member who observes misbehavior has a responsibility to correct the student and if necessary apply consequences. Below is a list of possible consequences to be used to correct misbehavior.

- Verbal reprimand ("Zach, you need to walk in the hall. Running is unsafe.")
- Redirection—for example, have the student go back and walk.
- Briefly delay the student. ("Tanya, this is the second time I have talked to you about running. You need to stand right where you are and wait. [Wait ten seconds] Now you can go, but remember to walk.")
- Use office referral only for insubordination or for dangerous or illegal situations.

Reinforcement Procedures

On an intermittent basis, students should receive acknowledgment for their efforts to behave responsibly in the halls. All staff are responsible for providing occasional encouragement to students. This expectation goes beyond reinforcing the students that a staff member is directly supervising and should also include reinforcing students from other classes.

1. Friendly interactions from adults.
2. Compliments to individual students on their safety, courtesy, and respect.
3. Compliments to a teacher (so students can hear) on the degree to which the teacher's class is following the rules.
4. Written compliments from the principal to a teacher on the class's behavior. Teachers should discuss the compliment with the class and post the note so students can see it.

Supervision Responsibilities of Staff

1. Each teacher is responsible for being out in the halls and supervising restrooms at least one day before school and one day after school. During at least one other morning and one afternoon, teachers should be out in the halls or in their doorways.
2. While in the halls or your doorway, interact positively with students as they pass. The goal is to supervise in a warm and friendly way rather than a cold and hostile way.
3. If a student violates a rule, use a respectful but firm voice to inform the student of what he should be doing. Point out the appropriate behavior the student needs to exhibit.

4. For repeated infractions, have the student go back and walk, or delay the student so she is not allowed to socialize with friends.
5. If a student refuses to follow your instruction, inform the student that he can choose to follow your instruction or be referred to the office for insubordination. If the student refuses to accompany you to the office, make no attempt to physically take the student. Simply inform the principal of the incident.
6. Support staff will assist in monitoring the halls but will not replace teacher supervision.
7. Teachers will be responsible for escorting their classes to and from recess, to and from music, and to the dismissal area after school.

Teaching Responsibilities

At the beginning of each school year, there will be a short lesson in each classroom on hallway expectations. These lessons should be conducted in a way that informs students of the rationale for the procedures (i.e., safety, respect, setting a calm tone for entering class, etc.), but should be presented in a way that implies faculty and students will work together. Teachers of primary students will also take students into the halls to practice appropriate procedures.

If there are recurring problems in the halls exhibited by a large number of students, the Hallway Committee will be asked to reconvene and will attempt to work out new procedures for improving the situation.

The principal or her designee will review hallway expectations with student teachers and aides.

SUMMARY

Historically, schools have operated without having a written discipline policy or a policy that defined severe offenses and the corresponding consequences. However, a comprehensive manual for staff, while difficult and time consuming to design, has many advantages. Developing a staff manual forces staff to identify their philosophical beliefs regarding how students should be treated in a school. The process also requires staff to specify the responsibilities of each and every participant in a school, from the students, to the parents, to each of the different job roles of the school staff. The process requires that staff think about and define the procedures for schoolwide programs that either recognize students or give consequences for misbehavior. Finally, the process forces staff to develop comprehensive procedures for teaching and managing the behavior of students in common areas such as halls or playgrounds.

CHAPTER ACTIVITIES

1. Visit a school and discuss with a teacher or principal what schoolwide discipline policies are used. Compare the schoolwide discipline policies of that school with the approach discussed in this chapter.

2. Discuss how severe behavior problems are managed in the schoolwide program presented in this chapter.

3. Identify and briefly discuss the major components of the five sections of a Schoolwide Staff Manual.

SUGGESTED READINGS

Comer, J. P., & Hayes, N. M. (1991). Parent involvement in schools: An ecological approach. *The Elementary School Journal, 91,* 271-278.

Duke, D. (1993). How a staff development plan can rescue at-risk students. *Educational Leadership, 50,* 28-33.

Sprick, R. (1992). *Foundations: Establishing positive discipline policies.* Longmont, CO: Sopris West.

References

Chapter 1

Albert, L. (1990). *A teacher's guide to cooperative discipline*. Circle Pines, MN: American Guidance Service, Inc.

Berman, P., & McLaughlin, M. (1977). *Federal programs supporting educational change (vol. 3): Factors affecting implementation and continuation* (Report No. R-1589/7-HEW). Santa Monica, CA: The Rand Corporation.

Boyer, E. (1990). Introduction: Giving dignity to the teaching profession. In D. D. Dill and Associates (Eds.), *What teachers need to know: The knowledge, skills, and values essential to good teaching* (pp. 1-10). San Francisco: Jossey-Bass.

Canter, L. (1989). Assertive discipline: More than names on the board and marbles in a jar. *Phi Delta Kappan, 71*, 57-61.

Carnine, D. W., Silbert, J., & Kameenui, E. J. (1990). *Direct instruction reading*, 2nd ed. Columbus, OH: Merrill.

Carnine, D. W., Stevens, C., Clements, J., & Kameenui, E. J. (1982). Effects of facilitative questions and practice on intermediate students' understanding of character motives. *Journal of Reading Behavior, 14*(2), 179-190.

Carroll, J. B. (1963). A model of school learning. *Teachers College Record, 64*, 723-733.

Chard, D., Smith, S., & Sugai, G. (1992). Packaged discipline programs: A consumer's guide. In G. Tindal (Ed.), *The Oregon Conference Monograph* (pp. 19-26). Eugene, OR: The University of Oregon, Behavioral Research and Teaching Group.

Colvin, G. T., & Sugai, G. M. (1988). Proactive strategies for managing social behavior problems: An instructional approach. *Education and Treatment of Children, 11*(4), 341-348.

Curwin, R. L. & Mendler, A. N. (1988). *Discipline with dignity*. Alexandria, VA: Association for Supervision and Curriculum Development.

Gibson, S., & Dembo, M. H. (1984). Teacher efficacy: A construct validation. *Journal of Educational Psychology, 76*, 569-582.

Glenn, S. M., & Nelson, J. (1987). *Raising self-reliant children in a self-indulgent world.* Rocklin, CA: Prima Publishing.

Kameenui, E. J. (1991). Publishing in research journals: Guarding against the false and fashionable. In J. F. Baumann and D. D. Johnson (Eds.), *Publishing professional and instructional materials in reading and language arts* (pp. 17-28). Newark, DE: International Reading Association.

Kameenui, E. J., & Simmons, D. (1990). *Designing instructional strategies: The prevention of academic learning problems.* Columbus, OH: Merrill.

Little, J. W. (1982). Norms of collegiality and experimentation: Workplace conditions and school success. *American Educational Research Journal, 19,* 325-340.

Nelsen, J. (1987). *Positive discipline.* New York: Ballantine Books.

Schwartz, B., & Lacey, H. (1982). *Behaviorism, science, and human nature.* New York: Norton.

Slavin, R. (1989). PET and the pendulum: Faddism in education and how to stop it. *Phi Delta Kappan, 90,* 750-758.

Smylie, M. A. (1988). The enhancement function of staff development: Organizational and psychological antecedents to individual teacher change. *American Educational Research Journal, 25*(1), 1-30.

Smylie, M. A. (1989). Teachers' views of the effectiveness of sources of learning to teach. *The Elementary School Journal, 89*(5), 543-558.

Sprick, R. (1981). *The solution book: A guide to classroom discipline.* Chicago: Science Research Associates.

Sugai, G. (1992). Instructional Design: Applications of teaching social behavior. *LD Forum, 17*(2), 20-23.

Toffler, A. (1990). *Power shift.* New York: Bantam.

Wong, K., Kauffman, J., & Lloyd, J. W. (1991). Choices for integration: Selecting teachers for mainstreamed students with emotional or behavioral disorders. *Intervention in School and Clinic, 27*(2), 108-115.

Wolery, M. R., Bailey, D. B., & Sugai, G. (1988). *Effective teaching: Principles and procedures of applied behavior analysis with exceptional students.* Boston: Allyn & Bacon.

Chapter 2

Albert, L. (1990). Cooperative discipline: *Classroom management that produces self-esteem.* Circle Pines, MN: American Guidance Service.

Anderson, R. C., & Armbruster, B. (1990). Some maxims for learning instruction. *Teachers College Record, 91,* 396-408.

Baer, D. (1988). Foreword. In F. Rusch, T. Rose, & C. Greenwood. *Introduction to behavior analysis in education* (pp. ix-xi). Englewood Cliffs, NJ: Prentice-Hall.

Canter, L. (1989). Assertive discipline: More than names on the board and marbles in a jar. *Phi Delta Kappan, 71,* 57-61.

Canter, L., & Canter, M. (1976). *Assertive discipline: A take charge approach for today's educator.* Los Angeles: Canter & Associates.

Chard, D., Smith, S., & Sugai, G. (1992). Packaged discipline programs: A consumer's guide. In G. Tindal (Ed.), *The Oregon Conference Monograph* (pp. 19-26). Eugene, OR: The University of Oregon, Behavioral Research and Teaching Group.

Dreikurs, R. (1974). *Discipline without tears.* NY: Hawthorn Books.

Dreikurs, R. (1982). *Maintaining sanity in the classroom: Classroom management techniques.* New York: Harper & Row.

Duke, D. L., & Meckel, A. M. (1984). *Teacher's guide to classroom management.* New York: Random House.

Engelmann, S., & Carnine, D. (1982). *Theory of instruction: Principles and applications.* New York: Irvington.

Gordon, T., & Burch, N. (1974). *Teacher effectiveness training.* New York: Wyden.

Rusch, F. R., Rose, T. & Greenwood, C. (1988). *Introduction to behavior analysis in special education.* Englewood Cliffs, NJ: Prentice-Hall.

Skinner, B. F. (1971). *Beyond freedom and dignity.* New York: Knopf.

Wolery, M. R., Bailey, D. B., & Sugai, G. (1988). *Effective teaching: Principles and procedures of applied behavior analysis with exceptional students.* Boston: Allyn & Bacon.

Chapter 3

Berliner, D. C. (1988). Effective classroom management and instruction: A knowledge base for consultation. In J. L. Graden, J. E. Zims, & M. I. Curtis (Eds.), *Educational delivery systems* (pp. 309-325). Washington D.C.: WASP.

Brophy, J., & Good, T. L. (1986). Teacher behavior and student achievement . In M. Wittrock (Ed.), *Third handbook of research on teaching* (pp. 328-375). Chicago: Rand McNally.

Engelmann, S., & Carnine, D. W. (1982). *Theory of instruction: Principles and applications.* New York: Irvington.

Evans, D. (1991). *An analysis of representations in mathematics instruction.* Unpublished doctoral dissertation, Special Education Area, University of Oregon, Eugene, OR.

Evertson, C. M. (1989). Improving elementary classroom management: A school-based training program for beginning the year. *The Journal of Educational Research, 83*(2), 82-90.

Gettinger, M. (1988). Methods of proactive classroom management. *School Psychology Review, 17*(2), 227-242.

Good, T. L. (1979). Teacher effectiveness in the elementary school: What we know about it now. *Journal of Teacher Education, 30,* 52-64.

Kameenui, E. J., & Simmons, D. (1990). *Designing instructional strategies: The prevention of academic learning problems.* Columbus, OH: Merrill.

Paine, S. C., Radicchi, J., Rosellini, L. C., Deutchman, L., & Darch, C. B. (1983). *Structuring your classroom for academic success.* Champaign, IL: Research Press.

Rohrkemper, M. M., & Brophy, J. E. (1980). *Teachers' general strategies for dealing with problem students.* Paper presented at the annual conference of the American Educational Research Association, Boston, MA.

Chapter 4

Kameenui, E. J., & Simmons, D. (1990). *Designing instructional strategies: The prevention of academic learning problems.* Columbus, OH: Merrill.

Wolery, M. R., Bailey, D. B., & Sugai, G. (1988). *Effective teaching: Principles and procedures of applied behavior analysis with exceptional students.* Boston: Allyn & Bacon.

Chapter 5

Canter, L., & Canter, M. (1976). *Assertive discipline: A take charge approach for today's educator.* Los Angeles: Canter & Associates.

Duke, D. L., & Meckel, A. M. (1984). *Teacher's guide to classroom management.* New York: Random House.

Gelfand, D. M., & Hartman, D. P. (1984). *Child behavior analysis and therapy,* 2nd ed. New York: Pergamon Press.

Kameenui, E. J., & Simmons, D. (1990). *Designing instructional strategies: The prevention of academic learning problems.* Columbus, OH: Merrill.

Mercer, C. D., and Mercer, A. R. (1989). *Teaching students with learning problems,* 3rd ed. Columbus, OH: Merrill.

Sugai, G. (1986). Recording classroom events: Maintaining a critical incidents log. *Teaching Exceptional Children, 18,* 98–102.

Chapter 6

Alberto, P. A., & Troutman, A. C. (1986). *Applied behavior analysis for teachers.* Columbus, OH: Merrill.

Darch, C. (1993). Direct instruction: A research-based approach for designing instructional programs. In R. C. Eaves & P. McLaughlin (Eds.). *Recent advances in special education and rehabilitation* (pp. 88–106). Boston: Andover Medical Publishers.

Darch, C., & Simpson, R. (1990). Effectiveness of visual imagery versus rule-based strategies in teaching spelling to learning disabled students. *Research in Rural Education, 7,* 61–70.

Kameenui, E. J., & Simmons, D. (1990). *Designing instructional strategies: The prevention of academic learning problems.* Columbus, OH: Merrill.

Rusch, F. R., Rose, T., & Greenwood, C. (1988). *Introduction to behavior analysis in special education.* Englewood Cliffs, NJ: Prentice-Hall.

Sprick, R. S. (1981). *The solution book: A guide to classroom management.* Chicago: Science Research Associates.

Whaley, D. L., & Malott, R. W. (1971). *Elementary principles of behavior.* New York: Appleton-Century-Crofts.

Chapter 7

Kameenui, E. J., & Simmons, D. (1990). *Designing instructional strategies: The prevention of academic learning problems.* Columbus, OH: Merrill.

Madsen, C., Becker, W., Thomas, D., Koser, L., & Plager, E. (1968). An analysis of the reinforcing function of sit down commands. In R. K. Parker (Ed.). *Readings in educational psychology* (pp. 27–35). Boston: Allyn & Bacon.

Rusch, F. R., Rose, T., & Greenwood, C. (1988). *Introduction to behavior analysis in special education.* Englewood Cliffs, NJ: Prentice-Hall.

Sprick, R. S. (1981). *The solution book: A guide to classroom management.* Chicago: Science Research Associates.

Walker, H. (1979). *The acting out child: Coping with classroom disruption.* Boston: Allyn & Bacon.

Wolery, M. R., Bailey, D. B., & Sugai, G. (1988). *Effective teaching: Principles and procedures of applied behavior analysis with exceptional students.* Boston: Allyn & Bacon.

Chapter 8

Kameenui, E. J., & Simmons, D. (1990). *Designing instructional strategies: The prevention of academic learning problems*. Columbus, OH: Merrill.

Sprick, R. S. (1981). *The solution book: A guide to classroom management*. Chicago: Science Research Associates.

Chapter 9

Colvin, G. T., & Sugai, G. M. (1988). Proactive strategies for managing social behavior problems: An instructional approach. *Education and Treatment of Children, 11*(4), 341–348.

Chapter 10

Leone, P. E. (1985). Suspension and expulsion of handicapped pupils. *Journal of Special Education, 19*, 111–121.

Sprick, R. S., Sprick, M. S., & Garrison, M. (1993). *Foundations: Establishing positive discipline policies*. Longmont, CO: Sopris West.

Index